CRITICAL ACCLAIM
FOR *TRAVELERS' TALES*

"The *Travelers' Tales* series is altogether remarkable."
—Jan Morris, author of *Journeys, Locations,* and *Hong Kong*

"For the thoughtful traveler, these books are an invaluable resource.
There's nothing like them on the market."
—Pico Iyer, author of *Video Night in Kathmandu*

"This is the stuff memories can be duplicated from."
—Karen Krebsbach, *Foreign Service Journal*

"I can't think of a better way to get comfortable with a destination
than by delving into *Travelers' Tales*...before reading a guidebook, before
seeing a travel agent. The series helps visitors refine their interests and
readies them to communicate with the peoples they come in contact
with...."
—Paul Glassman, Society of American Travel Writers

"*Travelers' Tales* is a valuable addition to any predeparture reading list."
—Tony Wheeler, publisher, Lonely Planet Publications

"*Travelers' Tales* delivers something most guidebooks only promise: a real
sense of what a country is all about...."
—Steve Silk, *Hartford Courant*

"The *Travelers' Tales* series should become required reading for anyone
visiting a foreign country who wants to truly step off the tourist track
and experience another culture, another place, firsthand."
—Nancy Paradis, *St. Petersburg Times*

"Like having been there, done it, seen it. If there's one thing traditional
guidebooks lack, it's the really juicy travel information, the personal
stories about back alleys and brief encounters. The *Travelers' Tales* series
fills this gap with an approach that's all anecdotes, no directions."
—Jim Gullo, *Diversion*

TRAVELERS' TALES BOOKS

Country and Regional Guides
America, Australia, Brazil, France, Greece, India, Ireland,
Italy, Japan, Mexico, Nepal, Spain, Thailand;
Grand Canyon, Hawai'i, Hong Kong,
Paris, San Francisco

Women's Travel
A Woman's Path, A Woman's Passion for Travel,
A Woman's World, Women in the Wild, A Mother's World,
Safety and Security for Women Who Travel,
Gutsy Women, Gutsy Mamas

Body & Soul
The Road Within, Love & Romance, Food,
The Fearless Diner, The Gift of Travel, The Adventure
of Food, The Ultimate Journey, Pilgrimage

Special Interest
Danger!, Testosterone Planet, There's No Toilet Paper
on the Road Less Traveled, The Penny Pincher's
Passport to Luxury Travel, The Fearless Shopper,
The Gift of Birds, A Dog's World, Family Travel,
Shitting Pretty, The Gift of Rivers,
Not So Funny When It Happened

Footsteps
Kite Strings of the Southern Cross,
The Sword of Heaven, Storm, Take Me With You

Classics
The Royal Road to Romance,
Unbeaten Tracks in Japan

TRAVELERS' TALES

GREECE

TRUE STORIES

TRAVELERS' TALE

GREECE

TRUE STORIES

Edited by

LARRY HABEGGER, SEAN O'REILLY,
AND BRIAN ALEXANDER

Series Editors
JAMES O'REILLY AND LARRY HABEGGER

TRAVELERS' TALES
SAN FRANCISCO

Credits and copyright notices for the individual articles in this collection are given starting on page 315.

We have made every effort to trace the ownership of all copyrighted material and to secure permission from copyright holders. In the event of any question arising as to the ownership of any material, we will be pleased to make the necessary correction in future printings. Contact Travelers' Tales, Inc., 330 Townsend Street, Suite 208, San Francisco, California 94107. www.travelerstales.com

Art Direction: Michele Wetherbee
Interior design: Kathryn Heflin and Susan Bailey
Cover photograph: © Yuri Lev
Map: Keith Granger
Illustrations: Page 1 - Parthenon; Page 87 - Mount Olympus; Page 161 - Vase illustration with Dionysos, satyrs, and mænads, by Panphæos; Page 255 - Combat of a Greek and a Centaur (Metope of the Parthenon); and Page 303 - Caryatides.
Page layout: Patty Holden, using the font Bembo

Distributed by: Publishers Group West, 1700 Fourth Street, Berkeley, California 94710

Library of Congress Cataloging-in-Publication Data

Travelers Tales, Greece: true stories/edited [by], Larry Habegger, Sean O'Reilly, and Brian Alexander.
    p. cm.
    Includes bibliographical references.
    ISBN 1-885211-52-X (alk. paper)
    1. Greece—Description and travel. 2. Travelers—Greece. I. Title: Greece: true stories. II. Habegger, Larry. III. O'Reilly, Sean. IV. Alexander, Brian, 1959–

DF728.T7 2000
914.9504'76—dc21   00-041786

First Edition
Printed in the United States of America
10 9 8 7 6 5 4 3 2 1

Wherever you go in Greece the people open up like flowers....
No country I have visited has given me such a sense of grandeur....
Greece is a little like China or India. It is a world of illusion.

—HENRY MILLER

Table of Contents

Part Four
IN THE SHADOWS

Part Five
THE LAST WORD

Greece: An Introduction

For those of us in the Western world, Greece is a lodestone, a wellspring, an idea as grand and compelling and romantic as the *Iliad* and the *Odyssey*. This idea of Greece is also simple: Greece represents the zenith of enlightened civilization.

Classical Greece provided the empires of Rome and Byzantium and all future Western systems a model of civic mindedness that inspires to this day. Thus who could not want to "return home" to the cradle of democracy, to the source of our political and moral philosophies, to the land that established the foundations of our civilization and spawned the myths that for centuries have provided us an intellectual and emotional compass? It is a legacy that cannot be ignored, and a force that pulls us to visit this hallowed land, if for no other reason than to walk in the paths of gods and heroes who preceded us.

We might say that it is just about every child's dream, upon hearing the adventures of Odysseus, to explore the islands he visited, the seas where he sailed, to see and conquer the Cyclops, to negotiate the razor edge of Scylla and Charybdis, to hear the Sirens' song and to return home a stranger but later to be recognized as the hero we all wish to be. Who could resist strolling the lanes where Socrates, Plato, and Aristotle pursued ideas for their own sake and laid the foundation for 2,400 years of political thought? Or walk in the footsteps of Philip of Macedon or Alexander the Great?

There are so many icons from Greece's rich history still here to explore: the Parthenon atop the Acropolis in Athens; Delphi, where the Oracle dispensed wisdom through maddening riddles; Mount Olympus, abode of the gods; Ithaca, the island home

Odysseus sought for twenty years; Lésvos, home of the revered poet Sappho; Crete, site of the sophisticated Minoan civilization that preceded classical Greece; and countless archaeological sites on just about every island strewn throughout the archipelago.

Greece is, of course, more than an idea or a collection of ancient sites bearing memories of the glory that once was. It is breathtaking seas, rugged islands, exquisite coastlines and beaches, arid landscapes, dramatic mountains. It is orthodox monasteries, hidden forests, traditional villages offering legendary hospitality from people genuinely happy to open their lives to visitors. It is also chaotic cities and tourist resorts overrun during high season so there is more northern European than Greek experience to be had.

This contrast is Greece's burden: it is a modern country with all the attendant challenges, but one with the weighty baggage of much ancient honor. How does that past color the present? How do modern Greeks view their predecessors, their own place on the historical timeline, their nation that is home, not a series of stops on a cultural tour?

The answers lie in the stories that follow. In "The Land of Light," Lawrence Durrell explains how Greece's magical light sets the country apart from other Mediterranean lands. Susan M. Tiberghien, in "*Yasas!*," uncovers poignant hospitality and a desire for connection through an encounter with an old man in Crete. Robert D. Kaplan traces the genesis of the modern myth of Greeks' earthy passion in "Teach Me, Zorba," and probes the darker side of the Greek soul in "Farewell to Salonika." Paul Theroux's "Taunting the Oracle" is a critical look at modern reverence at Delphi. Emily Hiestand explores the taverna as a metaphor for the Greek way of life, and Patricia Storace finds the secret to all things Greek in the cuisine. Garry Wills probes the reality behind the Arcadia of the Romantic Poets while Katy Koontz goes to the ends of the earth, and her wits, to get married in the Greek isles. Tom Joyce's pilgrimage to Mount Athos, Laurie Gough's strange dream-time encounter with a crone, Robert Peirce's confrontation with rebels and Nicholas Gage's heart-rending search for the truth behind his mother's death during the Greek civil war broaden the portrait and pull the reader into a vital, multihued world. Lastly, Donald W. George explains why it's impossible not to be "In Love, In Greece, In the Springtime."

The Greece that comes alive in these pages is the Greece that exists today: passionate, sensuous, slightly mad, dusted by the scent of sage and baked by the sun. It is a place that commands us to come, and go we must, if we want to close the circle back to our origins.

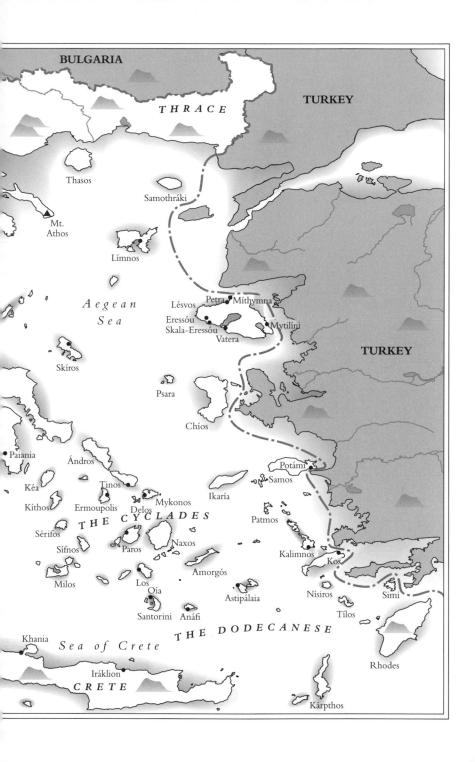

PART ONE

ESSENCE OF GREECE

LAWRENCE DURRELL

* * *

The Land of Light

A traveler arrives in Greece
and is bewitched.

THE TRAVELER AWAKES ABOARD SHIP AT DAWN, WITH LAND AHEAD of him and one shoulder of an island hunched up to the right of the vessel. It is an easy island to identify—those polished great fruity-looking mountains are Albanian. They are spacious and bare, and warmly painted in by the sun as it struggles up to shine over their shoulders on the sea. Corfu lies like a sickle beside the flanks of the mainland, forming a great calm bay, which narrows at both ends so that the tides are squeezed and calmed as they pass into it. So much is clear from the map. But for the moment the great ferry simply forges straight ahead, apparently going to crash straight into the screen of golden mountains before them. The northern shoulders of Corfu belie its reputation for luxurious beauty; they are craggy, penurious, and empty of villages—dull limestone, covered in scrub and holm oak. The traveler eyes them in some dismay, wondering if the stories he has heard of verdure and beauty were really fables. But gradually the main channel comes into view, and with it the old Venetian seamark which warns of shoals. Now the ship turns abruptly, as if on its heel, and heads due south, leaving Albania on her left. To the right is the channel, so narrow that the first few villages are, or seem to be, but a few hundred yards away.

In fact, at its narrowest point the northern end of Corfu is only separated from Albania by a stretch of sea two kilometers broad. The
general configuration of things becomes clear. The great serene bay
is like a punch bowl. The landmass is dominated by a big domed
mountain called Pantocratoras from which, later, he will be able to
stare out upon the two seas and upon a number of islands.

The maddening, yet reassuring, thing is that that rosy old satin
dawn, sending its warm pencils of light through the ravines of the
hills towards the island is really and truly "rosy-fingered." "Damn
Homer!" he thinks, determined to stay in the present. It is at this
early point that the traveler begins to recognize the distinctive form
and signature of things Greek. As the vessel bowls softly across the
smiling bay, as the coast with its dense, luscious lagoons unwinds in
the fashion of a spool, he sees the famous town coming up at him
with its small screen of decorative islands. The journey has not taken
as long as he thought—they will dock slightly before seven o'clock,
and climb up on to romantic quays lined with as yet empty cafés,
where yawning *douaniers* await them with their bills of lading and
maddening questions. There is a string of moth-eaten fiacres lined
up and waiting for him, with their horses wearing characteristic
straw hats that are pierced to let the ears of the animals pass
through. Hats which give them an arch and rather drunken appearance. But the beauty of the little town! He has been warned
that he will not find a prettier in Greece, and as time goes on this
will become more and more evident. At the moment his only ambi-
tion is to step ashore and into one of those carnival fiacres which
will draw him through the coils and loops of the old Venetian
fortress into the town of Corfu—where, doubtless, rosy-fingered
waiters will be waiting to ply him with breakfast.

Everything is indeed open, in spite of the early hour. The pave-
ments are being hosed down, and the warm earth releases choice
odors of lemon and wet dust. The old town is set down gracefully
upon the wide tree-lined esplanade, whose arcades are of French
provenance and were intended (they do) to echo the Rue de
Rivoli. The best cafés are here and the friendliest waiters in all
Christendom. This early morning animation is somehow an indica-

tion of the tempo at which Greece lives; you rise each morning to a new day, a new world, which has to be created from scratch. Each day is a brilliant improvisation with full orchestra—the light on the sea, the foliage, the stabbing cypresses, the silver spindrift olives...

Naturally the traveler, letting the eyes of his mind loose to browse among these bewitching shapes and colors, will find much to remind him of such other momentous places as Orta or Taormina. The tall, spare Venetian houses with their eloquent moldings have been left unpainted for centuries, so it seems. Ancient coats of paint and whitewash have been blotched and blurred by successive winters, until now the overall result is a glorious wash drawing thrown down upon a wet paper—everything running and fusing and exploding. But more precise, though just as eloquent, are the streets between the houses, each a deep gully made brilliant with washing hung out to dry from every balcony—bright as bunting. This great spread of color moves and sways in the light dawn breeze in a way that reminds one of tropical seaweed. The red dome of the Church of St. Spiridion shines aloft with its scarred old clock face; the church which houses the mummy of the island's patron saint. If he knows what is good for him, the traveler will make an indispensable pilgrimage to this dark fane, whose barbaric oriental decoration smolders among the shadows like the glintings of a fire opal. He will kiss the sacred slipper or a suitable icon and light a candle to place in the tall sconce as he utters a prayer—the subject of which he will confide to nobody. In this way his journey will be under good auspices and the whole of Byzantine, modern, and ancient Greece will be waiting with open arms.

Coming out of the dark church into the market he will be almost blinded by the light, for the sun is up; and it is now that the impact of this extraordinary phenomenon will begin to intrigue him. The nagging question, "In what way does Greece differ from Italy and Spain?" will answer itself. The light! One hears the word everywhere "To Phos" and can recognize its pedigree—among other derivatives is our English word "phosphorescent," which summons up at once the dancing magnesium-flare quality of the sunlight blazing on a white wall; in the depths of the light there is blackness, but it is a blackness which throbs with violet—a magnetic unwearying ultraviolet throb. This confers a sort of brilliant shine of white light on material objects, linking near and far, and bathing simple objects in a sort of celestial glowworm hue. It is the naked eyeball of God, so to speak, and it blinds one. Even here in Corfu, whose rich, dense forestation and elegiac greenery contrasts so strangely with the brutal barrenness of the Aegean which he has yet to visit—even here there is no mistake about the light. Italy has no such ray, nor Spain. Flowers and houses and clouds all watch you with a photoelectric eye—at once substantial and somehow immaterial. Each cypress is the only one in existence. Each boat, house, donkey, is *prime*—a Platonic prototype of a sudden invention; maybe an idle god's quite *arbitrary* invention, as if he had exclaimed, "Let there be donkey."

And in each donkey (by now they are braying all along the esplanades, waiting for their children) one sees the original, the archetypal donk: the essence, the quiddity of the *idea* of donk.

> What is the god singing in his profound
> Delphi of gold and shadow?
> What oracle for Thebes, the
> sunwhipped city?
>   —Sophocles, *Oedipus*

He is not of course the first visitor to be electrified by Greek light, to be intoxicated by the white dancing candescence of the sun on a sea with blue sky pouring into it. He walks round the little town of Corfu that first morning with the feeling that the island is a sort of burning-glass.

Later, sitting in a tavern built out over the Venetian mole with its somber lions of St. Mark, he thinks of other light-drinkers in the past who have, like himself, suddenly felt that they were moving about in the heart of a dark crystal.

The first impression of the country, from whatever direction one enters it, is austere. It rejects all daydreams, even historical ones. It is dry, barren, dramatic and strange, like a terribly emaciated face; but it lies bathed in a light such as the eye has never yet beheld, and in which it rejoices as though now first awakening to the gift of sight. This light is indescribably keen yet soft. It brings out the smallest details with a clarity, a gentle clarity that makes the heart beat higher and enfolds the nearer view in a transfiguring veil—I can describe it only in these paradoxical terms. One can compare it to nothing except Spirit. Things might lie thus in some wonderful intelligence—so alert and so lulled, so divided and yet so closely linked. Linked by what? Not by mood; nothing could be more remote from that floating sensuous soulful dream-element: no, by the Spirit itself.

Pondering these words of Hugo von Hofmannsthal, the traveler feels within him the first premonitory signs by which the heart recognizes the onset of a great love affair—the light in the eyes of the beloved. He is falling in love.

Lawrence Durrell's literary works span a broad spectrum from poetry and plays to novels, translations, and travel. He is perhaps best known for The Alexandria Quartet, *a series of four novels set in Alexandria, Egypt. Before and after World War II he lived for eight years in the Greek Islands, and he died in 1990 in Sommières, France. This story was excerpted from* The Greek Islands.

PATRICIA STORACE

Marble Girls

*An American poet finds
a home in Greece.*

ARKHE TOU PARAMYTHIOU, KALISPERA SAS, IS A TRADITIONAL BEGIN-
ning of a Greek fairy tale. The fairy tale begins, good evening to you.

I lived in Athens, at the intersection of a prostitute and a saint. It
was a neighborhood of mixed high-rises and a scattering of neoclassical houses, some boarded up while the owners waited to be
offered the right price for their inheritance. The neighborhood
hardware stores carried, along with screwdrivers and lengths of wire
and caulking pastes, icon frames with electric lights in the shape of
candles attached, so you wouldn't have to inconvenience yourself
with oil for the perpetual flame. All the neighborhood shops—the
laundry, the butcher's, the vegetable market, the TV and appliances
store, the cheap dress shop and the bridal gown shop, the school
supplies shop with its large-sized brightly colored picture books of
Greek myths and tales of Alexander the Great—were defended by
charms against the evil eye suspended over their counters. If you
took the evening *volta*, stroll, that provides most Athenians with
their exercise during the punishingly hot times of the year, certain
streets gave you glimpses of Mount Hymettus, smudged with darkening violet light, like a drawing someone had started and then
decided to cross out with ink.

The tiny cottage of an apartment I moved into yesterday has already begun to teach me what a different world I have come to, physically, socially, historically. It is no easy matter to find apartments with furniture and kitchen appliances here. In Greece, the tenant is supposed to supply these things. Until 1983, when the obligatory dowry—the *prika*—a woman brought to her husband was declared illegal, refrigerators and beds were components of the marriage agreement. And for the most part, unmarried people until fairly recently lived with their parents, and had no need for their own domestic equipment. Even now, when it is common for couples to marry later, and to live together before they do, many people I know from previous visits live in a kind of compromise between independence and family surveillance. Their parents or grandparents built family-only apartment buildings in which each child of adult age is housed on a different floor, along with members of the extended family, who wander in and out of each other's living rooms, dandling each other's babies, stirring each other's pots of *stifado*, hoping to catch a glimpse of the man Kiki has gone out with three times in the last month.

The miniature living room of this flat is dominated by a ballroom-sized chandelier, a persistent element of the middle-class Greek idea of grandeur in decoration, probably translated into homes from Orthodox churches, which usually feature monumental gilt chandeliers, their branches supporting a rain of votive offerings. There is also a glass-fronted trinket cabinet, which displays a blue-and-white Greek flag, some seashells, a souvenir china plate from the island of Paros, and a narghile, or hookah, the Middle Eastern water pipe. In the tiny kitchen, there is the ubiquitous, dull-white marble sink, and a bottle of Ajax cleanser, which promotes itself here through its claims to whiten marble. Marble is more common than wood in southern Greece, and an apartment building which takes itself at all seriously will have marble floors and steps, at least in the entrance. A narrow balcony runs the length of the two rooms, overlooking the courtyard, dotted with green trees in clay pots, an attempt at a city garden from the tenants of the ground floor. There is a balcony etiquette I will have to master, I realized yesterday, even through my jet lag. I suddenly understood the cliché about airing laundry in public, as the neighbors frankly scrutinized my lingerie and the patterns on my sheets as I hung them out to dry. The balconies are proportioned to the size of the apartment, and across the way, on a substantial balcony, a neighbor is handling her line, pins, and draped laundry with the grace and expertise of Madame Vionnet fitting a mannequin. She looks at me impassively. I know I am affording her an odd spectacle—I have never lost a freezing childhood fear of heights, and to lean out over a fatal drop to dry my laundry gives me a sudden image of the characters in *North by Northwest* as they scramble over Mount Rushmore with a gunman in pursuit. I have to close my eyes for each garment. A badly positioned dress drips a steady purple rain onto the balcony railing below, and a black lace bra spirals down into the courtyard when a clip pulls loose. The neighbor stares at me, and I leave the field, making a show of not clinging to the walls, disguising the symptoms of hyperventilation.

Recovering with a cup of coffee inside, I hear a scratching sound from the front room; a handful of leaflets has been thrust under the door. Greek apartments, I discover, are leafleted as thickly as American college dormitory rooms. The local movie theater offers a showing of a film starring Yuppy Goldberg, as she transliterates to Greek, and Italian. It takes no more than a drive from the airport to realize how critical the study of foreign languages is in Greece. One of the most common neighborhood sights is the colorful signs offering the teaching of *xenes glosses*.

I remember a drive I took across the United States a few years ago. From one end of the continent to another, I did not see a school for foreign languages. They were there, of course, but to be sought out. Here, though, they are ubiquitous; it is hard to walk more than a city block without seeing schools or posters advertising them, as if foreign languages were some kind of vital substance you needed constantly to replenish, a milk. In Greece, where every enterprise that involves language—publishing, entertainment, journalism, tourism—is dependent on the roughly 9 million people who speak Greek, knowing one or more foreign languages is a professional necessity. Businessmen, politicians who deal with European Community officials, doctors who must keep abreast of foreign research, writers who here largely make their living on translations, all need foreign languages in order to survive. There used to be an unanswerable Greek joke phrase, "What says meow-meow on the roof tiles?" the equivalent of "Is the pope Catholic?" But friends tell me that it now has an answer—"A dog who is learning foreign languages."

The status of the language affects the country externally, too, influencing how well a country is known, whether the outlines of its history become part of the stock of common knowledge. Browsing in bookstores outside Greece, I have much more easily found works on French or German or Spanish history and biography than on modern Greece. The scarcity probably begins with childhood circumstance; lessons in those other languages were readily available. I wonder how it affects people here to have to add the learning of languages to other everyday necessities, and I wonder how it affects native English speakers to be in possession of the current lingua franca, a status once held by Latin, and before that, by Greek. Being able to

---

As a child, my father heard adults tell strange tales about the *castingari*. All he knew about this creature was that it lived in America, where anyone wishing to immigrate had to confront it. The *castingari* was feared because it was capricious; not everybody was able to get past the beast. Angelo recalled one would-be immigrant, a simpleton, who sailed all the way to New York and then all the way back to the village again, where he climbed a wild pear tree and sat in it until his neighbors found him.

"What are you doing up there?" they asked him. "Why aren't you in America?"

"I couldn't go in because of the *castingari*."

It took Angelo many years to realise that the *castingari* was the customs gate on New York's Ellis Island.

—Katherine Kizilos, *The Olive Grove: Travels in Greece*

rely on the dominance of English may affect English speakers' ability to approach and imagine other cultures—as if they were rich children, who have inherited such an enormous trust fund that they can choose whether or not to go to work.

The third leaflet offers a six-volume set of the classics of modern Greek literature. It is promised, as if it were in doubt, that the introductions by prominent Greek scholars will "reveal to us the greatness of the deeds and spirits" of the founders of the modern nation. Pictures of the gilt-edge volumes are set against the backdrop of a nineteenth-century painting, showing romantic warriors wearing the *foustanella*, the pleated Greek kilt, in repose among the ancient columns of the Parthenon—the classical past defended by the creators of modern Greece. The books are the collected writings of Kolokotronis, Krystallis, Valoritis, Solomos, and Makriyiannis, all men of the nineteenth century, when the Greek nation violently entered history. It occurs to me as I look at the elaborately bound books offered by the leaflet that I have never heard them mentioned in speeches by tour guides I have overheard in museums, or listened to on bus trips. The emphasis is usually on Thucydides, Aristotle, or Sappho; paradoxically, it is the history of modern Greece that seems more distant. The past which can be remembered as well as imagined, the recent past which directly produced the manners, customs, and political situation of the nation we travel to, seems almost too complex to approach.

Kolokotronis and Makriyiannis were military leaders of the Greek War of Independence of 1821 against the Ottoman Turks—these two soldiers so despised each other that the Greek campaign against the Turks nearly became a civil war as well. The engravings show both men wearing oriental turbans and the highly prized elaborate oriental mustaches. In features, costume, and expression, they could be chieftains from any Near or Middle Eastern country. They could be Afghan. They could be Syrian. They could be Turks. All six of them display the self-consciously stern, imposing jailer's facial expression that means authority in Greece. Taki, a Greek friend of mine, shook his head once over a picture of Franklin Roosevelt that accompanied a review of a biography, and said irritatedly, "That face. I can never understand that face, that inane smile." In the Greek vocabulary of the face, smiling does not include the nuance of power that it does in the United States. Roosevelt's sunny optimistic smile had an air, for Americans, of invincibility, of mastery of both good and bad fortune, because to possess happiness is a kind of authority in America, barely comprehensible to Taki, who saw smiling as a kind of placation, a sign of submission, and in whose native tongue the verb "to laugh" also means "to deceive." This different language of the face begins at passport control in each country. The Americans smile in their booths with an easy self-assurance that enjoyment cannot threaten; the Greeks scowl theatrically, implacably, since a smile is not considered an impressive facial expression, and a male face is meant above all to impress, not to charm.

The group of men in conventional nineteenth-century European dress are men of letters. Solomos, whose poem to freedom was set as the national anthem, is considered the national poet. He and General Makriyiannis share a quality that makes them not only eminent personalities in the struggle to found the Greek nation, but symbols of it. Solomos, the bastard son of a Greek maidservant and an Italian count who lived on the Ionian island of Zákinthos, is the symbol of the Greece created out of the embrace of European and Greek cultures. Makriyiannis, who said that Greece and Europe could never learn each other's dances, and who was instrumental in bringing about the fall of the Bavarian king who had been dispatched to rule over the new nation, is the symbol of the Greece created out of the rejection of Europe. That simultaneous rejection and embrace of Europe shifts and collides still, like tectonic plates, under the surface of the country.

Makriyiannis and Solomos had another common quality which established them as symbols of modern Greece: their relation to Greek. Solomos, who was educated in Italian and had a child's imprint of the simple Greek of his mother, had virtually to teach himself Greek in order to write poetry in the language. Makriyiannis was semiliterate, and had to learn to write Greek as an adult in order to record his memoirs. In their rebirth as Greeks, they were seen as proofs of "the Greek miracle," resurrected. And in this nation, which sees itself as the true birthplace of Christianity, and whose national history is seen as a reenactment of the life of Christ, so that the Greek national holiday is deliberately celebrated on the day of the annunciation of Mary's pregnancy, resurrection is an idea with an erotic power over the national imagination, invoked, yearned for, caressed, an image as present in pop songs as it is on church walls. Yesterday, riding in a taxi, I caught a line on the radio through the chaos of Athens traffic: "And if you cut me in half, I'll love twice as much."

Most non-Greeks, in my experience, have never heard of any of these men. I hadn't myself until the first time I came here and felt the eerie sensation of disorientation I recognized from my childhood; I had grown up without knowing my parents, although intensely aware of their existence in my own body, made out of elements of theirs. So I knew something about beings who are powerfully present without being visible to others, and I knew something about lost worlds, even though my lost world was the past, and the lost world of Greece was the present. Greece, too, was preoccupied with questions of origins, however different the configuration. Having to use my imagination to understand the impact of tragically real events had made me aware of imagination's enormous force—for good and evil—in every aspect of our lives, even in realms supposedly free of it, in law, science, and politics, in history and economics, in learning and ignoring, in describing and in lying, in crime and in love. In Greece I saw a nation both tormented and exalted by imagination.

The doorbell rings, and I answer it a little uncertainly, not knowing quite how cautious to be. Standing outside is a small, sturdy woman with carefully architected gray curls. She is holding a tray of some unrecognizable cookies and is dressed in a flowered smock. The entire floor smells like a swimming pool, thanks to the heavily chlorinated cleaners popular in Greek households. "Welcome to Greece," she says, "I am Kyria Maro. If you have any questions, knock at my door. I am a friend of your landlady's, so if you cannot reach her for some reason you can come to me. Any questions at all. And," she adds in grandmotherly tones, as if she were imparting some domestic golden rule about doing the dishes or the frugal use of electricity, "you know, Macedonia is Greek." She hands me the china plate and tells me to return it whenever it should happen that I have the time, and clacks down the hall in her slippers.

I look down at the plate—I have never seen any confections in these shapes before, and I can't anticipate the flavor of any of them. There is one in quadrants, like a pastry kite, another like a ridged sausage, another like a piece of fried lace. I might as well be living on the moon. It seems I will need a new body in order to live here, that the demands of a new country begin as demands on the body. I feel the weight and alienness of the food, the light, this world where a day has a different geography, and a life moves through time and space differently. I feel the tug of Greek words as a change in the force of gravity, and as the plate of pastries in my hand posits a different conception of appetite than I know, and a different conception of pleasure, I begin to understand that this language will perceive the body, and the world itself, differently from my own. This is the moment when travel is felt most absolutely, when time and space and history and emotion exert a force on the body, and the distances you are traveling inside are as great as the distance you have traveled outside.

I have some basic household staples to buy and a bank account to set up before I meet some friends in central

> In classical Athens, whether the struggle was between you and the world's pleasures, or between you and your body, this state of conflict was normal and natural. What was abnormal was to put up no resistance, to be continually and instantly overwhelmed. Such feeble characters threw in the towel without a fight. They were defeated and enslaved by their desires. They were known as the *akolastoi*, the uncorrected, the unchecked, the unbridled, or the *akrateis*, the powerless, the impotent, the incontinent.
>
> —James N. Davidson,
> *Courtesans and Fishcakes*

Athens for lunch. It takes deep breaths and resolution to get myself down the three flights of stairs onto the neighborhood streets. The first month in a new country is an exhausting one; every object, every face, every incident comes at you the size of faces on a giant screen. You are exhausted from paying attention, and even sleep is sleepless, because the magnified days, the fifty-foot words, the towering new conventions insist their way into your dreams, too.

It seems almost impolite, somehow tactless, to notice how unlike any other neighborhood streets in any other country these are. I pass two or three icon stores in the space of six or eight blocks, hung with rows of sullen female saints, dead-eyed male saints, looking as if they are at the last moment of control before an explosion of anger. The more expensive images have ornate frames or silvered-over clothes. Women buy them and women tend them, lighting oil flames in front of them, burning incense, and misting them with holy water as if they were sacred houseplants. I never actually saw a man buy one, not during the year I spent in Greece; and I often remembered, as I walked by these stores, that during the two periods of fierce Byzantine iconoclasm, both times the revival of icon worship was sponsored by women, the empresses Theodora and Irene. There is something disturbing about all those blank pent-up-looking faces that demands propitiation, like a child's desperate attempts to please a remote, miserable parent. And there is something poignant, too, as if they are only so alike because they need to be rescued into individuality, they need the mercy of tending, one reason little girls play with dolls. I used to spend pocket money for small toys when I was little, not nearly so much because I wanted the toys for myself as because I wanted to release them. I remember buying a palm-sized monkey and the saleslady wanting me to exchange him because he didn't have the right tag. "They're all alike," she said, and threw him into the bin overflowing with the toy monkeys. "No, they're not all alike," I said, fishing him out. "Not anymore." Outside the shop, safe in my hand, he stopped being a movie tie-in.

I walk past yet another icon shop, past those bitter faces imprisoned in their silver cells. I look for a moment past the street of

Phryne, beyond a small green square, to the street of Ágios Fanourios, the revealer, patron saint of illumination, who finds lost objects and gives glimpses of the future. He is also famous for having had such a monstrous mother that on his name day, one formulaic prayer runs: "God pardon the mother of Ágios Fanourios."

At my intersection, Phryne, the prostitute, was a courtesan in the fourth century B.C., the lover of the sculptor Praxiteles, and the model for what seems to have been the first monumental statue of a female nude. She was also the only woman in antiquity to have won a lawsuit with only her own eloquent breasts. When she was about to be condemned by the Athenian court for immoral conduct, she pulled her dress from her shoulders down to her waist in front of the judges, who, transfixed, ruled in her favor. In a world where speech and thought were neither the rights nor the privileges of women, Phryne found a way to pose philosophical questions with her body. "Are you immoral?" she asked the judges. "Is desire immoral? What is immorality?"

This story may or may not be true. And all we know of the looks of this standard of female beauty in the Greek and Roman worlds is our dream of them. We only know the lost Aphrodite of Knidos from Roman copies and images on coins, made by artists who probably never saw the original statue, and certainly never saw the woman. In any case, the statue was rejected by the islanders of Kos, who had commissioned it; they considered its nakedness immoral.

According to Callistratus in his work *On Hetaeras*, Phryne became so rich that after the Macedonians had razed the city of Thebes to the ground she said she would pay for the city wall to be rebuilt, providing the citizens put up an inscription: "Alexander may have knocked it down, but Phryne the hetaera got it back up again," one of the very few occasions when these women gave themselves the label.
—James N. Davidson,
Courtesans and Fishcakes

Running parallel to the street of Phryne, forming a rough cross with it, flecked with small shops is the street of Fanourios, a saint, who was satisfied that as a Christian he had found the answer to Phryne's questions. Following the consequences of his logic, he submitted himself to the sacred suicide of virginity and martyrdom, instead of the profane suicide of sexuality. Greek polytheists were not "pagan," in the licentious interpretation of the word given by their religious rivals. The old Greek word for pagan is *ethnikos*, which is synonymous with "national," as in the national flag. I didn't know you were *ethnikos*, says a Christian to a polytheist in one of Cavafy's poems.

The Greek polytheists regarded the body with their own kind of mystical puritanism, believing that each sexual act diminished in some degree the vital force of the partners, and even shortened their lives. Their ideal was a highly stylized and controlled kind of sexual contact, in which the "passive" partner was always to some degree humiliated, and which looks from the scenes on vase paintings to have been really very dull. Perhaps it is no accident that the body of myths assembled, invented, reinvented, and anthologized from a variety of sources by the ancient Greeks is one of the least erotic of the world's mythologies, rivaled perhaps only by the mythology of the ancient Israelites. The source of sexual tension in ancient Greek myth is not so much the drive to the ecstasy of consummation, but uncertainty as to whether either or both partners will survive the sexual act. This thread runs through all the stories of the young men and women who are killed after lovemaking with each other or the gods; through all the stories of rape, a sexual act in which there is always an implicit threat of murder; and on a global scale, through the *Iliad*, in which generations and nations die because Helen and Paris lay down together.

I realize now how much being on the courtyard side of the building shields me from the noise of the streets. Athens streets are substantially noisier to my ear than New York's, because of the ubiquitous motorcycles and from the incessant gear-shifting here, where nobody drives automatic.

I am on my way to the *laiki agora*, the farmers' market, held on different days of the week in different neighborhoods throughout the city.

The traffic is anarchic, and walking here requires acute scouting attention. Cars simply drive over curbs; motorcycles wanting to pass weave through the pedestrians on the sidewalks; and often cars are parked directly on the sidewalks, further narrowing the slim margin of safety separating pedestrians from the onslaught. Traffic is worse today because there is a bus strike—the conservative Mitsotakis government and the bus drivers' union are struggling over the government's attempt to privatize the buses. There are hints that the trolleys and taxis will soon strike in sympathy. Walking everywhere doesn't trouble me, since I am used to some five miles a day, but I wonder what it will do to elderly people like Kyria Maro if they have heavy groceries or errands downtown. A red light halts me at the *periptero*, one of the kiosks for newspapers, aspirin, batteries, and the cold drinks that are crucial in the southern Greek summer, when thirst is felt more violently than hunger. I am caught in a crossfire of stares: a motorcyclist has turned his face away from the lights toward me and is staring with dedicated attention, while the *periptero* man has me covered from the other side. It is very hard to get used to, but there is no social prohibition against frank, assessing, concentrated staring, and my first pervasive sensation in Greece is of those eyes—the stares of the coffee-drinking shopkeepers, the gazing icons, the tin and glass eyes dangling from key chains and rearview mirrors and hung over doors as protection against harm from living eyes.

The *periptero* man waves me over. "You just move here?" he asks, framed by newspapers hanging over his head like national flags from wooden poles. There are the Everydays, the Afternoons, the Newses, the Free Presses, the Uprootings, as some of the dizzying range of Greek newspapers, journals usually openly affiliated with political parties, are called. There is *Estia*, named after the goddess of the hearth, which in the nineteenth century serialized many of the first modern Greek novelists, and is now one of the most vitriolic of right-wing papers, referring to Bosnia-Herzegovina as a "Turkish protectorate." There are the magazines named as if they were philosophical categories: *Images, It Is, She, Woman, One,* and the Greek satirical paper *The Mouse.*

"Yes, I'm here for a year," I answer, aware of the constantly shifting passage through Athens of diaspora Greeks, students, tourists, international scholars, and EU employees. I choose a carton of strawberry juice from the kiosk refrigerator. Except for certain wines and cold mountain water, I have never drunk anything as perfect as Greek fruit juices, each as distinct in timbre and character as the instruments of an orchestra.

"And you're Greek?" the *peripteras* asks.

"No," I say.

"But you speak Greek?"

"Yes, but I still talk a lot of *ardzi, bourdzi,* and *loulas,*" I say, using a Greek phrase for nonsense that amuses people when they hear it, a phrase that plays with the idea of being fluent in nonsense.

"So how much a week do you have to live on?" he asks.

"Enough for *horta,* greens, at the *laiki,*" I say, and catch the light to cross.

"Well, buy your newspapers here," he calls after me, "and you can practice your Greek, too. Here we speak

---

"**P**eople rush through Athens on their way to the islands," he said, "and take in nothing but the Acropolis." Antonis recited the words of a shepherd he'd encountered while lost in the mountains: "A foreigner and a blind man are the same. They don't see what's in front of them." And it's true—Athens has gotten a bad rap among travelers, for its traffic jams, overcrowded tourist sites, and seasonal air pollution. But there is another side to Athens, and those who focus only on the city's glorious past, Antonis says, are missing its seductive present: its sensual dry heat and sea light; its blue sky and bright flowers; the icy drinks, garlicky dips, and tangy cheeses served in cafés; the splashes of green and, everywhere, a citrusy smell; the startling hills that jut up heroically in the center of town.

—Alan Brown, "Athens, Look Closer," *Travel & Leisure*

Greek for absolutely nothing. Even though it is an expensive language to speak."

Just beyond, a shop window offers a new line of wedding and baptism invitations, all embossed with a gold Star of Vergina, the symbol marking some of the grave treasures of Philip of Macedonia, Alexander the Great's father. The vegetable and fruit stalls of the *laiki* are hung with the most beautiful agriculture I've ever seen: olives in many colors, grapes so real they make fancy grocers' bunches seem like Victorian wax ornaments, eggplants that are the royal porphyry that was the exclusive color of the Byzantine imperial family, branches of bay leaves that are called Daphne here, after the nymph who metamorphosed into the laurel tree to escape being raped by Apollo. "Wherever I go and wherever I stay," wrote the novelist Kazantzakis, "I grasp between my teeth, like a bay laurel leaf, Greece."

The sellers shout for the shoppers' attention "*Aromata kai khromata*," perfumes and colors, says one, scooping up handfuls of ruby-colored cherries. He gives me one to sample and enjoys my response. The fruit has something more than flavor; it evolves—it has drama. "It's the sun," he says. "We get more sun than any other country in Europe, and it concentrates all the sugars in the fruits and vegetables. And we pick them ripe, just before we sell them." The only other place I find with fruits and vegetables to equal this brilliance, when I travel there at the end of my year here, is Turkey.

I pass a stall with barrels of grains that are collectively called here *demetriaka*, after the Greek goddess Demeter, as we call them cereals, after the Roman goddess Ceres, a subtle reminder of complicated historical fissures and parallels. The Western world is called the Western world because it descends from the western Roman Empire, while Greece belonged to the eastern Roman Empire of Byzantium. The polarity of the relations between the two and the cultural dominance of one over the other are rarely as clear in their contrasts as they are often presented. These empires seemed not so much to face each other like black and white champions across a chessboard as to be enmeshed dynamically together, more a spiral than a chessboard, in a cultural struggle that could never be fully

resolved or completely clarified, because each side was so marked by
the characteristics of the other it had taken on. Each side at times
confronted the other in opposition, but at others adopted the more
insidious method of incorporating its rival, like two actors competing for the same role. It was even a common dream in the second
century for Romans and Greeks to have dreams of each other's
alphabets. The interpreter who recorded these dreams remarks, "If a
Roman learns the Greek alphabet or a Greek learns the Roman
alphabet, the former will take to Greek pursuits, the latter to
Roman. Many Romans, moreover, have married Greek wives, and
many Greeks, Roman wives, after having this dream." Elite Roman
children had Greek nurses, and Greek literature and decorative arts
had something like the prestige and elegance of French for nineteenth-century Russians or Persian for the Ottoman Turks. I remember having dinner with a teacher who worked at one of the most
prestigious Greek prep schools, who told me her high school class
had flatly refused to read Virgil's *Aeneid*. Greek high school students
have a reputation for being ungovernable; I heard teachers' stories
of classes who, en masse, refused exams, and of idle weeks passing
while students went on strike, attending school but doing no
schoolwork, in the service of various causes. These particular students held it as dogma that the *Aeneid* was a cheap imitation of
Homer, with a popular Platonism, present in both the ancient
Greek preoccupation with sculpture and the modern Greek preoccupation with icons, that insisted there was one ideal original, and
the rest of the genre increasingly false and bloodless. "It's as if they
accused Chopin of being a cheap imitation of Beethoven, without,
of course, having heard him," the teacher said frustratedly to me.
They were unable to see Virgil's poem as a radical reinterpretation
of the epic and the epic hero. It was an ironic thing to hear, since
the borders of influence were so permeable—the Byzantine
Empire, which evolved into an empire dominated by Greeks, was
founded by a Latin-speaking Roman, now one of the important
saints of the Greek church, and the language of this empire, later to
become Greek, was originally Latin, and remained Latin for an
ample number of centuries. Besides, the Greeks had called them-

selves, well into the twentieth century, Romans, and their word for quintessential Greekness had been Romiosyni, Romanness. This historical vertigo had been brought home to me by the title of a modern short story, which described a quintessential Greek Orthodox Easter. The title of the story was "Romaic Easter." Through the strange spiral of this history, the Greeks evolved into their conquerors.

The Byzantine emperors, though, in the eastern empire, were the emperors of the crossroads—not only did the Byzantines have to claim to Rome that they were the real Romans, but they had to declare to their rivals in the Middle East—the Persians, the Jews, the Arabs, and the Turks—that they were the Roman Empire. Partaking of both the cultures of the West and the East, but fully integrated with neither, Byzantium was a transvestite empire, partly both but also neither, the Empire of the Crossroads, whose preoccupation with dual natures of all kinds, from its man-gods to Diyenis

---

The Byzantine Empire left its traces in many more ways than the classical world of Pericles. What has puzzled the West for hundreds of years has been the huge contradiction of Byzantium. It was the first empire dedicated to a Christian god. And yet it was one of the bloodiest of empires if judged by wars, palace intrigues, and civil strife within its own shifting borders. The contradiction is real, but to focus only on this aspect of Byzantium is to miss the point of the longest lasting empire in history. Western Europe during this period— roughly A.D. 400 to 1453— developed as a territory of separate countries and kingdoms organized on feudal systems. In Byzantium, all territory was one empire under God. Beyond that level, the family emerged as the strongest unit, quite unlike the feudal development of Europe. God and family were the twin poles of a thousand years of rule, and still are, in many ways, the orientation of modern Greeks.

—Andrew Horton,
Bones in the Sea

Akritas, its own epic hero, the biracial knight of the border, is its most ineradicable legacy to modern Greece. Diyenis (of two races) Akritas, the medieval Greek hero, son of an Arab chieftain and an aristocratic Greek lady, was to have been the subject of the second part of Kazantzakis's *The Odyssey: A Modern Sequel.*

A boy calls for customers to riffle through this stock of used CDs—the one in his right hand has a picture of one of the finest current pop singers, and I go closer to read the title: *Our National Loneliness.*

Walking away from the perfection of the produce, I wander past stalls selling utensils of the worst possible design, waste bins with lids that don't fit, plastic colanders that would melt on contact with boiling water, cheap clothes in punitively ugly prints. I can't find the simplest glass mixing bowl, only greasy plastic, so I turn back, changing my plan for the eggplant and olives—in any case, the genius of the flavors will overcome the limitations of the cook, like a person thrust from private life into fame. My marketing is snatched from my arms suddenly by a wiry, sixtyish man, whose eyes behind his old-fashioned glasses are brown like weak coffee, and anxious. He shoves a hand under my elbow and pulls me toward the street. "You must come with me, you must come with me," he says urgently. My thoughts are of fire, riot police, terrorists. "What is happening?"

"Hurry," he says, "hurry up. I want to have coffee with you." A struggle ensues over my packages, which I win, thanks to my new height. Having stepped through the mirror to this country, I find that I am no longer small as I was in the United States, but have become magically taller than average. "Where are you going?" he calls after me. "You will be perfectly safe. I am a doctor."

"But I am perfectly healthy." I escape down a side street past a grim-looking restaurant full of men reading newspapers and eating hot food. It is a genre of restaurant you find tucked away in city neighborhoods, patronized by old bachelor and widower habitués, with no wives or mothers to cook for them. The men settle at their separate tables as if they were distinct worlds, eating in silence, in a kind of public solitary confinement.

Another person calls to me, this time a girl in blue jeans standing on the corner beside a stack of books piled on an upended crate. "Do you need a new one?" she asks.

"What are they?" I slow down, shift my packages, and climb toward her. Athens is all ascent and descent, like San Francisco, and readjusting your balance is what walking is about as much as covering distance. She holds up a volume and flips the pages. "Dream books. *Oneirokrites*."

Actually, I did bring one. But it was written in the second century, the *Oneirokritika*, a handbook of dreams collected by a professional dream interpreter named Artemidorus, who traveled in Greek cities, and recorded and classified the dreams people told him in order to make a manual of the art of dream interpretation for his son. It is a social history of shocking intimacy, a study of the unconscious lives of people of another world, trying to divine the future through their dreams, while we, so far away try to divine the past. The *Oneirokritika* was translated into Arabic in 873, and was an inspiration for the great dream book of Ad-Dinawari, published in 1006; in the West, it was an inspiration for Freud's *Interpretation of Dreams*.

"I do have one," I say, "but it's old."

"You are foreign?" she asks, and I nod. "How long have you lived here?"

"Two days."

"Then you will need a new one. You will have new dreams here."

Patricia Storace, a native of Mobile, Alabama, was educated at Columbia University and the University of Cambridge. She is the author of a book of poems, Heredity, *and the winner of a prize for poetry from the American Academy of Arts and Letters. Her essays have appeared frequently in the* New York Review of Books *and in* Condé Nast Traveler. *This story was excerpted from* Dinner with Persephone.

SUSAN M. TIBERGHIEN

Yasas!

Two visitors experience the
significance of a toast.

MY HUSBAND STOPPED OUR CAR, AND I LEANED OUT THE WINDOW
to ask a tall and imposing Cretan the way to a small Byzantine
chapel marked in our guidebook. Pierre and I were vacationing for
one week, away from the children, with time for one another.

We were high in the hills on the southern side of Crete, where
dittany and other wild herbs burst into pink blossoms in early
spring. It was in these flowering fields where Zeus courted the
beautiful Europa. We had gathered handfuls of the aphrodisiac pink
flower, perfuming our arms and saving some to make tea during the
cold winters back home.

Our impressive Cretan was dressed all in black—high leather
boots, wide breeches fitted at the knee, a hand-woven buttoned shirt
with long sleeves. He stood very straight, holding on to a sturdy cane.
He had thick gray hair and the strong noble face of Cretan men, the
men Henry Miller described as the most handsome in the world.

I first tried in English, then in French to make myself understood.

"No Greek?" he asked.

"No Greek," I replied with regret, but I held out the guidebook
and pointed to the picture of the Byzantine chapel.

He nodded his head and motioned to the back of our small

rented car, proposing to show us the way. I pushed aside the paper bag of black olives and goat cheese, the round loaf of bread and the bottle of Minos rosé. Our newly appointed guide folded himself into the little car.

He led us up a narrow dirt track, past a few farms and over a green hilltop, to another hilltop where he told us to stop and follow him on foot. We walked behind him into the grayish-green olive groves. The gnarled branches were stooped with age. Worn nets were still spread out on the ground to catch the last tiny purple olives.

Our Cretan continued and we followed, bending to pass under the low branches, stepping carefully over the nets. He soon stopped and lifted his walking stick to point out the chapel we had seen in our guidebook. The red, sun-baked roof was half covered with vegetation, and the white walls were almost buried in the ground. We walked closer. The door was open.

Inside the dusky church, candle wicks flickered in front of old icons, illuminating faded red and blue frescos behind the stone altar. Scenes of the Last Supper and of the Garden of Gethsemane wavered on the rounded wall. Earlier visitors had come before us that day, lighting the way.

Our guide found a thin, hand-dipped candle in a tin can and placed it near the others burning in front of an icon of Mary, with the infant Jesus in her arms.

"The Panayia," he said, bowing his head.

Pierre and I followed his example, each taking a skinny candle, lighting it, and finding room for it in front of the Blessed Virgin. She was looking directly at us. The infant Jesus was looking at her. We stood together for a long moment in silence.

When we went back out into the sunshine, the white walls gave off waves of heat. We retraced our steps under the tangled branches of the olive trees. Our guide slowed his pace, asking us questions, using English words and Greek words. He nodded when he learned we lived with our children in Switzerland, that our oldest child was married and living in France, and that we were soon to be grandparents.

"Good," he said. "For me, not good."

"For you?" we asked.

"For me bad. The war. Dachau three years." He held up his hand showing three of his fingers.

We continued walking. He used his cane to steady himself on the uneven ground.

"My one child killed here. The war. She fifteen." He held up once again his hand, showing five fingers three times.

He kept talking. Slowly we learned that his village had once been large and prosperous. Then the Germans came and the fighting. Now it counted less than one hundred people all dispersed in small farms over the mountainside.

It was springtime and bushels of blossoming dittany rolled down the hills. But soon the pink flowers would dry under the hot sun, the green plants would turn brown and disappear under the hungry herds of goats and sheep. It would then be difficult to imagine the hills as the blossoming love bed of Zeus and Europa.

When we arrived back near the car, our guide invited us to come to his home.

"Please, you come," he said. "Friends," he said, pointing back and forth to us, to him, to us.

We accepted and he directed us over another dirt track to the top of another hill, where close to the crest stood his house. The brick walls were whitewashed. The wooden beams and the wooden door were hewn and chiseled by hand. He managed to tell us that most of his house had burned during the war. When he returned from Dachau he rebuilt the gutted portions with fresh bricks. The courtyard was swept clean, with a stone oven in the corner where he baked his own bread.

Inside there were two rooms, the kitchen and his bedroom. He said his wife died some years back. He lived alone. On the wall over his bed hung his daughter's gun. She fought with the guerrillas against the Germans in the hills surrounding their farm.

Next to the gun was a blurred black-and-white photo of his young daughter. He wanted us to look at it. The glazed surface was cracked and uneven. She had a wide open smile and was wearing a schoolgirl's smock, checkered once in bright colors.

He spread out a clean white cloth on the kitchen table and told us to sit down. There were two chairs.

"Me, how old?" he asked.

"Seventy," we guessed.

He shook his head. "Eighty-five!" He traced the numbers on my husband's hand.

We watched as he put out plates, knives, forks, glasses. He gave each of us a white folded napkin, and with another he polished the glasses. Next he brought a dish of small red tomatoes and some feta, his own goat cheese still in a crock chipped with years. He got a bread board and cut thick slices of a loaf of brown bread baked in the outside oven.

Then he reached for a bottle of ouzo on the shelf by the window and filled our glasses. The aroma of the pungent aniseed spirit encircled us.

"Yasas!" said our friend, downing his glass.

"Yasas!" we answered.

Susan M. Tiberghien, an American-born writer, lives in Geneva, Switzerland. She is the author of Looking for Gold *and* Circling to the Center, *and her stories are widely published in periodicals and anthologies in the U.S. and Europe. She teaches creative writing and edits the literary review* Offshoots, Writing from Geneva.

KATHERINE KIZILOS

Sappho's Island

A traveler explores the stamping grounds
of Plato's "tenth muse."

IN A SQUARE NEAR THE BEACH AT SKALA ERESSÓU STANDS A SMALL white bust of the philosopher Theophrastus. He has a good view. The silver beach is long and sandy; its air of lonely wildness fulfils even an Australian's exacting standards of what a good beach should be. At one end of the beach is a bare, rocky hill, the acropolis of Ancient Eresos. In the long grass that skirts the hill you can find remnants of stone walls, built before the time of Homer. Strong and perfect still, they stand impassively in the goat paddocks, surrounded by thistles and thorny oak trees.

Theophrastus was born at Eressós in 372 B.C., more than a thousand years after the walls were built. Now considered a minor philosopher, he was well known, even revered, in his day. He taught and wrote in Athens just after its glory days, in the years when the Macedonians ruled Greece, and while Alexander was in the east conquering the Persians and becoming Great.

The teacher of Alexander's youth was the philosopher Aristotle. When Theophrastus left Lésvos, he went to Athens and also studied with the mighty philosopher. Theophrastus was known as Tyrtamos then, but he so impressed Aristotle with the beauty of his writing that Aristotle gave him a new name: Theophrastus means divine speaker. The young philosopher went on to succeed Aristotle as the head of his Athenian academy and inherited his library. He wrote about volcanoes, the weather, stones, plants, wine, smells, and animal behavior. But his longest surviving work is not philosophical or scientific: *The Characters* is a brief collection of sketches describing the range of scurrilous and ridiculous men then found on the streets of Athens. Each sketch begins with a definition, a display of precision and wit. (Of the Superstitious Man, for example, Theophrastus writes: "Ah yes, superstition: it would appear to be cowardice in the face of the supernatural.") The book is said to have been a great influence on the comic playwright Menander, one of Theophrastus's pupils, but it is chiefly remembered because it brings the scoundrels of his age so vividly to life. Pithy and reso nant, it can still make you laugh out loud.

It was Theophrastus's fate to have been born in the same town as the poet Sappho, who came into the world two and a half centuries before him, in 610 B.C. In Theophrastus's time, Sappho was so highly esteemed that Plato—who also taught Theophrastus—dubbed her "the tenth muse." She still has many followers. During the warm months, women from around the world would make the long pilgrimage to the beach at Skala Eressóu to honor her. But in the square—the place where logic and sentiment dictate that they should find a stone or plaque to Sappho—Theophrastus's bald head looks out instead. Not many visitors have heard of the philosopher and so he is mostly ignored; the women have come to give a garland to Sappho. Her statue, however, is a two-and-a-half-hour drive away, at the edge of the harbor in Mytilíni, the capital of Lésvos and the city where the poet spent most of her life.

Skala Eressóu is peaceful, out of the way. Tourism transforms it for a few months each year, but a sense of its winter quietness never completely leaves the town. Sappho's fame is responsible for many of the tourists who journey to its silver-gray beach, but I cannot remember even a sign in Skala Eressóu that mentions her. A hotel-keeper explained the omission: the townspeople had nothing against the immortal poet—it was the pilgrims they objected to. The hotel-keeper was a portly, timid man. When he mentioned the

women, he dropped his voice, squirming a little. The women were
so overtly, so demonstratively *lesbian*. They held hands and kissed on
the beach. They shaved their heads. Sometimes they fought among
themselves. It was distasteful, the town disapproved. If I intended
to write about Skala Eressóu, perhaps it would be best not to mention Sappho: it would only encourage the women.

At this, another resident, a professional man, nodded in agreement. A great deal could be written about the area without mentioning Sappho, he said. Besides, he believed that the lesbian pilgrimage to her birthplace was misguided, the result of an
unfortunate historical misunderstanding. There was no evidence
that Sappho was homosexual. The rumors about her sexuality
began with Menander, but her contemporaries had been silent on
the matter; satirists had enjoyed making ribald jokes about her and
now, so many centuries later, Skala Eressóu was suffering the consequences. As was all of Lésvos, indeed: its very name had become
an allusion to Sappho's supposed sexual orientation, which was why
so many Greeks called the island Mytilíni.

Legend has it that Sappho killed herself for love by throwing
herself off a cliff. She was short, dark and plain, and was known as
the nightingale because her drab appearance belied the beauty of
her song. Along with the female students in her school at Mytilíni,
she worshipped the goddess Aphrodite and honored her divine gift,
the sweet madness of love. Love was Sappho's religion and her muse;
she believed it to be greater than war and the quest for power.

Some say thronging cavalry, some say foot soldiers,
others call a fleet the most beautiful of sights
the dark earth offers,
but I say it's whatever you love best.

Only a fraction of Sappho's work survives. Much of it was only
discovered by accident, when members of the British Egypt
Exploration Society scratching in the sands of Oxyrhyncus at the
turn of the century came across papyrus fragments with lines of her
poetry written on them. Many of the Sapphic scraps are about the

same length as a haiku, and they have the same delicacy and emotional immediacy:

Eros the Limb-loosener shakes me again—
that sweet, bitter, impossible creature.

Then love shook my heart like the wind that falls on
oaks in the mountains.

The moon has set
and the Pleiades; it is the middle of the night
and the hours go by
and I lie here alone.

Much of Sappho's writing celebrates the beauty of women and her love for the girls in her school. (One unattached line says simply: "O beautiful, O graceful girl...") Talent rarely flourishes in a vacuum, and so it is believed that Sappho must have lived in a world in which women enjoyed a fuller, freer life than was allowed them in succeeding centuries. For how could Sappho alone have achieved the freedom of body and spirit that we can still glimpse in the broken mosaic of her work? So little is known about the other women of her time, however, that Sappho remains both a miracle and an enigma: the only female genius of the ancient world.

Meanwhile, it is a safe bet that Skala Eressoú's unease with the Sapphists is a continuing source of amusement for the lonely bust of Theophrastus, providing a daily demonstration that in the late twentieth century, human foibles have much the same texture as they did in his own time.

I arrived on Lésvos at 6 A.M. and, out of habit, took a taxi to Mytilíni's bus station. The cabbie, also acting out of habit, charged me an exorbitant amount for the short ride, causing me, in turn, to perform the now familiar ritual of cursing him soundly before slamming the door. A wispy-haired old lady, with one tooth left in her lower gum, watched me drag my suitcase to the seat beside her and, once I had done so, told me that the station would not be open for two hours. Then she asked brightly if I would walk to the other side of a nearby park to buy her a loaf of bread; she was particular about the kind of bread she wanted, describing it at some length.

This was not my first encounter with old Greek ladies of this type: Zen-like apparitions, they typically strike when their quarry is dazed and vulnerable. Once, when I was hitchhiking in Epirus, an old lady approached me as I clambered off the back of a utility truck; I had just endured a reckless downhill drive from the mountain village of Métsovon, during which the driver had taken hairpin bends from the wrong side of the road.

"*Herete,*" said the crone, "would you be so kind as to give me some Nivea cream?" Shaken and covered with sawdust, I automatically opened my bag and gave her the cream. She thanked me and disappeared. Similarly, I now did as requested, eventually returning to the bus station with warm bread and *tiropites*, cheese pies, for our breakfast.

It was now October. I knew the warm weather would not last much longer, that my journey around the islands was almost at an end. I stared balefully at my luggage. My case was so heavy that its handle had broken after a few weeks, so heavy that I was tempted to stay in substandard places rather than lift it, so heavy that I inevitably arrived at my destination tired, trembling and prey to anyone who offered to carry it for me. Gallingly, I knew all about the advantages of traveling light; but the pressure of time had turned me into a fool. Before leaving Australia, I had been too busy to pay attention to what I packed and so had crammed absurd, extraneous items into my case: two left thongs, heavy books, winter suits. I had abandoned some items in Athens; some, I had posted home; others, I had dumped. Even so, a millstone remained. I mentally rehearsed the routine ahead: dragging my case onto the bus to Skala Eressóu, dragging it off again, and then dragging it to my hotel room. This protracted folly—my clumsy metaphor for an overloaded life—had gone on for long enough. I brushed away my *tiropita* crumbs and fear of driving, and decided to hire a car.

Lésvos is one of the biggest islands in the Aegean. It has a permanent population, a private life, and its citizens produce excellent ouzo and olive oil, away from the insatiable eyes of the tourist. Mytilíni itself is crowded, grimy, and car-choked; an ugly incongruity on an otherwise lovely island, and one that is typically Greek. I wondered if the noise and chaos was an inevitable part of any Greek city because it represented an unconscious Greek ideal (the clamor, the sense of unforeseen possibilities), just as Australians can be relied upon to build towns permeated by a lonely, tree-lined hush.

Once I had left Mytilíni, I drove through a rolling landscape of densely planted olive trees. The topography of Lésvos lacks the drama of other islands: the steep peaks have the space to stretch out, to undulate and create more subtle allurements. Skala Eressóu was a ninety-kilometer drive away, to the west. The farther I drove, the flintier the landscape became, as the dark olive groves slowly gave way to spare, stony hills crowned with thorny-flowered oak trees; boulders occasionally thrust their way through the topsoil. The landscape took on an expansiveness, a mythic quality. I could imagine medieval pilgrims with their cloaks and long staffs walking over the rocky hillocks, under an immense sky.

This sense of a medieval quest was reinforced by the monasteries, which were the most substantial landmarks along the road. The biggest was the Leimonos Monastery, founded in 1523 by the metropolitan of Míthymna, St. Ignatius. From a distance, the monastery looked grand and imposing, but on closer inspection there were signs of dereliction everywhere. The main building was three stories high, with wings of monastic cells enclosing a courtyard, but what was once a thriving center had now largely been abandoned. Some of the cells, including that of St. Ignatius, were being restored, and the rubble and detritus around the site reinforced the sense of decay. I asked a woman at a souvenir stall how many monks still lived in the monastery; five, she said, and two of them were very old.

Leimonos had the third-largest collection of manuscripts in the Greek Orthodox world (after Mount Athos and Patmos), but its museum had the dusty, makeshift look of a converted scout hall. The remains of saints were stored in silver boxes in a glass case and labeled with a felt-tip pen. In the courtyard, a group of Greek tourists, mostly middle-aged women, were angrily dismayed to learn that their sex prevented them from entering the monastery's main church. "I've been in there before," one of them shouted, "and nothing happened to the church or to me!" But the monks refused to give way, even as the monastery gave way around them.

Just before I reached Skala Eressóu, I saw another monastery perched high on a stony peak. Moni Ipsilou was built from the same material as the mountain it stood upon. The mountain stones, the monastery walls and the clouds above them were all varying shades of gray, and it was difficult to tell where one ended and the other began. As the clouds parted, the building looked as though it was emerging out of the sky. It reminded me of a sorcerer's castle or a dragon's lair; a place that sprang from the earth, but fed the imagination.

Professor Ignatius P. Papazoglou arrived promptly at my hotel to take me on a walking tour of Ancient Eresos. The professor had responded to a call from my hotel owner, who had thought of him when I'd asked if he knew anyone who was acquainted with the history of the area. Professor Papazoglou was the ideal guide, he told me. The honorary director of the Teaching Academy of Mytilíni, he had been born at Eresos, he had written books about it, he had been instrumental in setting up the small local museum and he had attended the town's only archaeological dig.

The professor's goddaughter worked as a maid at the hotel. She greeted her godfather cheerily, and remarked that she had not once visited any of the town's historic sites, even though they were just outside her door, and wasn't it funny how all the foreigners were so crazy about them? She was interrupted by a man in the lobby, who proclaimed that Eresos was steeped in history, and that the great Sappho herself had taught on Vigla, the very hill before us on the beach.

No, said Professor Papazoglou, that was not true; Sappho never taught at Eresos. He seemed a cheerful man, lacking in self-importance, and was presumably accustomed to the historical indifference of the villagers. But when the man in the lobby began to argue the point, the professor's temper frayed.

"They'd know what they were talking about if they'd read my books," he muttered as we set out for the archaeological museum. On the way, we collected his brother-in-law, Tassos, a furniture salesman from Mytilíni, who was washing his car on the street.

"Forget that and come with us," said the professor abruptly, "you might learn something." Tassos, a smiling, ironic fellow, dropped his sponge and obeyed.

The museum was a small building filled with artifacts: inscribed tablets, broken columns, little ceramic vases, measuring cups from an ancient grocer. A grave stele from the classical period was the prize exhibit: a husband's solemn farewell to his seated wife, made in a time before mourners found consolation in dreams of heaven. Next door was the archaeological dig: the early Christian Basilica of St. Andrew, occupying the site where it is believed a temple of Apollo once stood.

The isles of Greece, the isles of Greece!
Where burning Sappho loved and sung,
Where grew the arts of war and peace,
Where Delos rose, and Phoebus sprung,
Eternal summer gilds them yet,
But all, except their sun, is set.
—Lord Byron, "The Isles of Greece"

Professor Papazoglou told me that Ancient Eresos had also boasted temples to Poseidon and Dionysus, as well as an agora and a stadium. The town had been one of the great cities of Lésvos, famed for its wine and as the place where Hermes was sent to gather wheat for the gods. The professor gestured to Vigla and the surrounding fields. The area was sure to be full of archaeological treasures, lying just a meter or so below the surface, but the lack of funds kept them in the ground.

We picked our way along goat tracks and over grassy fields, in brilliant sunshine. The oak trees that were a common feature of the western part of the island shed their thorny flowers on the ground; they grew in the loneliest spots, usually in formation. I had asked a number of people about them, but no one knew why the trees had been planted. I picked up a dried oak flower, with an acorn in its heart, and listened to the professor. He was a natural teacher: he enjoyed an audience, enjoyed explaining what he knew. His enthusiastic commentary was occasionally interrupted by Tassos, who was concerned about grass burrs in his socks. "Ignat?" he'd say plaintively. "Where are we going? Where are you taking us, Ignat?"

Our last stop was a tumbledown farmhouse, erected in part from marble scrounged from the ruins. A foundation stone from the basilica lay underneath the stair, its engraved cross placed upside down; a broken column supported the veranda; and the backyard tap dripped onto what appeared to be a Doric capital. The professor rapped on one of the wooden window shutters, but there was no one home; only a goat bleated a reply.

The morning ended at Mitso's bar, where I often ate my breakfast. Mitso served good coffee and pancakes, and played Nat King Cole and Peggy Lee, music that had been popular in Sydney when he lived there. He was a melancholy soul. Whenever I praised Skala Eressóu, he would respond with a sardonic smile: *if only I knew*. And yet, despite his sadness—or perhaps because of it—he had an oddly compelling charm. He told me he often regretted returning to Greece, but the cause of this regret was hard to fathom. In Sydney he worked in a metal factory, in a food-processing plant and in a restaurant, where he had spent his days scrubbing saucepans. He described all this in dour, self-mocking tones; he knew that he could hardly be said to have left the big time behind.

Mitso now joined the professor and me for coffee. As he sat down he picked up the thorny flower that I had gathered from beneath the oak trees. "How many years has it been since I saw one of these?" he said, cradling it in his hands.

His voice expressed both bitterness and tenderness. When he was a boy, his family had cultivated the oak flowers, which he called *velonyes*. He had picked them, sorted them, stacked them, and had finally fled to Australia to escape them. The acorns were fed to the pigs, while the flowers were sold to be used in the dying and preservation of leather.

"Now they use chemicals and poison the earth," he said with a grimace, "and that is what will end us all."

Mitso gazed at the flower in his hands, but when I asked him if he wanted to keep it he looked at me as though I were mad, and dropped it on the ground. "I've seen enough of them to last me a lifetime," he said.

I wanted to return to Míthymna, a village I had visited with a girlfriend one August, thirteen years before. My memory of our week there had brought me back to Lésvos: the gray stone buildings on a hillside with their views of the water; the steep, narrow main street covered in wisteria vines; and, most of all, the night when there were no beds to be had in the village, and we had slept in a field of stubble, under a full moon, listening to the sea.

Having overcome my fear of driving, I had decided to keep the car for the duration of my stay. On a whim I took a detour to Ancient Andissa, because I believed the sign that said it was only three kilometers off the main road, and because I was enjoying meandering around the island. I soon found myself driving behind the sand dunes of a long, deserted beach. The site, when I eventually reached it, consisted chiefly of a derelict fort standing on a raised promontory, with a beach on one side and a protected cove on the other. Wild fennel, oregano, and a luxuriant fig grew between the rocks, and in the distance I could see farmers burning off nettles in their fields. Although not far from Skala Eressóu, I'd left the tourist belt way behind me; I felt like a time traveler, heading back into the island's rural past.

The roads were now unsealed: I had driven off the map. I drew up beside a farmer and his wife sitting stoically on rush-bottomed chairs, one on either side of their farmhouse. They bustled up to the car, eager to give me directions back to the main road. They had been sitting there, alone with their thoughts, just waiting; our brief chat in the fading light was their afternoon's diversion.

I spent that night in the heart of the olive-growing district. I had intended to stay in Mytilíni, but had impulsively followed the signs to Agiásos on Mount Olympus, inspired by an acquaintance in

Athens who had described Agiásos as "one of the beautiful villages
left in Greece."

The village was really a small town, steeply situated on the
mountainside. The road narrowed as I approached the dense cluster
of stone houses and shops, leading me to a vine-covered, brightly lit
square, where meat hung on hooks outside the butchers' shops and
men stood around the newsstands, smoking and gossiping. It was
Saturday evening, the shopping hour—*volta* time. The men stared
openly as I drove by, giving me the uncomfortable sensation that I
had intruded upon them.

The only pension I could find was at the top of the hill. It was
unlit; no one answered the door. As I walked back to the car, an
old lady with a scarf around her head greeted me warmly: "And
so you have come to us," she said, taking my hand in the dark,
"welcome to our village." She told me that the pension was not
closed, but merely unattended; the owner lived nearby. She walked
with me to his house, smiling sweetly all the while, before bidding
me good night.

After I had settled into my room, I walked back into the town,
passing a butcher's shop that displayed cows' heads, pigs' trotters,
sides of pork, and a huge lump of beef bleeding slowly onto an
enamel plate. Agiásos was a constricted, old-fashioned place. The
men in the square lacked the old lady's grace and made no effort to
disguise their curiosity about me. Trying to ignore their stares, I
bought a bag of apples and some pomegranates before entering a
small restaurant.

All the other customers were men who had gathered to watch a
soccer match on television. My entrance caused a hiatus in their
talk, and when their chatter resumed I felt that I was still under
covert surveillance. A man at a nearby table suddenly began talking
loudly in German, to the amusement of everyone else. At first I
couldn't tell whether he was trying to say something serious to me
or was simply making fun of a stranger. I told him in Greek that I
was Australian, and that I didn't understand German; but as he was
having some success with his performance, he ignored me and
continued his German routine, his voice and gestures unnatural,

exaggerated. He reminded me of the man in my father's village who had threatened to kill my husband when he'd first seen us in the street; later, we'd learnt that the man, a returned emigrant, was crazy; the trauma of living abroad had left him unbalanced, and with a lifelong grudge against foreigners. The man in Agiásos may well have had a similar story, but in this case his resentment had spread around the room. The waitress smiled at me, trying to make amends, but whenever she withdrew to the kitchen an atmosphere of subdued hostility remained.

That night my sleep was infected with dreams of claustrophobia, impotence, and failure. I woke wanting to escape from Agiásos, convinced that the place had infected my dreams. But that impulse was balanced by a desire to leave with a good impression of the village. It was Sunday, so I decided to attend the service at the village church; I walked down to the square as the bells rang out.

The church was full of women; this was their domain, just as the square, the restaurant and the cafés were male territory. Greek churches are usually social places: a low murmur of greetings and chat hums over the congregation, children run up and down the aisles, and men cluster around the doorway, finishing their cigarettes. But a heavy, self-conscious piety hung over the women at Agiásos; the atmosphere was as unwelcoming as the mood in the square had been the night before.

Most of the women were sitting on the left side of the church; a few men sauntered in during the latter part of the service, taking the less crowded pews on the right. Their studied casualness made a sharp contrast to the intense, emotional mood that surrounded the women. About halfway through the service, a middle-aged woman stood up and systematically genuflected before all the icons of the iconostasis. Then she walked down toward the entrance, only to turn around and make her way back up the central aisle on her knees. A much younger woman followed suit, bearing a tall candle and trailed by her mother, who was blind. The mother, in turn, clung to the arm of her son, who guided her with an air of smiling unconcern, as though unconnected with his family's fervor.

Later I learned that pilgrims visit the Agiásos church because they believe that its icon of the Virgin has healing powers. To make their way up the aisle on their knees is an act of devotion, or *tami*, a type of spiritual payment performed by those whose prayers have been answered and by those who hope that they will be. Men may also perform a *tami*, but it is traditionally women's business. Knowing nothing of this at the time, however, I took the ritual humiliation I witnessed that morning at face value; it saddened and disturbed me.

It was a relief to step outside into the sunshine, but the square held its own oppressions, I sat down outside a café to order a morning coffee, and immediately regretted it: what I really wanted to do, with a rising sense of urgency, was to get up and leave town.

The olive is a blessed tree. Hardy and long-lived, with fruit that is nourishing and useful, it is an intrinsic part of Greek cuisine and of Greek domestic life. The oil is used in delicate filo pastry; in bean and lentil soups; in sweet *kourambyedes*. It is used to dress salad, to baste meat, to moisten bread, to soften the skin, to make soap. Olive oil feeds the lanterns in roadside shrines and in grand cathedrals; it polishes the red eggs of Easter and anoints the baby in baptism. In myth, the olive tree was wise Athena's gift to the people of Attica. The olive branch is an ancient symbol of peace, but for Greeks, more particularly, the olive is also a symbol of domestic harmony. Olive oil is sacred, as bread is sacred. Like bread, it represents both poverty and wealth; the most meager rations include it, and no feast would be complete without it. The olive is a sign of modest attainment, for it is said that the smallest landowner will get by if he can produce enough oil for his table. The olive also stands for the land. The tree has been cultivated for as long as people have lived in Greece; both survive on stony ground. To a patriot, the olive is as bitter and necessary as Greek history: a reminder of hard times; a source of sustenance and continuity, of comfort and inspiration. The trees spring wild from the Greek soil; the roots go deep. Olives are a winter crop. By mid-October, the residents of Míthymna and the neighboring seaside town of Petra were beginning to spread their tarpaulins in the olive groves to catch the falling fruit. The sight reminded me immediately of my father's village. The olive groves brought back memories of the farming routines and the domestic entanglements that awaited me there, and nostalgia for the place rushed back with a familiar ache. I also noted—approvingly—the civilizing effect the olive tree continues to have in Greece. In these coastal villages on Lésvos tourism is intense and reliable, and yet the olive harvest continues. The olives slow the winter migration to Athens and Mytilíni; they provide a balance to the year.

As it was the tail end of the season, hotel prices were low. I found an elegant, self-contained apartment in a block bordering a newly planted olive grove. My room was opposite the beach at Eftalou, just out of Míthymna, with views of the sea and of the Turkish coast. Ever since I left Patmos, I had been skirting Turkey. Although its territory was so close, it was also absurdly remote: ferries traveled across the border, but ticket prices were inflated by steep customs fees; the Turkish-controlled islands of Bozcaada and Gökçeada were nearby, but excluded from Greek maps and ferry routes; Greek ferries did not make the trip up the Dardanelles to Istanbul (although Greek chartered yachts did).

In Míthymna's archaeological museum, the most touching exhibits were only eighty-three years old: framed black-and-white photographs of the Turks leaving Lésvos in November 1912. The deposed occupiers piled into wooden boats crammed with bedrolls and packs; Greek soldiers stood along the waterfront in front of a building's burned-out shell. The Turks wore balaclavas and scarves to keep warm. Although they were making just a short trip across the strait to what was notionally their homeland, the journey signaled the beginning of a lifelong exile. Already, each passenger had the hollow, worn look of a refugee.

The museum was in the basement of a neoclassical building that also served as Míthymna's town hall. Upstairs, in a cool, shuttered room, was the office of the mayor, Vathis Dimitrios, a dark-haired, dark-skinned, dark-browed man, handsome and articulate. A native of the town, he had returned to Míthymna after an exile of his own making. For fifteen years he had studied and worked as an electrical engineer in the United States, where he had been employed by

General Electric's scientific research center in North Carolina. His hunger for an intellectual challenge had driven him abroad.

"I couldn't pursue what I wanted to do in Greece. My job in the States was something I would not have left for anything. But,"—and here he spread his hands and smiled—"I came to the point where I did leave it."

He left because his daughters were ready to begin high school. He had been alarmed by the example of his sister's daughter, who had been born in the States and married an American. His niece still spoke Greek, but her children did not; he did not want his own grandchildren to share that fate.

Back in Míthymna Mr. Dimitrios had built a hotel on the outskirts of town, on land he had inherited from his family; the hotel was his livelihood now. He said he had no regrets about his decision to return: the Greek way of life made more sense to him. In the second half of his life, Míthymna offered him what the States could not: simple conviviality. "To go out regularly with your friends at night—now that is group therapy, something that doesn't exist elsewhere. That is why there are no psychiatrists here. We talk about our problems, our plans, our children. We talk about what troubles us, and what do we see? That our problems are shared by other people, that they are not ours alone; and that knowledge helps us not to worry."

But he admitted that the transition back to life in Greece had not been entirely smooth; bureaucracy had been a constant bugbear, particularly in the early years of setting up his business. The effects of lifelong tenure for public servants and the hazards inherent in any bureaucracy combine hellishly in Greece; only the wealthy and powerful are immune. Smiling thinly, Mr. Dimitrios said that in order to build his hotel, "I had to navigate the forty waves, as they say." His chief tormentor had been a clerk in the Greek National Tourist Organization, who had the job of approving the architectural plans for his hotel. Mr. Dimitrios sent the plans, with all the requisite specifications, to Athens and then telephoned to ask how long approval would take. He was told that his plans were number 1,000 on the list, and that they were now processing application number 80. They suggested he ring back in a month. And so, "like a good little American," that is what he did. And he rang the month after that, and the month after that, and the month after that. Finally, in the fifth month, Mr. Dimitrios set off for Athens to inquire about his plans in person.

"I'm sorry, I still can't help you," the clerk told him. "I am still not up to number 1,000." But, as luck would have it, Mr. Dimitrios happened to see the application on the public servant's desk: it was number 1,015.

"What's this?" he asked.

"I just pulled it out for a quick check," said the clerk.

"Well, pull mine out for a quick check."

"I will in due course."

"Good, I'll wait for you." Mr. Dimitrios then pulled up a chair and watched the man work. He stayed there for three days.

"Eventually, he couldn't work with me sitting there. By which I mean that he was accustomed to not working very hard, but with me there he had to put on a show of working. And so, finally, he said to me, 'I'll look at your file.' And do you know how long it took him? Fifteen minutes. He opened it, he read it, he signed it, and I left."

Mr. Dimitrios told me that his daughters were both studying abroad: the older girl was in the United States, pursuing her aptitude for mathematics, while the younger one was in England studying business administration. He was confident that the younger girl would return, as she would be able to find tourism work in Míthymna; but he feared that his elder daughter would stay away, as he had, and for much the same reasons.

Míthymna was as charming as I remembered, but it had also become a different place. The fishing village had metamorphosed into a wealthy and sophisticated resort; only a skeleton of the village fleet remained, and serious fishing was supplemented with moonlight fishing cruises for the visitors. Although the historic old town was protected by government decree, big hotels proliferated in the surrounding countryside. Mr. Dimitrios told me that he believed development in the district had reached a critical point: further construction would make the town too crowded, and whatever charm it still retained would be lost. The transformation of the town was already irreversible; the fields of stubble where I had once spent the night now existed only in memory.

I wanted to return to my father's village, but at the same time I was reluctant to leave Míthymna and Lésvos and the sea. In planning this leg of my journey, I had imagined that visiting the islands would be like choosing between so many pearls on a string, and I had deliberately chosen a route that would take me farther and farther out over the Aegean. I had wanted to be satiated by the sea; to know how it felt to sleep over it, to eat by it, to swim in it, for days and weeks on end. And when the time came to say good-bye to the islands, what I regretted most was not leaving a particular person or place, but letting go of this watery fancy. Despite the wind and the heedless crowds and the crazy ferry routes, I did not want to give up the world of the sea.

I left Mytilíni on the *Theophilos*, a big ferry incongruously decorated with large color photographs of Tasmania; my blue-and-red cabin featured a photo mural of the Hobart casino. The ferry pulled out at dusk, to the accompaniment of a German jazz band playing on the cruise ship moored next to us. Our siren sounded, and the Germans stopped dancing on the deck and lined up to wave: good-bye, good-bye. It was ridiculous, but touching too. People were waving at us from the harbor as well, and some of the passengers began to cry. Caïques bobbed in the stretch of sea beyond the port, black outlines against the setting sun. I strained my eyes to count them, unwilling to lose sight of the men in their little boats who would always have that view, who belonged there, in the fading light of the purple Aegean.

Katherine Kizilos was born in Australia in 1960. She has lived in Greece and now resides in Melbourne, where she works as a journalist. This story was excerpted from The Olive Grove: Travels in Greece.

RACHEL HOWARD

Hector's Bread

It is the stuff that builds community

DRIPPING WITH THYME HONEY, DRIZZLED IN OLIVE OIL AND oregano, dunked in octopus *stifado*, I couldn't get enough of the bread. Waking to the teasing aromas of Koula's kitchen, I'd lie in bed trying to guess what Corfiote delicacies she was conjuring to complement that giant loaf. Eventually, the smell of fried onions would lure me downstairs, and there was Koula, beaming, stirring a *briki* of Greek coffee. And there, like a ripe fruit waiting to be cut open, was Hector's bread. Crunchy crusts, insides like hot crumpets, a faint flavor of ash…

It wasn't just the bread that was amazing. It was the story of the baker himself. Hector Kondos has been baking since age twelve. His father established the first bakery in the village of Gastoúni in 1926. When he was prematurely killed by a raging bull, his teenage son Hector took over. For a while, Hector's uncle Achilles ran a rival establishment but was outbaked by his mythologically correct nephew. Hector was the last baker in Corfu to use a traditional wood oven. "Corfiotes travel miles for one of his loaves," Koula boasted. "Many are turned away empty-handed. Hector will not part with a single crust until all his villagers have been given their daily bread."

I had to pay homage to Hector. I found him dusting off the counter with a broken broom. A fine layer of flour coated him like a second skin, misting his spectacles. The little room was bare but lively with a flux of regulars who exchanged greetings and wisecracks. "My pregnant wife is having terrible cravings. Go on, just half a loaf!" joked a crumpled geriatric with a bloodshot twinkle in his eye. "This bread has been all the way to Australia!" bragged another whose relatives had emigrated to Melbourne. A barrel-shaped *yiayia* reminisced about leaner years as a factory worker in Germany, sustained with no more than a crust of bread stashed in her pocket. "If it had been Hector's bread, it wouldn't have been so bad," she chuckled. Hector scowled modestly, the long-suffering curmudgeon reveling in his role as village benefactor.

Most customers bought their loaves *bistiou*, on credit, paying a monthly bill. Hector marked off their names on a register, row upon cryptic row of crosses and numbers. "I have about 300 families to take care of. This way I guarantee nobody goes without. The old folks depend on me. Someone might be held up in

---

I'd been thinking about spinach pies for days. I'd take the early bus so they wouldn't be sold out. The sole off-season bakery with spinach and cheese pies on the island was a good hour away, but there were nine bus stops between my house and the pies, and the bus was traveling on Greek time.

The bakery finally came into sight. To my relief, there was no line out front. My mouth was watering.

Without so much as a friendly good morning, I ordered my spinach pie and Costas nodded. His metal tongs scooped up one. "*Oxi.*" At the next, he shrugged and told me it also was too dry to sell.

It happened so fast. Costas found all to be unsatisfactory and in one swoop he had dumped the entire batch. And that, as they say, was that.

—Roberta Beach Jacobson,
"Pie in the Sky"

the fields; it's my responsibility to make sure their loaf is waiting when they get home tired and hungry."

For fifty-three years, Hector's life had followed the same unbroken pattern: up at three, bake till noon, close for lunch, open again for latecomers in the afternoon. Sundays were spent cleaning the ovens. "It took months to persuade my father to close for a few days to have an operation," sighed his son Spyros, a mathematics professor. Neither Spyros nor his elder brother, a croupier, were prepared to shoulder the commitment of running the bakery. Both had moved out of the small family home upstairs because of their parents' unsociable hours.

Their grandmother, eighty-eight and stone deaf, was still in the back slapping dough. "She'd shrivel up and die if we made her stop working," Hector shrugged. Approaching retirement age himself, Hector had just signed the business over to his wife. "So we have a few more years left. After that, who knows…?" He trailed off and his smile evaporated. Beside the smoldering wood oven squatted another testimony to encroaching modernization: a brand-new electric oven.

In Greece, where the *papara* is practically a national dish, breaking bread is the ultimate symbol of shared experience. Hector was the soft, warm dough that held his community together. Whenever I pass a fancy Athenian bakery, piled with buns, brioches, and croissants, I long for the simple sustenance of Hector's smoky loaf.

Rachel Howard was born in London but raised in Athens. She cooked, taught, and acted her way around the world before discovering that the best way to travel was by writing about it. She did a stint as special advisor to the foreign minister of Greece, was managing editor of Greece's first national Web site (www.greece.gr), and is a regular contributor to National Geographic Traveler *and* High Life. *Currently she lives in London.*

ROBERT D. KAPLAN

Teach Me, Zorba

*Greece is a land of myth, both
classical and modern.*

IN THIS AGE OF PACKAGED TRUTH, MANY LANDS, PARTICULARLY
those of the Mediterranean, have tourist myths associated with
them: a calculated blend of images, involving history and landscape,
that form a slick vision of romance under exotic circumstances. But
unlike the other tourist myths, the Greek myth was born out of a
movement in twentieth-century literature that was eventually crys-
tallized by one of history's most memorable films.

The year 1935 is as good as any to mark the beginning of this
process. That summer, twenty-three-year-old aspiring novelist and
poet Lawrence Durrell, his wife, his mother, two brothers, a sister,
and a dog named Roger traveled from England to the Greek island
of Corfu to take up residence. The Anglo-Irish Durrells had lived
in India, where Lawrence's late father had worked as an engineer.
Upon the father's death, the family moved to England, where they
never quite struck firm roots. This led to the somewhat eccentric
and off-the-cuff decision to try Corfu.

"Our life on this promontory has become like some flawless
Euclidean statement," writes Durrell in *Prospero's Cell*, a diary-cum-
memoir of his four-year stay on Corfu. *Prospero's Cell* was a fresh
kind of travel book: a travel-in-residence guide to the "landscape

and manners" of an island, that openly combines real and imagined events in a magical setting—magical because Greece was somehow different from other places in the Mediterranean. What this difference was Durrell could describe, but he could not as yet define it, because he had never been this far east since leaving India at age ten.

Durrell wrote enthusiastically about Greece to his friend in Paris, Henry Miller, who paid Durrell a visit in 1939. A writer of unmatched exuberance and ego but little restraint, Miller, like Durrell, went through a kind of spiritual rebirth in Greece. *The Colossus of Maroussi* may be the least flawed of Miller's handful of great but flawed books. A work of uncanny power and inspiration, it reads like a nonstop series of aphorisms that have become clichés, only because Miller's phrases have been the grist for two generations of copywriters in the Greek tourist industry: "Greece had made me free and whole.... Greece is of the utmost importance to every man who is seeking to find himself.... It [Greece] stands, as it stood from birth, naked and fully revealed.... It breathes, it beckons, it answers."

But Miller also noticed "confusion, chaos.... The dust, the heat, the poverty, the bareness," all of which he realized were necessary ingredients for this atmospheric magic act that he, too, could describe but not quite define. There was a missionary zeal to Durrell's and Miller's books about Greece that was absent in other travel books, and it was linked to an enjoyment of the physical senses that bordered on annihilation. Here is Durrell, entering the water in Corfu:

> I feel the play of the Ionian, rising and falling about an inch upon the back of my neck. It is like the heartbeat of the world.... It is no longer a region or an ambience where the conscious or the subconscious mind can play its incessant games with itself; but penetrating to a lower level still, the sun numbs the source of ideas itself....

Durrell and Miller were selling Greece in almost the same way that the hippie movement would later sell California and India: as a place to escape from the world and get in touch with your inner

self. But in the 1930s, as fascism spread across the map of Europe—
and during the war that followed—the world had no use for such
self-indulgence. Only after the dehumanizing horrors of World War
II did the hedonistic message of these authors suddenly acquire an
urgency. Due to the Greek Civil War, however, Greece remained a
devastated country that was not ready for tourism.

In the mid-1950s, Durrell began writing a series of novels, to be
known as The Alexandria Quartet. At the same time, a New York
City filmmaker, Jules Dassin, went to live in Greece with his new
wife, a Greek actress, Melina Mercouri. Dassin, in a conversation
with me at his home in Athens in 1989, explained what happened
next: "Melina's mother had just returned from the movies and was
talking about this film she had seen. We got into some argument—
I can't remember it exactly—that made me realize what I was: just
some American telling everyone here in Greece how to live their
lives. My original concept was a film about a busybody. But because
Greece at the time, as an actual place, was practically unknown in
America, the movie became something else."

Never on Sunday was a low-budget, ninety-four minute, black-
and-white film in Greek, with English subtitles. "We spent as much
on a publicity party at Cannes in 1960 [where *Never on Sunday* won
the Grand Prize] as on the film itself."

The movie begins in the port of Piraeus, where a group of boor-
ish sailors accept a dare from a prostitute, Illia (played by Melina
Mercouri), to join her in a swim in the harbor. At that moment, a
cruise ship appears. Seeing the prostitute in the water, a Greek on
board yells: "Where is the American, the intellectual, he should
see this." A tourist wearing a baseball cap is brought on deck. His
name is Homer, and he is played by Dassin himself. Eyeing the nude
woman swimming in the sea surrounded by men, this amateur
philosopher is overwhelmed with inspiration and jots in his diary:
"There is the purity that was Greece!" As the camera moves in on
the diary page, the rousing bouzouki music strikes up and the film's
title flashes across the screen.

Rather than Periclean perfection, what Homer quickly finds is a
sleazy world of seaside bars, where rude waiters serve thick, syrupy

coffee and an aniseed-flavored spirit, ouzo; where men stub unfil-
tered cigarettes out on the floor and dance and smash plates to
the sounds of bouzouki music (written especially for the film by
the since-famous Greek composer Manos Hadjidakis). Homer, an
expert on Greek classical drama, realizes he knows nothing about
the strange country he finds himself in. He laments to Illia, the prostitute, whom against his better instincts he has fallen in love with:
"I don't understand it, Greece was once the greatest country in the
whole world." And she, sensuously beckoning and stretching her
arms out on a bed, replies: "It still is."

What Homer found, of course, was not classical Greece, but
something better, or at least more fun, and certainly much more
unexpected. He found the Orient and the Balkans, with their
harshest edges softened ever so slightly by the Mediterranean.

The success of *Never on Sunday* came during the same year,
1960, when Durrell published the last volume of The Alexandria
Quartet, whose complex plot, sensuous prose, and overt sexual
themes made it a best-seller. Although the Quartet is ostensibly
about the Egyptian Mediterranean port of Alexandria, it is also
about Greece. The narrator lives in peaceful reflection on an un-
named Greek island in the Cyclades. The Alexandria that Durrell
remembers is a Greek city, whose most memorable characters are
Greek or Greek-influenced. A recurrent theme in the four books is
humanity's need for a pagan counterpart (which Durrell associates
with Greece) to the ethical rigors of Judeo-Christian morality.

The popularity of the Quartet chain-reacted with *Never on
Sunday*. "There are probably no statistics, but someone told me that,
in one year, tourism to Greece shot up 800 percent," Dassin told
me. In the early 1960s, Miller's *The Colossus of Maroussi* and Durrell's
Prospero's Cell were rediscovered and went into one reprint after
another. The high point came in 1964, with the release of *Zorba the
Greek*, Michael Cacoyannis's film of the Kazantzakis novel.

Zorba the Greek portrays Greece in the same stark, black-and-
white realism as *Never on Sunday*, only more so. The film also begins
in Piraeus, but in this case it is winter and there is a rainstorm. The
hero, Zorba, played by Anthony Quinn, sings Klephtic tunes from

Macedonia and confesses to raping and looting "because they were Turks or Bulgarians." Zorba's companion is a shy Englishman of Greek origin, played by Alan Bates, shocked by what he sees and hears after he and Zorba arrive on the island of Crete.

There, villagers loot a house before the occupant, an old Frenchwoman, has even finished dying. A widow is stoned and then has her throat slit outside an Orthodox church, for the sin of enticing a younger man. In the background, always, are the vindictive stares of peasants, and men unloading their bilious hatred of women in miserable coffee shops. In place of Hadjidakis's bright, explosive bouzouki tunes from *Never on Sunday*, *Zorba the Greek* introduced the world to another Greek composer, Mikis Theodorakis, who worked with a darker and more mysterious strain in Greek music. While Mercouri fluttered across the dance floor in a wildly exhibitionist *syrtaki* step, Quinn danced a slow-motion, meditative *zeimbekiko* to the drumroll of a Theodorakis melody. When Quinn wheeled his body around on one foot, ever so slowly, his eyes fixed toward the sky, it was like the earth turning on its axis.

After watching the peasants ransack the Frenchwoman's house, after watching the widow have her throat cut, for the first time in the life of Zorba's introverted and Westernized companion, a well of emotion breaks down his protective cerebral wall. "Teach me, Zorba," he begs, suddenly overtaken by a fit of comprehending madness. "Teach me to dance!"

What these books and movies said was essentially the same: there was a certain something about Greece that Spain, Italy, and other poor, sun-drenched lands lacked: something unique and inspiring precisely because it was so harsh and unforgiving; something beautiful because it was so ugly; something happy because it was so sad; something unique yet simultaneously familiar.

Greece was where you came to lose your inhibitions. The sea and the sun-scorched stone performed as your guru. Nothing more was needed. The islands—petrified gray forms lifting magnificently out of an inky-blue sea, and sleekly graced by the blindingly white walls of cubist villages—became a terrain of lust and passion and hallucination. The Greek tourist boom of the early 1960s was a precursor of the drug cult and the sexual revolution. Leonard Cohen was a little-known Canadian poet and songwriter when he first came to Greece and settled on the island of Hydra, where he composed many of the songs for his second album, *Songs from a Room*, including "Bird on a Wire," that helped make him an icon for introverted hippies.

The early and mid-1960s constituted the golden age of Mykonos, after that island had been discovered by *Vogue* magazine and an "in" group of performing artists—Jean Seberg, Yul Brynner, and Yehudi Menuhin (a friend of Durrell's)—had acquired houses there. Elizabeth Herring, a columnist for *The Athenian* magazine in Athens, telescoped Mykonos's history for me: "When I first sailed into the island, in 1961, at the age of ten, I recall extreme poverty. There were skinny, naked kids, and you couldn't even buy pasteurized milk. By the late 1970s, the streets were filled with gold jewelry shops and on the beach I had to step over a couple making love."

We order gin and tonics, place our towels on a rocky outcrop. The water ranges from indigo to emerald green, reflecting the gradations in the sea-floor. Dimitri takes a sip of his drink and tells me about the gift that the tourists in their bikinis and the producer of the film Zorba unwittingly bestowed upon the women of Crete.

"Years ago," he says, "when the families passed land to their children, they gave what they thought were the most worthless pieces to the girls. That land was along the sea coast because the best plots inland were saved for farming. Then, the tourists starting coming. They wanted hotels on the beach. So the developers had to bargain with the women for the shoreline and some of the women became very rich."

—Joy E. Stocke, "In the Footsteps of Zorba the Greek"

The certain something that Greece had that other countries lacked—that was unique yet so familiar—was a faultlessly proportioned, atmospheric mix of East and West. The ululating quarter tones of bouzouki music, the raw material for Hadjidakis's theme song for *Never on Sunday,* are, in fact, siblings of Bulgarian and Serbian rhythms, and are close cousins of the Arab and Turkish music that, heard in its pure form, gives most Western listeners a headache. Yet run through a Mediterranean musical filter, these monotonous and orgasmic sounds of the Orient appeal perfectly to Western ears, especially when they are heard in the setting of a Cycladic island like Mykonos. The abstract grace of Cycladic island sculpture and architecture in the third millennium B.C. was the seminal force behind the artistic values that, 2,000 years later, created the Parthenon. Architecturally, what we label as "Western" first appeared in the Cyclades. This was principally why Western tourists felt so comfortable on the Greek islands while listening to that strange music whose roots they could never identify. The fact that this music was often very sad—because for the Greeks it is meant to evoke memories of the loss of Byzantium, Hagia Sofia, and Smyrna—made it no less beautiful.

The Greek tourist myth depended on this fragile yet subtle recipe: of Greece being a summation of the Balkans, yet also being something apart; of Greece being only ninety minutes by plane from the tiresome and dangerous hatreds of the Middle East, yet also being millions of miles away.

Robert D. Kaplan has reported from more than forty countries for The Atlantic Monthly *and* The New Republic, *among other publications. His magazine articles of the 1980s and early 1990s were the first by an American writer to warn of the coming cataclysm in the Balkans. He is the author of several books, including* The Coming Anarchy: Shattering the Dreams of the Post Cold War, The Arabists: The Romance of an American Elite, Soldiers of God, *and* Surrender or Starve. *This story was excerpted from* Balkan Ghosts: A Journey Through History.

JOHN FLINN

Forever on Strike

When in Greece, be prepared for anything.

THE ATHENS SHOPKEEPER PUFFED OUT HIS CHEEKS, GAVE ME ONE of those whole-body Mediterranean shrugs, and began reciting a dauntingly comprehensive roundup of the city's current labor strife: "The trains will be back running tomorrow, but the subways, the banks, and the garbage collectors will still be on strike. And, my friend,"—he leaned closer and lowered his voice—"word is that the postal service is going out—if not tomorrow, then definitely the next day."

He was translating the television news, which, from what I could gather, broadcast a nightly strike forecast, right after the weather report.

At any given time, it seems, a worrisomely large portion of Athens's work force is either walking off the job or threatening to shut down whatever slice of the national infrastructure they control. Greeks habitually use strikes as weapons in economic and social disputes the way Californians file lawsuits.

The owners of those little kiosks you see on every corner have shut down their stands over proposed tax increases. Construction workers regularly put down their jackhammers to get the jump on the next forty-eight-hour nationwide strike called by public-sector employees. Taxi drivers shut down their cabs over government antipollution proposals. Soccer teams refuse to take the field over betting-pool money they say the government owes them. Internet users have even formed virtual picket lines, refusing to log on in protest over telecom charges.

Last spring tourists were turned away from the Acropolis after employees there walked off the job to protest the transfer of a few colleagues. This came just days after the workers had returned to their jobs after a previous three-week strike. Just for good measure, Greek teachers and university lecturers went on strike the same day over a new law requiring them to take tests.

My all-time-favorite labor dispute, though, came in 1990. The Greek government enacted a tough antistrike law, and workers throughout the country responded by...well, I think you can guess.

Inevitably, news accounts describe Athens as being "paralyzed" by these strikes. That's a little like saying Seattle was brought to a standstill by its 138th consecutive day of drizzle. When the banks close for a day or two, when the ferries or post office take an extended holiday, Athenians respond with a weary, whole-body shrug. Things will be back to normal tomorrow, or the next day, or the day after that, they say. No big deal. The only ones paralyzed are visitors who fail to take this into account in their trip planning.

People like, well, my wife Jeri and me.

We were already down to our last few drachmas due to a bank strike that prevented us from cashing traveler's checks or drawing a cash advance on our credit cards. At the railway station in Lithoro, at the foot of Mount Olympus, word spread up and down the platform that the trains were on strike that day.

I cursed Zeus and every other Greek god I could think of, and threw in a few Roman gods for good measure. We had to be in Athens by evening to use our prepaid, nonrefundable tickets on the overnight ferry to Crete, where we had prepaid, nonrefundable hotel reservations. Only a fool, I was beginning to realize, tries to keep to a tight schedule in Greece.

Well, it turned out that one train did run in Greece that day, apparently at the behest of the military, which filled virtually every seat with soldiers on their way from Thessaloníki to Athens. The rest of us crowded shoulder-to-shoulder into the aisles, doorwells and toilets, and heaved a collective groan as yet another horde forced its way aboard at each station. Picture your worst nightmare commute on the bus, and then try to imagine enduring those conditions all the way from San Francisco to Bakersfield.

In Athens, we discovered that the subway to the port city of Piraeus was also on strike. With less than an hour before our ferry's departure and no empty taxis in sight, I sat down on the curb to have a good cry.

And then a miracle happened. A taxi pulled up and disgorged its occupants right in front of us, and we were able to jump in ahead of half a dozen shoving businessmen. Hearing our story, the driver took it as a personal challenge to get us to the port on time. It was rush hour, a time when Athens's creeping traffic grinds to a horn-honking, exhaust-belching standstill, but our driver zipped through back alleys and under flapping clotheslines, scooted the wrong way down one-way streets, and made gravel-spraying detours onto unpaved shoulders.

We screeched to a halt at the dock just as they were beginning to pull up the gangplank. And then a jolt of panic shot through me. We hadn't discussed how much this cab ride would cost, and as I turned my pockets inside out I realized that whatever the fare was, I didn't have it.

I smiled weakly and held up a pathetic little wad of crumpled, small-denomination drachma notes, but the driver waved it off. He gave me one of those whole-body Mediterranean shrugs and said, "Welcome to Athens. Now go catch your ferry."

John Flinn is the travel editor of the San Francisco Examiner. *He lives in the often foggy coastal town of Pacifica south of San Francisco.*

Taunting the Oracle

*The author visits Delphi and finds
a riddle of modern Greece.*

WE HAD SAILED SOUTH OF THE LARGE ISLAND OF CEPHALONIA, AND passed Missolonghi, where Lord Byron had died, into the Gulf of Corinth, anchoring off the small Greek village of Galaxídion, on a bay just below Delphi. Indeed, beneath the glittering slopes of Mount Parnassus.

Tenders took us ashore, where we were greeted by the guides.

"My name is Clea. The driver's name is Panayotis. His name means 'The Most Holy.' He has been named after the Blessed Virgin." The driver smiled at us and puffed his cigarette and waved. "Apollo came here," Clea said.

Near this bauxite mine? Great red piles of earth containing bauxite, used to make aluminum, had been quarried from the depths of Itéa under Delphi to await transshipment to Russia, which has a monopoly on Greek bauxite. In return, Russia swaps natural gas with Greece. Such a simple arrangement: we give you red dirt, you give us gas. Apollo came here?

"He strangled the python to prove his strength as a god," Clea went on, and without missing a beat. "The yacht *Christina* came here as well, after Aristotle Onassis married Jackie Kennedy, for their honeymoon cruise."

Through an olive grove that covered a great green plain with thousands of live trees, not looking at all well after a three-month drought, we climbed the cliff to Delphi, the center of the world. The navel itself, a little stone toadstool *omphalos*, is there on the slope for all to see.

"I must say several things to you about how to act," Clea began.

There followed some nannyish instructions about showing decorum near the artifacts. This seemed very odd piety. It was also a recent fetish. After almost two thousand years of neglect, during which Greek temples and ruins had been pissed on and ransacked — the ones that had not been hauled away (indeed, rescued for posterity) by people like Lord Elgin had been used to make the walls of peasant huts — places like Delphi were discovered by intrepid Germans and Frenchmen and dug up.

Delphi had not been operational since the time of Christ. In the reign of Claudius (A.D. 51) "the site was impoverished and half-deserted," Michael Grant writes in his *Guide to the Ancient World*, "and Nero was said to have carried 500 statues away." Delphi was officially shut down and cleared by the Emperor Theodosius (379–395), who was an active campaigner for Christianity. It is no wonder that what remains of Delphi are some stumpy columns and the vague foundations of the temples — hardly anything in fact except a stony hillside and a guide's Hellenistic sales pitch. Anyone inspired to visit Delphi on the basis of Henry Miller's manic and stuttering flapdoodle in *The Colossus of Maroussi* would be in for a disappointment.

The Greeks had not taken very much interest in their past until Europeans became enthusiastic discoverers and diggers of their ruins. And why should they have cared? The Greeks were not Greek, but rather the illiterate descendants of Slavs and Albanian fishermen, who spoke a debased Greek dialect and had little interest in the broken columns and temples except as places to graze their sheep. The true philhellenists were the English — of whom Byron was the epitome — and the French, who were passionate to link themselves with the Greek ideal. This rampant and irrational philihellenism, which amounted to almost a religion, was also a reaction to the confident dominance of the Ottoman Turks, who were widely regarded as savages and heathens. The Turks had brought their whole culture, their language, the Muslim religion, and their distinctive cuisine not only here but throughout the Middle East and into Europe, as far as Budapest. The contradiction persists, even today: Greek food is actually Turkish food, and many words we think of as distinctively Greek, are in reality Turkish—kabob, *doner*, *kofta*, meze, *taramasalata*, dolma, yogurt, moussaka, and so forth; all Turkish.

Signs to the entrance to Delphi said, "Show proper respect" and "It is forbidden to sing or make loud noises," and "Do not pose in front of ancient stones."

I saw a pair of rambunctious Greek youths being reprimanded by an officious little man for flinging their arms and posing for pictures. The man twitched a stick at them and sent them away.

Why was this? It was what you would expect to happen if you put a pack of ignoramuses in charge of a jumble of marble artifacts they had no way of comprehending.

One should not race along the Sacred Way in a motorcar—it is sacrilege. One should walk, walk as the men of old walked, and allow one's whole being to become flooded with light. This is not a Christian highway: it was made by the feet of devout pagans on their way to initiation at Eleusis. There is no suffering, no martyrdom, no flagellation of the flesh connected with this processional artery. Everything here speaks now, as it did centuries ago, of illumination, of blinding, joyous illumination. Light acquires a transcendental quality: it is not the light of the Mediterranean alone, it is something more, something unfathomable, something holy. Here the light penetrates directly to the soul, opens the doors and windows of the heart, makes one naked, exposed, isolated in a metaphysical bliss which makes everything clear without being known.

—Henry Miller, *The Colossus of Maroussi (1941)*

They would in their impressionable stupidity begin to venerate the mute stones and make up a lot of silly rules. The "Show proper respect" business and "No posing" was an absurd and desperate transfer of the orthodoxies of the Greeks' tenacious Christianity, as they applied the severe prohibitions of their church to their ruins. Understanding little of the meaning of the stones, they could only see them in terms of their present religious belief; and so they imposed a sort of sanctity on the ruins. This ludicrous solemnity was universal in Greece. Women whose shorts were too tight and men wearing bathing suits were not allowed to enter the stadium above Delphi, where the ancients had races stark ballocky naked. In some Greek places photography of ruins was banned as sacrilegious.

In spite of this irrationality, the place was magical, because of its natural setting, the valley below Delphi, the edge of a steep slope, the pines, the shimmering hills of brilliant rock, the glimpse of Mount Parnassus. Delphi was magnificent for the view it commanded, for the way it looked outward on the world. The site had also been chosen for the smoking crack in the earth that it straddled, that made the Oracle, a crone balancing on her tripod, choke and gasp and deliver riddles.

"What kind of child will I give birth to?" someone would ask the Oracle," Clea said. "And the Oracle was clever. She would say, 'Boy not girl,' and that could mean boy or girl, because of the inflection."

There is a statue in the Delphi museum of Antinous, lover of the Emperor Hadrian, which is surely one of the finest sculptures of all time. Henry Miller refers to Antinous as the "last of the Gods." I couldn't have agreed more, although I hadn't read Miller at the time. I gaped openly at the statue, astounded by the beauty of the human form as rendered by an unknown master.

—Sean O'Reilly, "Footloose in Antiquity"

"I don't get it," someone said. "If the Oracle could see the future, why did she bother to speak in riddles?"

"To make people wonder."

"But if she really was an Oracle, huh, why didn't she just tell the truth?"

"It was the way that oracles spoke in those days," Clea said feebly.

"Doesn't that mean she really didn't know the answer?"

"No."

"Doesn't that mean she was just making the whole thing up?"

This made Clea cross. But the scholar Michael Grant describes how the prophecies were conservative and adaptable to circumstances, and he writes of the Oracle, "Some have...preferred to ascribe the entire phenomenon to clever stage management, aided by an effective information system."

Clea took us to the museum, where one magnificent statue, a life-sized bronze of a charioteer, was worth the entire climb up the hill. As for the rest I had some good historical sound bites for my growing collection.

—The Oracle sat on this special kettle and said her prophecies.

—Pericles had very big ears, which is why he is always shown wearing a helmet.

On the way back to the ship, while the guide was telling the story of Oedipus—how he got his name, and killed his father, and married his mother, while frowning and somewhat shocked *Seabourne* passengers listened—I began to talk to my friends, who told me about their recent win at the Kentucky Derby.

Paul Theroux is the author of many books, among them travel classics such as Riding the Iron Rooster, The Old Patagonian Express, The Great Railway Bazaar, The Happy Isles of Oceania, *and* The Pillars of Hercules, *from which this story was excerpted.*

Lessons from the Taverna

There is no better window on the
world than a taverna.

"I DEFY YOU TO FIND POVERTY ANYWHERE IN GREECE AS wrenching as what you see on Washington Street in downtown Boston, any hour of the day." Kostas Gavraglou makes the claim in his quiet professor's voice, at the Taverna Psarra, where Katherine and I are about to be treated to untempered Greek hospitality. Kostas and his wife Anne have been alerted to our arrival by a mutual friend, a philosopher of science with whom Kostas and I have both studied in America; the courtliness the Gavraglous shower on us is an extension of their regard for him. One goes to a taverna for dinner not before eight-thirty at night. Nine is better, ten o'clock prime time. Out of deference to our recent arrival from Boston where restaurants often *close* at ten o'clock, the Gavraglous come to our hotel at eight and lead us on a winding walk up the hill, through courtyards, shops, and tavernas seamed together by stairs, arbors, and strings of lights, until we reach the Psarra.

The name means fish. Outside the fishing villages, where, as we soon learn, the price scarcely shows up on the bill, fish is quite expensive in Greece. But Psarra is a rare city taverna that serves fresh, affordable fish. In other ways, too, Psarra betrays village roots, its clock slow as a sleepy town. It is the one taverna in the foothills of the Acropolis that makes no special appeal to the tourists flowing up the hills, leaving to other eateries the practice of lining the cobbled streets with *soi-disant* sauve men who perform like crosses between maítres d'hôtel and carnival barkers, calling out price, quality, and invitations in whatever tongue they suspect a visitor might speak. At the Psarra, a sloe-eyed, plump fellow subliminally notes one's arrival from his chair by the door, nods (possibly in sleep), and sometime later lumbers over with the standard taverna issue: paper tablecloth, a basket holding the mediocre bread, and silverware wrapped in napkins. To call the bread mediocre is no slur against Psarra. All the bread in Greece is mediocre—of refined flour, white, neither textured nor flavorful—and this is a surprise in a country of village-scale agriculture. In America, we have watched the migration of good, whole-grain breads into the boutique markets for the rich, and the peddling of something called "Wonder" to the poor, but I had imagined alive and satisfying bread to be a birthright of a people who live close to the land.

A vast tree grows in the center of the Psarra café: the roots have erupted between stones, causing the sloped dining plateau to be forever uneven. Limbs and leaves shade thirty tables, the kitchen structure, and nearby leather shop. Logging and stock-grazing severely deforested Greece as early as A.D. 300, and since these practices have relentlessly continued and there is today but slight interest in (and neither government nor private money given for) reforestation, tree and spring are welcome events of the landscape. Within hours of driving down the eastern prong of the Peloponnese, one knows viscerally why shade and water, and their sources, are revered and have been since the time of the bucolic and pastoral poets. It is an excellent sign when a taverna, or anything else, is located under a tree.

Under the Psarra's tree is scattered a medley of chairs and tables, bound in common only by their wobble. Most city tavernas have molded aluminum or plastic chairs, but the Psarra uses wooden tables and wooden chairs, and, like the country tavernas, paints them blue: teal, navy, dark, baby, light, or sea. Blue, one soon realizes, is the national hobby. (Another day, in a bright midday June sun, a woman of perhaps eighty-six, in widow's weeds, slowly repaints ten of

Psarra's wooden chairs; she uses a two-inch brush and a half-pint can of blue enamel, no drop cloth, merely semicareful strokes, and a tolerance she shares with her culture for the splatters of color that land on floors and stucco walls. Boats and chairs, windows, walls, and the hook-necked gourds hung to decorate the undersides of arbors are some of the things painted annually in Greece; the painting places are easily found, marked by layers of polychrome speckles.)

For dinner for four at Psarra, Kostas orders the following: fried squid; gopas, a large bony fish from the sardine family that is easily filleted, leaving a limber Fritz-the-Cat cartoon skeleton; greens similar to the collards of Alabama; thick ovals of fried potatoes; Greek salads; plates of steamed zucchini; bread; wine; and a plate of cut lemons. Twelve plates are crowded onto the table and, while small individual plates are handed to each diner, it is clear that to use them as more than a staging or boning platform is gratuitous, even rude. Over a long, courtly, and warm evening, Kostas and Anne demonstrate that the host/guest tradition celebrated in the *Odyssey* has endured. And they show us how to eat in a taverna, that is, they initiate us into the foods, the manners, and, without speaking of it directly, point us toward the secret of the village taverna.

Three weeks later, by the time our consorts Peter and Tony have arrived and we have all come upon the remote fishing village of Skala Sikiminias on the northern coast of Lésvos one mile from Turkey, we have learned just enough to enter into the communion that occurs throughout Greece in the great ritual of the village taverna. The conditions of the communion are not inevitable, nor spontaneously or easily achieved, nor, once found, enduring, nor even, I should think, apparent and meaningful to all participants, native or foreign. The intricacy and fragility of the conditions belie the notion that a spontaneous harmony is the natural estate of our species. For this particular communion to arise, Skala Sikiminias must have a climate and soil for vegetables and melons, and a fertile patch of the sea; it must be remote enough so cruise ships don't swarm, and close enough so that a few will come to be harvested like sardines. It must have an enormous boulder just offshore that provides the anchor for a harbor wall, a broad enclosure and promenade which snugs the fleet of fishing boats and accepts the wheel of infant prams, gangly courtship, working nets, and the labored climb of the old to the minute chapel perched on the rock. It must have a family-run taverna that serves, from dawn until early in the dark new morning, as the public living room of the village. The village must have inhabitants who are both ingenious and willing to mix their ingenuity into one soil; a people who may moon for faraway lands, but who come home after Athens, after life on the cruise ships, to tend *this* olive grove, *this* chapel by the sea—*Panayia Gorgona* it is called, the chapel of the mermaid.

Should these conditions— unique to this one village on Lésvos, different in every other place—be achieved and reachieved by each genera- tion, the taverna is a clock where the very rich hours turn their rounds. Through- out the long Mediterranean day, foods stream into the liv- ing room in baskets, sacks, plastic containers, and shop- ping bags. A back door exists in the taverna building and is used for taking out garbage, but suppliers to the commu-

> B
> ut when the artichoke is in flower…
> one might have the shadow
>   under the rock,
> and the wine of Biblis,
> a curd cake, and all the milk that
>   the goats
> can give you,
> the meat of a heifer bred in
>   the woods,
> who has never borne a calf,
> and of baby kids also. Then, too,
>   one can sit
> in the shadow
> and drink the bright shining
>   wine, his heart
> satiated with eating…
>   —Hesiod, *Works and Days*

nion make their deliveries by crossing the shaded front apron of the taverna among the tables and chairs and diners, entering the wide front doors. A typical early morning delivery begins when a Dutch couple place an order for yogurt with honey; minutes later a woman brings four containers of fresh-made yogurt from her neighboring house. A wiry farmer lugs in a lumpish burlap bag of onions; the taverna owner strolls up from the shore with a round basket brim-ful of glinting sardines. By ten o'clock, the first of a daylong pro-cession of six-year-old boys scampers in with limp octopus and an eel held by the gills. The baker sends his assistant down the small hill with a shopping bag of hot, fresh, mediocre rolls. Not only sup-pliers to the feast, but diners also are expected to come into the kitchen; one orders by repeatedly admiring and pointing to the array of hot dishes and chilled fishes. Next to the food cases, on a shelf amidst a stack of ripe red tomatoes, sits the village radio-tele-phone. The one telephone of the village sits in the tomato harvest like a tiny, perhaps friendly, alien craft landed in an Iowa cornfield, and its light-emitting diode pulses out resonant tomato-red numer-als. Overhead, the wall is crusted with snapshots, all curling, of the owner's family linking arms with tourists, cousins, and returnees from Athens and Kos.

Sitting is a constant and important activity in the taverna com-munion. Early-morning sitting is done by fishermen returned from lamp-fishing at night; after unloading the catch, they sit astraddle baskets three feet in diameter, each of which holds one taxi-cab-yellow-nylon or pale-yellow rope net. The nets are laced with corks and hooks, and after each use the men rearrange them, smoothing all the hooks in one direction. Even earlier morning sitting is done by clusters of women at the work tables in the taverna: peeling skins from braised tomatoes, chopping garlics and onions into rolling foothills, turning the mounds with their shiny, flavored hands. Even earlier morning sitting is done by dozens of cats, motionless medi-tators before the bows of unloading fishing boats until a silver fish comes flying from the deck to land on the dock, compelling them into a flurry of fur and claws.

Greek cats are thin, foxlike affairs, with ears large in proportion to delicate heads and jaws. The cats are not pets but hard-working members of the chain of being that involves legumes, olives, kelp, clams, fishes, rats, cats, amphibious children, fishermen, crones, tourists, the evil eye, and saints. The cat population is very large and fends for itself. When a fish-delivery truck pulls away one early morning from the dock of Skala Sikiminias and runs squarely over

the legs of a young marmalade dozing under its axles, neither the
driver nor any of the nearby fishermen, nor shopkeepers setting up
postcard racks, nor backgammon players, nor kitchen workers, nor
children even faintly move to tend it. Nor had the villagers stirred
to shoo the cat from under the wheels as it became clear to all
within eyeshot that it would likely be squashed. Only three
American tourists having tea and breakfast rolls at the far end of the
square leap up and start toward the unfolding accident. Too late; and
the wounded cat itself seems to expect neither warning nor first
aid, but soundlessly drags itself into a nearby shed.

No miserable sitting still is done by children in or near the taverna; they play under and between the table legs, chase cats, jump
stone walls, squash plants, prance by with aquatic things. Midafternoon sitting is done by the old men, who emerge in their places at
the old men's tables much the way mushrooms arrive on the lawn,
soundlessly, without any apparent motion. Wonderfully, the word for
"occupied" in Greek, as in "I am occupied just now," includes the
meaning "I am sitting." The old men have reached this purest meaning, for although they can be drawn into political talk and sliding
checkers across a checkerboard, most often the sitting of the old
men appears to be entirely unsullied by any motion, telos, or
worldly distraction. Late-night sitting is done by the oldest women
in the village, who sit flat on the floors of their porches and courtyards, in gangs of six or more, their black-stockinged legs straight
out, crocheting curtains and napkins on the round shelves of their
stomachs, eating massive bowls of popcorn and, it must be said,
cackling, until two o'clock in the morning. Just before the old
women emerge for night sitting, and periodically during their
tenure, the smell of hot oil and corn rises, and the street smells like
a disembodied Bijoux movie theater.

Some sitting is episodic; an old peddler with watery eyes appears
in town, lays out tin plates, nicked Swiss army knives, key chains,
cigarette lighters, and pictures of the Madonna on a stone wall, and
sits for one week, drinking coffee in a chair under a nearby awning.
Some sitting is hard-won: in an ongoing pas de deux, waiters vigorously shoo gypsies away from the taverna with roughly the same

success one meets when shoo-
ing away a housefly, and then,
once or twice during the
hottest swath of the day, re-
lent, allowing three chubby
gypsy women peddling bun-
dles of one-dollar tablecloths
to settle on a shady bench and
slowly drink glasses of water.
Tourist sitting is more desul-
tory, done at all times of the
day. A German woman sits for
hours reading Kierkegaard.
Alone. At noon, a cruise ship
drops anchor beyond the harbor and by launch brings 400
traveling souls to the taverna.
To one side of the taverna
there is a huge, unshaded side
terrace created for just this
purpose. Normally this terrace is empty, even ignored as
though it were a non-terrace;
during the hour-long swarm,
its chairs are briefly occupied
to bursting.

At nine-thirty or ten o'-
clock on weekend nights,
beautifully dressed clusters of
former native sitters and relatives of native sitters arrive in
the taverna from their homes
in the city. After the Second
World War, the horrendous
civil war in Greece continued,
with much bloodshed in the

Patrick Leigh Fermor, his
wife, Joan, and their friend
the writer Xan Fielding sat
down to eat their taverna dinner
at a table set out at the water's
edge on the flagstones that
"flung back the heat like a
casserole with the lid off."
Suddenly they decided to pick
up their iron table, neatly laid
out, and set it down a few yards
out to sea, followed by their
three chairs, then by the three
of them sitting down with the
cool water up to their waists.
They weren't the first or the last
to offer that kind of challenge
to the heat at a Greek shore, but
they were unusual in that they
were fully dressed. Yet the really
significant action occurred when
the waiter came out, gazed in
surprise at the space they'd left
empty on the flagstone quay,
then, "observing us with a
quickly masked flicker of pleasure," stepped without further
hesitation into the sea and
"advanced with a butler's
gravity" to put down their
meal before them.

—Edmund Keeley, *Inventing
Paradise: The Greek Journey*

countryside. The prevailing regime found ways to round up villagers and persuade them into Athens. The city was swollen within
a few years to four times its former population, and many villages
shriveled. The migration into Athens continues, and among the
professional and working classes of Greece are many city dwellers
who have left their childhood villages. They often drive back on
Friday and Saturday nights: they come in couples, in groups of six
or eight, and cluster around one long table, perhaps visiting with a
fisherman brother who stayed, ordering the catch of the day and,
in mid-June, *kolokithia lololuthia*—the small folded squash-blossom
pockets of rice, rosemary, onions, and cheese that taste like chloro-
phyll and color. After eating, the fisherman brother, who lamp-
fishes during much of the night, leaves the others at the table and
motors his boat out of the harbor to work. In a while you will see
his lamps set out in a string, like Christmas tree lights, bobbing on
the surface of the sea. The others linger: one young man has
brought his guitar, and one of the women, who is plump and pretty
in a tight red dress, gets him to play it and stirs her friends into
singing Greek folk songs. Some in the group are embarrassed, some
not at all. The scene appears to be the equivalent of young
American financial consultants sitting around a Vermont inn wearing new Bean boots and ironed chamois shirts, singing "Green
Grow the Rushes Ho." After the singing starts in earnest, the taverna owner's flushed, handsome son, Nikos—who manages the
table service and talks exuberant if not smooth English with the
customers—lowers the taped Theodorakis that comes from a
walnut-veneer speaker wired in the tree, and the returnees have the
floor to harmonize for the night.

In June, at the harbor taverna of Skala Sikiminias the evening air
is reliably balmy, breezy. Each night, we gather during the early
evening hour that bathes boats, cats, trees, faces, and stones in an
intense coral light. We sit at a blue table on blue chairs and tell of
divergent field trips. Peter, who spends his day in a mask and flip-
pers underwater, draws a detailed picture of a fish who flies along
the bottom with blue wings and eight legs. After the orange-red sun
grows too heavy for the sky and slides behind Turkey, the lights

strung through the trees come on. Humans and leaves collaborated in darkening patterns; speech emerges from the tables on a murmuring continuum with sounds from the sea. We order food in the manner of Kostas: marrow lolls in a shallow pond of lemon juice, the greens wade in greens liquor, and fishes yield their flesh from supple bones like fossils. Now and then our forks, approaching the same potato oval, clink in midair. Of the Penan Urun tribe's wild boar feasts in East Malaysia, the poet Carol Rubenstein has written that the sharing of their hunt meat "unites the group and binds it in communion with the forest animal whose life force and flesh they have ingested." Surely the people of Skala Sikiminias are bound with the zucchini blossoms and gopa fish of their biome; even we brief visitors can feel the molecular tug, and our conversion, if allowed to continue, would require no ideology other than greens and things with blue wings. The communion occurs not only among different species along the fluent chain, but among the several layers of the human brain; particularly, the old reptilian brain of instinct courts, and is well received by, the outer rind, the big frontal cortex full of ideas. One afternoon I watch two tiny, slippery-wet boys splash in the water near a manta ray that their father has caught and put in a shallow box for safekeeping. The boys are so nearly aquatic that they easily recall the evolution of the human brain—that onion at the top of the spinal cord—from origins in the salty sea.

The ongoing ordinary communion of the rural Greek taverna is, after all, a form of travel in which individual boundaries become transluscent, allowing for an expansion of the self into a larger gyre of being. As the expansion of the narrow into the great occurs, I wonder if we can also follow Blake's maxim to infuse the great with the particularity of the small. Can we take love of the particular place with us to the foreign regions where our bodies and spirits must go? I suppose this is to ask, Can we expand the notion of what *home* is? As we understand through our knowledge of global warming et al., the village of Skala Sikiminias and a Kentucky farm community are one geography. Moreover, the landscapes that matter most to us occur in patches all over the planet: a wooden porch in

Tuscaloosa, Alabama, with sulfur winds blowing in from the paper mills; a cement terrace on Lésvos ringed with gardenia bushes.... On our earthly travels, we encounter a being whose diversity and vastness challenge our emotional and intellectual assumptions about both self and home.

For the cautious, there can be no better place to begin to take the pleasures of ecological communion than in a Greek village taverna. Here, the tender fish taken into one's body is an enactment of the process by which any individual enters into a larger whole. In the case of the fish dinner, one welcomes with gratitude the end of the fish as fish, the beginning of fish as oneself. Moreover, by the immediate communion with other humans, sea creatures, trees, and time—the knowledge that this experience has occurred and reoccurred, here, over a great round of years—one may experience the analogous motion: in ritual time, one may take one's place in the full circle of life and sense less with dread than with calm that other passage that leads into the Earth. These yieldings occur lightly—as a story is told, a plate passed. The secret of the taverna is to make one a conscious member of a being of complexity and beauty. This ongoing naturally erotic encounter with our world, with our species and the creatures with whom we participate in a being called Earth, is our common wealth. In whose interest is it that wealth has been defined otherwise?

Emily Hiestand is a visual artist and writer, author of Green the Witch-Hazel Wood, Angela the Upside Down Girl, *and* The Very Rich Hours, *from which this story was excerpted. Her writing has appeared in* The Nation, The New Yorker, *and* The Atlantic Monthly, *among other publications. She has received the National Poetry Series award, "Discovery"/The Nation, and the Whiting Writers Award. She lives in Cambridge, Massachusetts with her husband, the musician and journalist Peter Niels Dunn.*

PIPPA STUART

Sweat and Sage on Samos

Some things only live as olfactory memories.

WE ALMOST LOSE COUNT OF THE TIMES WE HAVE TRAVELED TO THE
green isle of Samos. Years ago we had our first flight from Athens in
a small propeller plane: we went over the isles of Paros and Ikaría,
with Turkey rising up on the horizon, then down above the
wooded hills of Samos, over Mount Kerkis, and swooped at last
along the small runway at Pythagorio (ancient Samos). As we drove
from the south to the north of the island, there was an almost-
instant impression of a leisurely, donkey's-trot pace of life.

The village we came to was quite unsophisticated, with friendly,
old-fashioned family shops and no supermarkets. When the fruit-
seller's donkey walked in the door of the Hellenic Bank, the clerks
rushed out, not to chase it away but to buy grapes and peaches.
When we came that first time the season was over, we were the only
guests in the newly opened hotel, and almost the only tourists. We
sometimes used the erratic bus service but mostly went by foot
along to the great sweep of shore at Potámi.

Back then the new road leading along the cliffs toward Mikro
Seitani and Megalo Seitani was, happily, not even thought of. We
climbed a narrow stony track, up and up into the olive groves.
Everything then was a voyage of discovery. We walked over a carpet

75

of russet grasses, under pines, and past the century-old, dry-stone olive terraces. The hazy autumn light enfolded us like a golden garment, and hoopoes called along with blackbirds.

One day, into the stillness came a far-off swishing sound, a tinkling and jingling. Following it, we came upon a man cutting swaths of sage; two donkeys were tethered beside him, snuffling, shaking their ears, and clinking their harnesses. The man was so absorbed in his work that it took a while for him to become aware of the presence of strangers. He was lean and brown, with a face creased and furrowed by the seasons and outdoor living, yet he looked somehow ageless.

His first act was one of Grecian hospitality: he poured water for us from a flask, watching us while we drank as if sizing us up. We had arrived from Scotland, weary and longing for a leisurely holiday of walking and swimming, but mostly we wanted to just sit under the olives, reading and writing.

The water we drank must have had something in it of perpetual youth, for never before or since have we had so energetic a holiday. This Greek, Dmitri, had no idea of where we came from; tourists were to him an unknown breed. He only knew the race of toilers. His conception of life was summed up in one word—*doolya* (work).

He might look ageless but he was not young, and he could do with helpers. We fitted the bill. There was no point in saying that we were on holiday and wanted to rest. What were holidays? What was rest? They had no meaning for him.

There we were, Ariel or Caliban to this Samotian Prospero, cutting sage, rosemary, lavender, thyme, oregano, wild marjoram, and a host of herbs that were unknown to me. Farewell to all thoughts of sweet idleness. We were taken up into a world of blazing sunshine; of mingled fragrances; of blue and golden light, birdsong, and the tranquil munching and jingling harnesses of Ariera and Arietta, the donkeys.

We were allowed brief rests to drink the spring water of Samos. We knew very little Greek then, and Dmitri not a word of English, but somehow or other, wonderfully, we communicated. As we talked on those breaks, we began to understand his dreams of those ships that would sail from the port of Vathí or from the little harbor at Karlovasi and go over to Piraeus, and then all over the world, carrying his herbs—"our herbs," he sometimes added magnanimously. Then, remembering, he would spring to his feet and shout "*doolya!*" We would repeat Ariel's "I must obey, his art is of such power." He smiled, not understanding a word but liking the sound of it.

Every day we were ready to climb the steep track from Potámi, up to the olive groves and the fields of sage. We became increasingly skillful, tying up bundles of thyme, marjoram, and lavender and stuffing them into sacks that hung from the donkeys' wooden saddles. The final proof, if one was needed, of the power of Dmitri's art was that, forgetting a lifelong terror of heights, I was able to ride side-saddle on Arietta as she descended the sheer rocky tracks along the cliff's edge. With Dmitri holding the bridle, there was no danger of flying over Arietta's tall ears and falling down to where the sea churned on the rocks far below.

We rode along to the bay at Mikro Seitani, then, finally, to the loveliest shore of all at Megalo Seitani. The rare monk seals still bred there in those days. Here Dmitri lit a driftwood fire and boiled water in a black pot, stirring in sprigs of sage and brewing up *ptisan*. We drank it along with fresh-baked goat cheese, tomatoes, and olives. We had time to swim, then "*doolya!*"—back to cutting sage and thyme.

In the late afternoon, with the mysterious blue twilight gathering, we returned to what Dmitri called his "pharmacy." It was a large barn filled with hay and herbs, where, in the last war, Italian soldiers had slept. One of them, sick for home and for peace, had written, ironically, on the walls: *Dulce et decorum est pro patria mori*….(It's sweet and proper to die for one's country.) We piled up our perfumed packs, the latest cuttings, and called, in parting from our Prospero, "Till tomorrow!"

"*Doolya!*" was his unfailing reply.

When we got back to our hotel, bedraggled and sun-scorched, our host stared at us incredulously. "Where have you been all day? Working? That's no way to spend a holiday! Who is this Dmitri?"

Days passed. Our vacation time was running out, and Dmitri had begun to take on a thoughtful look. We had managed to convey to him that we had to return to our country. He had quite other plans for us. Where was *Skotia* anyway? He had never heard of this small, cold, sunless land in the north. Far better to stay on for the warm winter in Samos. Besides, there was the grape harvest in Idroussa, the olive crop to gather in Pagóndas, sage still to cut in Kalívia.

On our last evening, just when we had begun to pack, we were called down to the reception desk: someone wished to speak to us. We hardly recognized our Greek Prospero in a fine brown jacket.

"I have come to give you your pay, since you insist on leaving," he said grandly, looking around the shining, brand-new hotel, unimpressed. Our pay was a bulky, sweet-smelling bundle of herbs. "I'd like to buy some of your sage," the hotelkeeper said, his hand moving toward his pocket. Dmitri halted it in midmovement. "You *work* for these," he said. "You don't *buy* them!"

We walked with him as far as the barn, which stood on the shore. A storm was brewing and the sea was rising. "Poseidon is at work," Dmitri said with satisfaction, as if he and Poseidon had been weaving spells together.

Waves came surging over the breakwater, soaking us in spray. "If by your art you have put the wild waters in this roar, allay them!" we said. Dmitri smiled, as always, at our quotations with their fine strange sound.

When we shook hands, bidding him good-bye, we sensed that he was sorry to lose not his most skilled workers but perhaps his most willing. "*Poli doolya!*" he called back to us, adding something else. But he had vanished, swallowed up in darkness, and his voice was carried away by the howling gale. He could have been repeating Prospero's farewell to Ariel: "I shall miss thee, but yet thou shalt have thy freedom." We would miss him; we had grown used to one another in those autumn weeks, bound closely together in the joy of shared work. The next day our plane was delayed. We sat waiting in the little airport at Pythagorio. Perhaps Dmitri was right after all: we would winter in Samos; no plane or ship would ever venture forth at this season. Toward evening the wind dropped, and a tiny black speck appeared above Mount Kerkis, flying nearer and nearer. Soon we were off, across the storm-tossed Aegean.

Over the years we have come again and again to Samos, finding quite different delights, but none so wonderful as that first encounter with a magician in the fields of sage. We had the good fortune to know the island before the great wave of tourism invaded it: a time when the rough old tracks twisting among the hills were the only ones; when donkeys were the best and surest means of transport; when monk seals safely bred, untroubled by speedboats and the noise of transistors; when jackals might still be glimpsed high on Mount Ambelos.

We were lucky to have enjoyed those gentler days, that simplicity of living, lost perhaps forever. We need only the faintest sniff of sage to be transported back to that enchanted season of working for our Greek Prospero, and to hear again the echo of his relentless "*Poli doolya*." For there's more work.

Pippa Stuart has an obsession for European languages and birds, which she attributes to her good fortune in being born to a father with a love for birds and poetry and a mother whose special passion was for those human birds known as "lame ducks." She has traveled extensively throughout Europe and Russia and now makes her home in a village in Scotland where she devotes her time to poetry.

HENRY MILLER

* * *

The Soul of Greece

A heat wave sheds light on
Grecian character.

I WOULD NEVER HAVE GONE TO GREECE HAD IT NOT BEEN FOR A girl named Betty Ryan who lived in the same house with me in Paris. One evening, over a glass of white wine, she began to talk of her experiences in roaming about the world. I always listened to her with great attention, not only because her experiences were strange but because when she talked about her wanderings she seemed to paint them: everything she described remained in my head like finished canvases by a master. It was a peculiar conversation that evening: we began by talking about China and the Chinese language which she had begun to study. Soon we were in North Africa, in the desert, among peoples I had never heard of before. And then suddenly she was all alone, walking beside a river, and the light was intense and I was following her as best I could in the blinding sun but she got lost and I found myself wandering about in a strange land listening to a language I had never heard before. She is not exactly a storyteller, this girl, but she is an artist of some sort because nobody has ever given me the ambience of a place so thoroughly as she did Greece. Long afterwards I discovered that it was near Olympia that she had gone astray and I with her, but at the time it was just Greece to me, a world of light such as I had never dreamed of and never hoped to see.

We had hardly gotten through the gate at the dock in Piraeus when we fell into the hands of a wily Greek guide who spoke a little English and French and who promised to show us everything of interest for a modest sum. We tried to find out what he wanted for his services but in vain. It was too hot to discuss prices; we fell into a taxi and told him to steer us straight to the Acropolis. I had changed my francs into drachmas on the boat; it seemed like a tremendous wad that I had stuffed into my pocket and I felt that I could meet the bill no matter how exorbitant it might be. I knew we were going to be gypped and I looked forward to it with relish. The only thing that was solidly fixed in my mind about the Greeks was that you couldn't trust them; I would have been disappointed if our guide had turned out to be magnanimous and chivalrous. My companion on the other hand was somewhat worried about the situation. He was going on to Beirut. I could actually hear him making mental calculations as we rode along in the suffocating dust and heat.

The ride from Piraeus to Athens is a good introduction to Greece. There is nothing inviting about it. It makes you wonder why you decided to come to Greece. There is something not only arid and desolate about the scene, but something terrifying too. You feel stripped and plundered, almost annihilated. The driver was like an animal who had been miraculously taught to operate a crazy machine: our guide was constantly directing him to go to the right or the left, as though they had never made the journey before. I felt an enormous sympathy for the driver whom I knew would be gypped also. I had the feeling that he could not count beyond 100; I had also the feeling that he would drive into a ditch if he were directed to. When we got to the Acropolis—it was an insane idea to go there immediately—there were several hundred people ahead of us storming the gate. By this time the heat was so terrific that all I thought of was where to sit down and enjoy a bit of shade. I found myself a fairly cool spot and I waited there while the Argentine

_____ ※ _____

For 1,000 years—up to 1456—the Parthenon was used by the Greeks as a Christian church. Then the Turks captured Athens. *They* made of it, for the next 400 years, a Muslim city. They turned the Acropolis into a fort. Over there by the porch of the Marble Maidens, they raised a minaret which stood for 200 years. Here, inside the Parthenon, the Turks stored their gunpowder.

And so it came to pass, in 1687, that the Venetians, at war with the Turks, attacked the Acropolis and shot a cannon ball through the roof into the powder kegs. Flames burst forth and caused a terrible explosion. The roof was blown into the air, half the walls hurled down, many of the columns smashed.

This was one of the most tragic art losses the world has ever suffered. After it had stood in all its beauty for 2,100 years, after it had survived a dozen invasions by the Romans and the barbarians, this matchless temple had to meet destruction from a single cannon ball at so recent a date as 1687.

—Richard Halliburton, *Book of Marvels: The Occident*

chap got his money's worth. Our guide had remained at the entrance with the taxi driver after turning us over to one of the official guides. He was going to escort us to the Temple of Jupiter and the Thesion and other places as soon as we had our fill of the Acropolis. We never went to these places, of course. We told him to drive into town, find a cool spot, and order some ice cream. It was about 10:30 when we parked ourselves on the terrace of a café. Everybody looked fagged out from the heat, even the Greeks. We ate the ice cream, drank the iced water, then more ice cream and more iced water. After that I called for some hot tea, because I suddenly remembered somebody telling me once that hot tea cools you off.

The taxi was standing at the curb with the motor running. Our guide seemed to be the only one who didn't mind the heat. I suppose he thought we would cool off a bit and then start trotting around again in the sun looking at ruins and monuments. We told him finally that we wanted to dispense with his services. He said there was no hurry, he had nothing special to do, and was happy to keep us company. We told him we had had enough for the day and would like to settle up. He called the waiter and paid the check out of his own pocket. We kept prodding him to tell us how much. He seemed reluctant as hell to tell us. He wanted to know how much we thought his services were worth. We said we didn't know—we would leave it to him to decide. Whereupon, after a long pause, after looking us over from head to foot, scratching himself, tilting his hat back, mopping his brow, and so on, he blandly announced that he thought 2,500 drachmas would square the account. I gave my companion a look and told him to open fire. The Greek, of course, was thoroughly prepared for our reaction. And it's this, I must confess, that I really like about the Greeks, when they are wily and cunning. Almost at once he said, "Well, all right, if you don't think my price is fair then you make *me* a price." So we did. We made him one as ridiculously low as his was high. It seemed to make him feel good, this crude bargaining. As a matter of fact, we all felt good about it. It was making service into something tangible and real like a commodity. We weighed it and appraised it, we juggled it like a ripe tomato or an ear of corn. And finally we agreed, not on a fair price, because that would have been an insult to our guide's ability, but we agreed that for this unique occasion, because of the heat, because we had not seen everything, and so on and so forth, that we would fix on thus and such a sum and part good friends. One of the little items we haggled about a long time was the amount paid by our guide to the official guide at the Acropolis. He swore he had given the man 150 drachmas. I had seen the transaction with my own eyes, and I knew he had given only 50 drachmas. He maintained that I had not seen well. We smoothed it out by pretending that he had inadvertently handed the man 100 drachmas more than he intended to, a piece of casuistry so thoroughly un-Greek that had he then and there decided to rob us of all we possessed he would have been justified and the courts of Greece would have upheld him.

An hour later I said good-bye to my companion, found myself a room in a small hotel at double the usual price, stripped down and lay on the bed naked in a pool of sweat until nine that evening. I looked for a restaurant, tried to eat, but after taking a few mouthfuls gave it up. I have never been so hot in all my life. To sit near an electric light was torture. After a few cold drinks I got up from the terrace where I was sitting and headed for the park. I should say it was about eleven o'clock. People were swarming in all directions to the park. It reminded me of New York on a sweltering night in August. It was the herd again, something I had never felt in Paris, except during the aborted revolution. I sauntered slowly through the park towards the Temple of Jupiter. There were little tables along the dusty paths set out in an absent-minded way: couples were sitting there quietly in the dark, talking in low voices, over glasses of water. *The glass of water*...everywhere I saw the glass of water. It became obsessional. I began to think of water as a new thing, a new vital element of life. Earth, air, fire, water. Right now water had become the cardinal element. Seeing lovers sitting there in the dark drinking water, sitting there in peace and quiet and talking in low tones, gave me a wonderful feeling about the Greek character. The dust, the heat, the poverty, the bareness, the containedness of the people, and the water everywhere in little tumblers standing between the quiet, peaceful couples, gave me the feeling that there was something holy about the place, something nourishing and sustaining. I walked about enchanted on this first night in the Zapion. It remains in my memory like no other park I have known. It is the quintessence of park, the thing one feels sometimes in looking at a canvas or dreaming of a place you'd like to be in and never find. It is lovely in the morning, too, as I was to discover. But at night, coming upon it from nowhere, feeling the hard dirt under your feet and hearing a buzz of language which is altogether unfamiliar to you, it is magical.

Marvelous things happen to one in Greece—marvelous *good* things which can happen to one nowhere else on earth. Somehow, almost as if He were nodding, Greece still remains under the protection of the Creator. Men may go about their puny, ineffectual bedevilment, even in Greece, but God's magic is still at work and, no matter what the race of man may do or try to do, Greece is still a sacred precinct—and my belief is it will remain so until the end of time.

Henry Miller was the acclaimed author of many books, including Tropic of Cancer, Tropic of Capricorn *and* The Colossus of Maroussi, *from which this story was excerpted.*

PART TWO

SOME THINGS TO DO

MARK JENKINS

*　*　*

Going to Hell

There really is a Hades, but the gift
shop closes at half past two.

IT WAS RAINING WHEN I SET OFF THROUGH THE MOUNTAINS IN A
rental Fiat little bigger than a go-cart. The windows fogged up
immediately. I swabbed the glass with my sleeve. The road
corkscrewed along cliffs and beneath overhangs like all semipaved,
one-lane roads in the backlands of Greece. For some reason—hope
perhaps, fear, curiosity—I was driven by a sense of urgency. The
wheels of my matchbox car were so tiny and treadless I almost
skidded off a misty, precipitous hairpin turn before realizing I
shouldn't be in any hurry to get where I was going.

Through the drizzle, I noticed that at almost every airy turn
there was a metal box with a cross welded on top. At first I thought
they might be mailboxes for gnarled farmers or taciturn shepherds,
but they were too big, too ominous. I finally pulled over to exam-
ine one. It was two feet square, painted a faded sky blue, with a plate
glass window on one side. The box contained an unlighted candle
in a bronze dish, a box of matches, a bottle of olive oil, a bottle of
wine, a framed picture of the bloodied, beatific Jesus, and a photo
of a man with a drink in his hand, grinning wildly, toasting some
unknown occasion.

Back behind the wheel, I slowed down to peer into each shrine as I passed by. In a few the candle was burning. Others contained personal effects: a pocket watch, a necklace, or a book. In three hours of mountain driving I passed more than thirty reliquaries. Where the road dropped down onto the plain of Achéron, I pulled off beside one of these small monuments to lost life, reached across to the passenger seat, took up my college copy of the *Odyssey*, and read Circe's words to Odysseus: "You must go to the house of Hades and awful Persephoneia, to ask directions from Teiresias the blind Theban seer."

Travel long and far enough, physically or metaphysically, and you'll eventually lose your bearings. It can't be helped. When it happens, no matter where you are or what you're doing, all you really want to do is go home.

It happened to me in Switzerland. I had come to climb the north face of the Matterhorn, but the day I arrived in Zermatt it started snowing, and it dumped nonstop for almost a week. Every morning I went trudging into the mountains hoping against hope, and every night I slunk down to the North Wall Bar, played chess with the local climbers, and did pull-ups on the door frame to win free pints of lager and pans of pizza. Then I'd stumble back to the Bahnhof Hotel and read Homer.

On the sixth day, the day I flew out, it was still snowing. But I didn't fly home. I could have—should have, perhaps—but Homer had gotten to me.

Most people pitch Homer five seconds after taking the final exam. I did. At a certain age, however, you start thinking you might have learned something when you were young if you hadn't already been so smart. I was rereading the *Odyssey* because it is arguably the world's first novel, the original thriller, composed 700 years before the birth of Christ. It's also the seminal adventure book, chronicling the surreal travels and travails of an alpha adventurer, the hubristic yet humble Odysseus, who sails away from Ithaca to fight the good fight, sneaks into Troy and dismembers his enemies, blinds the Cyclops with a burning pole, has all-night sex with Calypso. But his most daring adventure is a visit to Hades. Why did he go there? For answers only the underworld could provide, and for directions home. After years of sailing beyond the edge of the known world, Odysseus had lost his bearings.

Days of unconsummated mountain climbing are not unlike windless days at sea. You eventually grow weary and frustrated, and you also come up against questions that experience can't answer. On the fifth day of snow in Zermatt I bought a map of Greece. Odysseus got answers when he visited the underworld. I thought the place might be worth a visit.

Homer, like all learned Greeks, freely mixed geography and cosmology. Hence he was quite specific about the location of hell on Earth: It could be found at the confluence of the Achéron, "river of pain," the Pyriphlegethon, "blazing with fire," and the Cocytos, "resounding with lamentation, which is a branch of the hateful water of the Styx." Where the three rivers merged there was a great stone, and beneath the stone, a cave—the entrance to the underworld.

I found the Achéron on the map. Almost 3,000 years later and it was still right there, doglegging through the Pindus Mountains just south of the Albanian border.

Odysseus sailed to Hades; I flew. Nonetheless, my journey began as any proper trip to hell should. The plane sat on the tarmac for over an hour, with jet fuel fumes seeping into the cabin and passengers starting to faint. There was a heart attack on board somewhere over the Alps, and the flight was diverted to Milan. We arrived in Athens a half-day late. Naturally I missed my connection north, and naturally my rucksack was sent to baggage purgatory— somewhere in eastern Slovakia. I hiked around Athens in the polluted heat for three days before giving up on my bags and flying up to Ioánnina with just the shirt on my back and enough cash to get a rental car.

In a village where the old men wear black berets, sit at an outdoor café, smoke, play cards, and stare disapprovingly at slowmoving vehicles, I drove right up to a half-hidden blue sign with an arrow and the word "Nekromanteio." Turned right, chugged up a steep cobblestone path lined with whitewashed cottages, passed into a sparse wood, and parked behind two European tour buses disgorging crowds of frumpy bluehairs and bony-kneed husbands of all nations. I should have known. It figured that hell would be just one more stop on a package tour.

I paid the entrance fee at the iron gate, bought the color brochure, and began wandering around the ancient ruins and taking snapshots in the rain with all the other camera-clicking idiots. The site itself lies atop a small knoll surrounded by scarred poplars. Fanning out in all directions is the floodplain of the three dark rivers I'd read about. The ruins consist of the shell of an eighteenth-century Greek Orthodox monastery defiantly built right atop hell. Beneath the monastery is a labyrinthine passageway that leads to a hole in the stone floor. Below is a crypt—a chamber purported to be the cave that Homer described in the *Odyssey* as the entrance to Hades.

I circled through the wet ruins and the labyrinth and got in line, ready to descend into the mouth of hell, when a nasal Texas drawl screeched up from the hole: "Lemme out. Lemme OUT! It smells down 'n here." Then another voice, blasé and male: "Aw, honey, go ta hell." A roar of cackling.

Suddenly I realized this wasn't right. This wasn't the way to visit Hades, the sacred Land of the Dead—in broad daylight with tour guides wearing too much makeup shouting at their bespectacled sheep. It was heretical. Blasphemous. I turned around and left, noting on my way out that hell closes every day at 2:30 P.M.

I drove back into the village, parked at the café of old men, ordered a bottle of retsina and a plate of *yemista*, and began studying the brochure. It was written by an archaeologist and included an account of Odysseus's visit, as well as photographs and intricate diagrams. I committed the floor plans to memory.

On the second bottle of retsina I remembered the first time someone told me I was going to hell. It was three decades ago in Sunday school class with the medieval Mrs. Teuful. I was having problems with this idea of a merciful God in a world full of suffering. If God was so merciful, why didn't he just help us out?

"Young man!" Mrs. Teuful admonished. "You'll go to hell for asking such questions."

Some years later, as should happen to every young man, I was told to go to hell moments before receiving a stinging, Hollywood-worthy slap. More years later, as should happen to every young writer, I was told to go to hell by someone who read what I had written about him and believed I should be punished.

That's what hell is for most modern-day Christians: a netherworld where the skeptical and the wicked are punished. It hath been such since the time of the Apostles. St. Peter described hell as a place of "unquenchable fire" where there was a "great gnashing of teeth among the children" and sinners were "hung up by their tongues" or "by their loins" and tormented by worms and venomous beasts. Charles the Fat, Holy Roman emperor in the late 800s, described hell as a place of "inextricable punishments" where infidels suffer in "boiling rivers and…liquid metal." The clergy of the Dark Ages loved this stuff. So did Hieronymus Bosch.

But the Hades of Homer was less vengeful. There were those who were punished—Sisyphus forever shouldering the great stone uphill, Tantalus chin-deep in water and dying of thirst, Tityos with his liver repeatedly torn out by vultures—but most were there only because they were dead. For the Greeks, Hades was simply where the soul went when the body expired. And these souls, no longer bound by the shackles of time, had one tremendous gift: They could see into the future. Hades was a realm of oracles. Odysseus went there not only to find his way home, but to discover his destiny.

I returned to the Nekromanteio at dusk. The rain had stopped and a purple shroud hung over the valley as I came up behind the ruins through the trees and encountered a stone wall. I had expected a fence of some kind, but this section of the ruins was set upon a high rampart. Since there probably was a night watchman at the front entrance, my only choice was to scale the wall.

It was near dark as I began climbing. The stones were covered in moss and dripping with phlegmlike liquid. I moved as quickly as possible. Near the top I lost my footing and only by the luck of a desperate lunge managed to clutch a stanchion above my head.

Adrenaline poured into my blood as I pulled myself up and surreptitiously flipped over a spiked fence.

I had to feel my way along the broken walls to find the opening to the labyrinth. I could see nothing. With my arms stretched out before me, I glided along the twisting path—as if by coming here at night I had become a phantom myself. I found an iron rail and traced it. I knew I was standing above the crypt when I felt and smelled a dank, almost putrid air exhaling upward from the orifice. My feet found stairs dropping steeply into the abyss.

At the bottom of the stairs I stopped and stared sightlessly into nothingness. A damp chill touched my face. The stench of wet dirt filled my nostrils. I tried stepping forward but the ground was slick, as if still wet with the blood of ancient sacrifice.

When Odysseus was here he saw the ghost of his mother and spoke with her. He met the fathers of his fellow warriors and told them of their sons' adventures and great deeds in battle. He spoke to Achilles, the doomed hero of the *Iliad*.

I waited in blackness. It had all seemed like a lark, really, until that moment. Then something strange began. A primeval desire welled up inside me, and as I stood blind and silent above the bowels of the Earth I realized I honestly did want what Odysseus had wanted—answers. I wished with all my heart for those I'd lost to return, to speak with me, to share their cosmic secrets, for the light of their faces to illuminate this inky pit. But no one came to see me. Not the too-many dead friends and lovers with whom I'd drunk and slept and struggled and whom I could not save from falling in the wars of life; nor my dead relatives, men and women who carried me upon their shoulders or in their hearts or in their stories. I strained with my eyes wide open in hopes of making out kith or kin in the impenetrable, eternal midnight—but nothing.

I don't know how long I waited in darkness, but no mysteries were revealed to me. Odysseus was more fortunate. His mother told him that his wife, Penelope, was still faithful, and that his son, Telemachos, had become a brave prince. Teiresias instructed him how to find and fight his way back home, and assured him that he would complete his journey and live a long, contented life. "Death ever so peaceful shall take you off when comfortable old age shall be your only burden," the blind seer said, "and your people shall be happy round you."

Odysseus was the luckiest of great travelers, perhaps because he was also the most courageous, but more likely because he believed. He had faith. For me, one of the multitudinous modern-day agnostics, it would have been asking too much to be given answers to the mysteries of life. The faithless are forever searching.

I retraced my steps back up out of the crypt, back through the labyrinth, and out into the night of ruins in the valley of the Styx.

If going to hell was easier than I had expected—which is what I should have expected—getting out turned into a nightmare.

Some days later I dropped off the rental car in Ioánnina to fly back to Athens. The plane, of course, was late. One hour, two hours, four. Eventually a woman behind the ticket counter announced that the plane was not coming. The waiting room exploded. Huge Greek men with bellies hanging over their pants began bellowing, women began screaming, little children started crying.

In the pandemonium I bumped into a Canadian surgical-supplies salesman named Terry and his Greek partner, Marina. They specialized in replacement parts for hearts. Terry and Marina had decided to hire a taxi and drive the length of Greece in one night. Why not?

It was raining again, but the taxi was a Mercedes and the driver inexplicably cautious. We ate at a roadside café at one in the morning and pushed on to the Gulf of Patras, where we changed taxis and drivers and took a ferry across the dark waters to the Peloponnesian peninsula. As soon as we docked, our taxi shot out of the ferry like a bat out of hell. The new driver had demonic eyes, a torturer's smile, and a death wish. The road was slick as black ice, and he loved it. Curves posted at fifty miles per hour he took at no less than eighty. I kept involuntarily grabbing the dashboard. At one point, in desperation, I glanced up at the license strapped to the visor, but the photo was a chiaroscuro blur, and the letters of his name were smudged. C-H-A-R-O-something....

Back on a straightaway, he gunned the engine, and we were soon going so fast that the rain flew straight over the windshield without getting it wet. As we went flying around the next black bend, starting to hydroplane—obviously about to smash through the guardrail, sail off the cliff, and be dashed upon the jagged rocks stabbing up out of the ocean—the headlights caught, for the briefest possible moment, the ghostly image of a dripping metal box with a cross on top and a dim, guttering candle within.

Mark Jenkins is a regular contributor to Outside *and the author of* To Timbuktu: A Journey Down the Niger.

G. C. KEHMEIER

The Lions of Delos

The spirit of Apollo can still be felt
on the island of his birth.

NINETY MILES EAST OF ATHENS NEAR THE CENTER OF THE Cyclades lies a graveyard twenty-one centuries old, the island of Delos. It lies very low on the water with only the small hill of Mount Cynthos to hold it down. Sapphire seas wash its shores, and in May the winds are fresh and sweet. It is a mass of flowers, whole sheets of anemones flooding the meadows filled with gleaming columns and ruins glittering like white bones. On Mount Cynthos barley grass grows among the ruins. There is hardly a square foot of the island that does not lie under the shadow of some broken columns or a broken wall. The only inhabitants are lizards which hide under the broken stones and butterflies dancing in the spring sunshine among the flowers.

In the sixth century B.C. the people from Naxos built a thirty-foot high statue of Apollo. It had been standing for 150 years when the Athenian General Nicias, at the height of the Peloponnesian War, visited Delos and paid homage to Apollo, hoping to improve his luck. Thus fortified, he sailed for Sicily where his luck ran out. He was killed before the walls of Syracuse and his army captured. The Athenian Empire came to an end in the marble quarries of Syracuse.

About this time the statue of Apollo fell over in a storm. There, lying where it fell near the sacred lake, the broken pieces have remained for twenty-three centuries. The great torso of the god, headless and without arms, broken at the waist, lies in the open, where the rains will eventually reduce it to powder. My daughter stood by it while I took her picture.

Once fourteen lionesses stood thirty feet apart facing the low plain. Today only five remain. A sixth stands in Venice. Lions should be heavy shouldered, austere, powerfully built, and ripe with wisdom like those at Forty-first and Fifth Avenue in front of the New York Public Library. These lionesses are female cubs, and they sit on their haunches watching the sun.

There are no legends to account for their presence. Perhaps the influence of Egyptian, Assyrian, and Persian monarchs who had stone lions guarding their tombs had spread to Delos. They were carved about the time that Apollo was carved, and they face west toward Europe. In them we see the expression of the spirit of the Western world with its unparalleled eagerness and thirst for adventure, its mockery of all accepted conventions, and its rage for destruction.

At the height of its empire Athens used Delos as a treasury. It reached its zenith as a free port and slave-trading center between 138 and 88 B.C. when it was

> I head up Mount Cynthos, the only peak on Delos. I'm drawn to a second-century-B.C. Doric temple on the slope: peaked roof, four columns, symmetrical. Graceful Isis, decapitated and armless, waits between two columns. Beneath the pleats of her cracked marble robe I can make out the slant of her hips, the bend of her knee. Inside the temple, brittle leaves scuttle across the stone floor, the only sound in this cool, hushed place. Here the ghosts of holy maidens, prayerful and promising, whisper their silent devotions and sailors past seek protection from the roiling seas.
>
> —Lisa Moskowitz,
> "Season's End"

plundered by Menophanes, an officer serving in the army of King Mithridates of Pontus, who put all the citizens to death. When Pausanias visited the island in the second century A.D. it was deserted. During the eighteenth and nineteenth centuries, English lords and Ottoman Turks collected and plundered. During the past century the French have carried on systematic archaeological exploration.

There are places on earth where holiness dwells, where crimes innumerable have been committed, yet holiness remains. The lion gate at Mycenae, Temple Four at Tikal, the Wailing Wall at Jerusalem are good examples. So it is with Delos, birthplace of Apollo. He has ruled it for twenty-five centuries and his presence can still be felt. Excavators are at work and their wheelbarrows wander among the ruins of the temples that were built when the worship of Apollo was young.

Wildflowers grow by an abandoned well, and jet planes fly overhead pulling white contrails before beginning their descent for a landing at Hellinikon Airport in Athens. A laborer draws water from a well once owned by Cleopatra. He offers us a drink. The water tastes cool and sweet. Cleopatra must have liked it.

G. C. Kehmeier was born in 1918 and grew up on a farm near Eckert, Colorado. He flew C-87s in the South Pacific during World War II. A retired airline pilot since 1978, he has visited 115 countries.

God as *Pâtissier*

*Metaphysical lessons emerge from
a hunt for culinary miracles.*

I HAVE A PALM-SIZE ICON THAT I FOUND ONE EASTER ON CORFU in the shop of an impulsive, affectionate woman named Mrs. Gift-of-God. The painting shows three angels dressed in ruby-colored caftans, sitting together at a round table covered with a beautiful sea-green tablecloth just the color of the Aegean in certain lights and depths. You can tell they have come a long way; they have the slightly weary, relaxed posture of people who have arrived at their destination after a long flight, and their bare feet are propped on soft cushions. They look cheerfully hungry; on the table are three tiny forks and three golden goblets, the same gold as their wings and halos. They are talking together with delicacy and wit, to judge from the inclinations of their heads and the appreciative smile of the angel on the right. It is obvious that the cool wine in their glowing goblets and the aromatic scent of their dinner cooking is inspiring them. I know they represent the angels who visited Abraham in the desert and that, theologically, they are supposed to prefigure the Holy Trinity, but I don't care. For me they are the angels of the table, presiding over one of the arts of peace, the arts in which the sensual and the spiritual, and physical and metaphysical love, are fused into one substance, far more difficult to accomplish than any of the arts of war.

My gastronomic guardians, who traveled with me throughout Greece, are the patron saints of the answered prayer, which every good meal is, and they remind me of one of the most important elements of Greek cooking. If French cooking is an ongoing inquiry into the ultimate rules of cuisine and Italian cooking explores the nature of impulse and improvisation, Greek cuisine, with its combination of frugality and richness and its transformation of scarcity into plenty, is a demonstration of the miraculous. Think of the olive, a bony-looking tree with a fruit no bigger than a fingertip, which can be turned into pies, sauces, fuel, and even light itself.

In Greece, when you go to the herb and spice seller for a handful of bay leaves, what you ask for is Daphne, the name of the nymph who gave this flavor to the world, the legacy of her flight from Apollo and her transformation into the laurel tree. Greek life is thoroughly entangled with myth, but nowhere more intimately than in the kitchen, where someone wielding a wooden spoon is always sure to remind you that the Greeks like to say that their words for cooking and magic are related. And one of the most charming double entendres I know I learned when I was searching for a rolling pin, called a *plastis*, which is another name for the Creator of the Universe. I was delighted to think of God as a breadmaker, perhaps even a *pâtissier*—at last we had something in common.

Greek cooks are past masters of the loaves-and-fishes method of cooking, feeding a full table of hungry guests and children with expandable handfuls of beans or a scant pound of meat that turns into a voluptuous moussaka or a *pastitsio*. But the dishes that seem closest to the Greek ideal of food, appearing in different combinations through each season, are the *yemista*, stuffed vegetables with different fillings. These demonstrate the two principles of the best Greek cooking: the love of freshness and the appetite for the miraculous. The *yemista* are edible treasure chests, trompe l'oeil main courses. Probably the most famous are stuffed grape leaves (*dolmathes*), but in the fall there are golden quinces stuffed with lamb and pine nuts (*kydonia yemista*), food out of fairy tales, and eggplant stuffed with rice and quail (*melitsanes yemistes me ortykia*), for which the island of Mytilíni, otherwise known as Lésvos, is famous. In the winter, there are onions encasing rice, meat, and currants (*kremidia yemista*), and in Macedonia, *yiaprakia* for Christmas dinner (pickled cabbage leaves surrounding pork and dill). In spring, there are artichokes heaped with meat and cheese (*anginares yemistes me kraes kai tyrî*) and delicate leaves of romaine enfolding rice and scallions and served with egg and lemon sauce (*maroulo dolmathes*). But my private passion is for zucchini blossoms filled with rice or bulgur, either gently sautéed or simmered in white wine and herbs. They have a flavor as indescribably rare as truffles and a texture that combines the melting with the crackling, like good kisses, a dish as erotic as summer itself.

Last July, over dinner with a friend at one of my favorite restaurants in Greece, Prinkiponisia of Thessaloníki, which specializes in the food of Greek Constantinople, I begged for advice about where to spend August 15th, the great feast of the Greek summer, celebrating the Dormition of the Virgin Mary.

"Every place celebrates a little differently," my friend said. "Do you know what you want?" I jumbled together pilgrimages, beautiful beaches, miraculous icons. "Miracles?" he said, "You want miracles? You want zucchini flowers. Where you want to go is Mytilíni. In my home village there, we have a miraculous icon; we make the best ouzo in all of Greece at the distilleries in Plomárion;

Chefs in tavernas and seaside resorts, mothers in remote villages and in bustling cities, monks in Varlaam, Meteora and nuns in Pantanassa, Mystrás—all speak to me of their foods.... While they are explaining, however, they urge care and caution, and my mind buzzes back over the centuries, recalling the advice of a Greek mentioned by the comic poet Damoxenus, of the third century B.C.: "When you see them making a pickled sauce out of fish of contradictory qualities and grating a dash of sesame into it, take them in turn and tweak their noses."

—Vilma Liacouras Chantiles,
The Food of Greece

and as for food, the Virgin Mary herself got hungry on Mytilíni. One August when she was passing through and the heat was getting to her, she regained her appetite and her health eating our August mackerel and grapes. This is a fact everyone from the island knows."

So, later in August, a month known in some parts of Greece as the Banquet Bringer, I took the ferry to Mytilíni.

I went first to Vatera, a village on the southern coast of the island, bound for the Vatera Beach Hotel, a place with a promising reputation for good food, which boded well for people in search of zucchini flowers. I drove down the main road toward the southern peninsula, through caramel-colored mountains and stunning pine forests.

Vatera turned out to be utterly refreshing; the hotel overlooked a crescent of sandy beach and a clear, jewel-colored sea, ample for contemplative walks at sunset. Every day you would see the guests waiting to read through the new lunch and dinner menus before their first swims, as if they were anticipating a new chapter in an irresistible serial novel. There were thrillingly fresh grape leaves, the best *tzatziki* I tasted in the country, stuffed eggplant that had the sweetness and fleshiness of a peach, rabbit *stifado*. The seasoning—herbs from just outside the back door—was an elegant heightening, like slightly darker pencil strokes defining a sketch's outlines. It was the food of artists—but there were no zucchini flowers.

On the day of the feast of the Dormition of the Virgin, the mountain village of Ayiasos, with its miraculous icon, was crowded with pilgrims. It smelled richly of pine and lamb roasting on the spit. I saw a boy with a shaved head, an earring, and a leather jacket stamped with the image of a skull and crossbones carrying a large candle into church to light before the icon of the Virgin Mary. I bought a homemade bottle of the most romantic liqueur I have ever encountered, with jasmine buds floating in it. But there were no zucchini flowers.

I gave up expecting them; like so many of the best Greek dishes, they were probably the privilege of home kitchens. I went to Petra to see its famous church, madly placed on a jagged cliff—Our Lady of Vertigo—and to the stately fortress town of Molyvos, with its castle overlooking the sea. From there, I had a personal pilgrimage to make to Skala Sikamia, a little fishing village where the novelist Stratis Myrvilis had written a dreamlike novel about Mytilíni called *The Mermaid Madonna*, in which he describes an icon of the Virgin portrayed as a mermaid. I had been told he had written it in a tiny chapel overlooking the sea, where the icon itself was preserved. Skala Sikamia was miniature and perfect: a square shaded with plane trees and grape vines and smelling of honeysuckle, a pride of brilliantly colored fishing boats, and a chapel seemingly set in the sea itself, more like a caïque than a chapel.

I went right away to the little chapel of the Mermaid Madonna; a family was inside, peering intently into the bare corners, fanned out to look for the image. But there was no mermaid.

Below the chapel I saw a woman sitting in the courtyard of her shop, reading a novel, and went to ask her about the icon. She smiled and said, "There is no icon." I was puzzled, because I had been shown a picture of it. "Yes," she said, "there are pictures, but the icon itself does not exist. There are pictures inspired by the novel, pictures of what Myrvilis dreamed. So you have learned in Skala Sikamia the difference between Greek art and the art you know in the West. In the West you paint reality in all its details; in Greece we struggle to paint what doesn't exist."

Metaphysical lessons are best followed by lunch. I sat under the trees at a taverna called the Cuckoo's Nest and drank a flowery white wine, looking across at the coast of Turkey. And the waiter said that they were making zucchini flowers in the kitchen. I asked if I could watch, and followed him to a corner where a woman was sitting with two chairs in front of her, one holding a wooden trough of zucchini flowers, the other a bowl of filling, one I hadn't encountered before, of feta and egg seasoned with shreds of fresh mint.

"They should be picked the same morning you are going to serve them," said the cook, "and if possible, before the sun comes up, when their throats are more open. You can see how delicate they are," she said, and handed me a weightless blossom and a teaspoon of filling. Coaxing the filling into the flower was like feeding a hummingbird with an eyedropper.

"Some people dip them into fritter batter," she said. "I don't. You'll taste why." I thanked her and went back to the table under the sweet shade. The first plate of zucchini flowers came out, with another carafe of white wine—elusive, dreamlike blossoms transforming a fleeting August afternoon into the unspoken goal of every traveler, an immortal day.

Patricia Storace also contributed "Marble Girls" in Part One.

Easy Rider

Born to be wild? Try this on for size.

YOU'VE TRUDGED TO THE ACROPOLIS, WANDERED THE PICTURESQUE streets of the Plaka, sipped Greek coffee among the chic patrons of a Kolonaki taverna, discovered that Omonia Square is actually a circle and danced until dawn at one of the city's many nightclubs. What's left to do in Athens that you haven't done?

If you've got a sense of adventure, you might try seeing the city the way many Athenians see it—from the back of a motorbike.

Notice I said the *back* of a motorbike, one that's driven by a Greek driver. This is the only way to experience an authentic motorbike sightseeing tour of Athens, because all Greek drivers are much more maniacal than you are, and without a Greek driver, you will probably never know the sublime sensation of driving fifty miles per hour through a gap in traffic only slightly larger than your average souvlakia.

This, I can assure you, is something not to be missed. First, find yourself an experienced driver, a motorcycle or reasonable facsimile thereof, straddle the seat and hang on for dear life. You'll discover that sightseeing by motorbike will provide an exhilarating, heart-pounding and bone-chilling new way of looking at Athens for two primary reasons:

1) There are too many cars in Athens. They tend to be very small cars, but still, there are far too many of them.

2) All of the cars are driven by maniacal Greeks.

Everyone drives in Athens because public transportation is confusing (Athenians themselves don't understand the bus routes), and the Metro won't be finished until sometime in the twenty-first century. Even though only half the city's cars are allowed on the streets on even-numbered days, and the other half on odd-number days, Athens seems to be just one car short of complete gridlock, kind of like those Chinese puzzles with one square missing.

Just getting from one side of the city to another requires the determination of a road warrior, the finesse of an Indy 500 champion, and the patience of Job. Greek drivers have only one of these qualities. Exactly which quality they have I will leave to your imagination, mentioning only that the Mad Max School of Driving is located in an alleyway two blocks south of the "Large Collection of Really Old Stuff Found in the Ground" Museum in Kifisia.

Even if you have a high regard for Greek drivers, I would advise against entering into a debate about Greek driving skills, since any argument with a Greek lasts for hours. On principle, Greeks will not reach an agreement with anyone about anything, with one exception: to a person they will declare that they are devoutly individualistic, and dislike following rules, regulations, or each other.

Which certainly explains their anarchic driving habits. Red lights are considered more of a suggestion than an actual imperative, and when you turn onto a main street in Athens, you'll find five or six cars staggered side by side and jockeying for inches of space, a create-your-own-lane philosophy of driving. When the rare half block or so of road opens up, everyone races ahead, attempting to be the first to lodge themselves into the next traffic jam.

Hence the great popularity of motorbikes. They're the fastest way to navigate the city streets, since motorbikes follow an even more liberal set of traffic laws than do automobiles, meaning that bikes are allowed to drive on any section of pavement not occupied by another vehicle—although, considering the number of traffic accidents in Athens, apparently this is a custom to which no one rigidly adheres.

Perhaps aware that Greece's unusually high number of mishaps is a bit of a deterrent to a tourist's enthusiasm for a motorbike sight-seeing tour, Greeks will be the first to inform you that it is Portugal and not Greece that ranks Number One on the European Traffic Fatality Chart, which simply places Greece firmly in the position of Number Two. This is the only instance I know of in which Greeks concede another nation's superiority.

Riding a motorbike in Athens is a lot like being a character in a Nintendo game, in which you negotiate a death-dealing obstacle course of thousands of autos, buses, trucks, hundreds of other motor-bikes, and suicidal, jaywalking pedestrians. And the maniacal dri-vers, both bike and auto, are Nintendo contestants all, constantly beeping their high-pitched horns and flashing their headlights with the rapid dexterity of pinball wizards. It seems ridiculous, until the terrible truth sinks in: they actually believe that all this beeping and flashing will prevent them from crashing into each other.

The other bit of commonly held wisdom, if it can be called that, is that you (or, in this instance, your driver) must drive very, very fast to avoid the slow drivers, who are the ones who cause all the accidents.

It is important to wear a helmet for your motorbike tour of Athens, although it will not save your noggin should you be thrown from the bike: once you hit the street you will be instantly run over by another vehicle. You must wear a helmet so that your driver will not overhear and thus be offended by any of your comments, which, with the expletives deleted, will sound something like this:

"We're going to be crushed by a bus!"

"Why are you driving into oncoming traffic?!!"

"My leg was almost ripped from my body by a Fiat!"

"You can't drive between those two trucks—Oh, my God!"

"Watch out for the...!" (Pick one)

    a. Dog

    b. Child

    c. Taverna

    d. Child walking a dog in the taverna!

As you are riding around Athens, you may notice that there are other people who are also riding on the backs of motorbikes, and they are not wearing helmets, screaming at their driver, or trying to pull out his spleen with their bare hands. Apparently oblivious to their risk of life and limb, they manage to converse, eat, study, begin relationships, have dinner parties, raise families, etc., while on the back of motorbikes. These people are Greeks and, unlike us, they love to flirt with tragedy.

Cultivating this Greek sangfroid is the mark of a master motor-bike rider, and it can be done in a number of ways. I first attempted to control my overwhelming excitement (fear) by closing my eyes, but found that my imagination could easily conjure up scenes of dismemberment that did nothing to promote my own comfort nor that of my driver, who was soon gasping for breath from the choke-hold I had on him. At least I believe it was the chokehold that had him gasping for breath, because no one except myself seemed to be aware that we were sucking in great lungfuls of the pungent Athenian air, also known as car exhaust, a rather intoxicating blend of diesel and carbon monoxide fumes that is available on your motorbike sightseeing tour at absolutely no extra charge.

Ultimately, I discovered that the best way to fully enjoy the experience was to direct my eyes away from our numerous near-death encounters, take in the sights of Athens, and window-shop. Athenian shopkeepers have graciously placed price tags on all items in store windows, so you can spend your time on the back of a motorbike planning exactly how you will spend your million-drachma insurance settlement, should you be lucky enough to survive the inevitable collision.

Yes, a collision probably is inevitable, because, as I've already told you, there are more traffic accidents in Greece than in any other European country (with the exception of Portugal, of course). But this is precisely why careening around the streets of Athens is so exciting and generally all-around, big-time fun. A brush with death is probably not something you should be thinking about while on your motorbike sightseeing tour of Athens, however. It's probably better to be thinking this:

"Boy, am I glad I'm not in Portugal."

✳

Christi Phillips's travel stories have appeared in numerous magazines, newspapers, and anthologies, including Travelers' Tales Food. *Her recently completed book,* Working for Rubles, *is a travel memoir set in Moscow.*

GARRY WILLS

The Real Arcadia

A scholar traces the lineage of
the Romantic Poets.

TO EUROPEAN POETS AND PAINTERS, ARCADIA WAS FAMILIAR territory, the home of all pastoral imaginings. But few who wrote about the place had ever been there. This was true even of Virgil, who put the place on the literary map. My own quick survey of a dozen classicist friends turned up none who had spent time in Arcadia, even though some of them lead tours of the Greek mainland and islands.

Is this because the region is uninteresting? The owner of a Greek restaurant in my neighborhood, whose family came from Arcadia, assured me that its scenery is majestic. Is it hard of access then? When I asked that question in Athens, I was told that an easy two-hour drive on a modern superhighway would get me there, to the mountainous core of the Peloponnese. Were the poets just vague in their gestures toward the region? On the contrary, their geography was very specific. In "Arcades," for instance, Milton managed to crowd the names of four of the area's mountains and one of its rivers into the lines that Ruskin mocked as "airy syllabling":

Nymphs and shepherds, dance no more
　By sandy Ladon's lilied banks.

On old Lycaeus or Cyllene hoar
    Trip no more in twilight ranks.
Though Erymanth your loss deplore,
    From the stony Maenalus
    Bring your flock and live with us.

If Milton never saw Arcadia, neither did most ancient Greeks.
They thought it a region to be avoided, a spooky, even repulsive,
place with mentally retarded inhabitants. The area's principal rites—
the sacrifices to Wolf-Zeus atop Lycaeus (Wolf Mountain)—were
thought to involve human sacrifice, not as an old legend like
Agamemnon's sacrifice of his daughter to get a wind for Troy, but
as a contemporary and annual occurrence. Even the historian
Polybius, the one famous writer born in the region, apologized for
his countrymen's savagery, though he noted that music softened
them. So rough and resistant was the land, so hard was it to wrest a
living from the soil, that Arcadians (or so went the joke) made good
soldiers for hire because they were so eager to get out of the place.
The comic poet Hermippus, listing famous exports in the fifth century B.C., said: "Egypt for papyrus, Syria for incense, Libya for
ivory…and Arcadia for mercenaries."

Then what turned Arcadia's savage gorges into the pastoral
poets' sweet vales, a land of serenity populated by singing shepherds with winsome milkmaids? How did the dim view held by
Polybius and Hermippus metamorphose into the starry-eyed
enthusiasm of Milton, Spenser, and Sidney, who gave the
Arcadian pastoral a major role in the history of English poetry, and
of Boccaccio and Sannazaro, who did the same in Italy? How did
the Arcadian myth filter down in such a dulcified form to Marie
Antoinette, who played the rural shepherdess in her deer park,
imitating the fair nymphs of pastoral painters from Luca Signorelli
to Poussin?

The man responsible for Arcadia's transformation from wasteland
to utopia was Virgil. In the *Aeneid* he would use a myth that
Arcadians had colonized the site of Rome before the Trojans
reached it. He made those proto-Romans stand for virtuous sim-

plicity. In his pastoral *Eclogues*, Virgil seized on the fact that Pan was, in Pindar's words, "Arcadia's ruler." The region was sometimes called Panland—in Greek, *Pania*. Pan was as rough as the country, half goat, half god, but Virgil preferred to idealize him by concentrating on a single aspect of his complex powers: the fact that he had invented the syrinx, now called the panpipe, and taught shepherds to play it and sing to it. Pan's invention has miraculous effects in Virgil's poetry, in which the harsh Arcadian landscape dances attendance on human flirting. When a swain is disappointed in love, two of the most forbidding mountains of the Peloponnese (including the very peak on which those human sacrifices were said to have taken place) boohoo along with him:

He lay there, crushed, beside a lonely rock,
And Maenalus, clothed with pines, wept over him,
While chill Lycaeus' barren rocks wept too.

Alexander Pope picked up the conceit in his *Pastorals*, where a smitten shepherd:

Taught the rocks to weep, and made the mountains moan.

How would these lines impress one in their real (supposed) setting? I wanted to put together the rebarbative geography and the emollient verse, so I went down from Athens to spend a week in Keats's "dales of Arcady."

The first thing I learned is that on a modern map, Arcadia does not mesh with the far larger region the ancients called by the same name. Today's Arcadia is a political unit (a nome), trimmed back from its ancient realm to strike a balance with other representative districts in the Peloponnese. I took as my guide Pausanias, who wrote Greece's first travel book. Touring his known world in the second century A.D., he marked out Arcadia by three overlapping norms: ethnicity (all Arcadians claimed descent from a common ancestor named Arcas); language (they spoke a very old dialect);

and religion (they had special rites, too primitive for most Greeks' tastes). I also used the wonderful map of all the discovered ancient sites in Madeleine Jost's *Sanctuaires et cultes d'Arcadie*.

Two of the mountains named by Milton are now in the nome of Corinth, but Pausanias noted that Erýmanthos and Cyllene marked, respectively, the northwest and the northeast corners of Arcadia. So I began with them. Mount Cyllene (modern Killini) is the highest peak in Arcadia, a place jammed with mountains shouldering each other about in jumbled ranks. The *Homeric Hymn to Pan*, written in the fifth century B.C., addressed the god this way:

Cyllene, holy to him, is his haunt.

The god had as a cult title "Cyllenean Pan." Sophocles, made the chorus in *Ajax* summon Pan "from rocky Cyllene flailed with snow." The snow was gone by the time I reached Cyllene in June, though traces had lasted on the north peak in May. The *Blue Guide* says climbers can go up the east approach in a "difficult" twelve hours. I settled for a stay at a lodge on the south slope that was said to offer "a good area for walking and for botanists."

The walk, along a dirt road girdling this sector of the mountain, was impressive; glimpses of other mountains opened through the trees like keyholes to infinity. But I was stopped in less than an hour by a dog fiercely guarding the sheep under its care, which had straggled across the path on their way back from pasture. Arcadia's up-and-down landscape is, by and large, for pasturing, not plowing. Ancient Greeks called the Arcadians "acorn eaters," a scornful epithet meaning they were so agriculturally primitive that they did not know how to grow staple grains. (Eating sheep was also considered backward by the Greeks, who were not regular meat eaters.) When northern Arcadians called their region Azanry (after Azan, a son of Arcas), other Greeks said it should be Brazenry—meaning its land was as uncultivable as brass.

What I found this first evening while walking I would afterward experience whenever I drove the rough little back roads of Arcadia: one must be prepared, early and late in the day, to wait for the sheep or goats to get where they are going. On the very next morning, while stopped behind a bickering flow of horned billies and horn-less kids, I glanced to the right, into the low sun of morning, and felt my heart stop a second as Pan himself returned my gaze. A care-ful second look reminded me of something I once knew but had long forgotten—that goats can stand on their hind feet, like dogs. But they have a higher, slimmer profile when they do. What I had seen was a kid on it hind legs slowly pawing a branch as it grazed its buds. This trick of turning biped, along with the sly look some goats contrive at times, no doubt contributed to a vivid apprehen-sion of Pan's nearness in the Arcadian cult. In the iconography of the god, he is often shown as "spying Pan," turning a quick intense glance on the viewer, lifting at times a hand (or hoof) to shade his eyes from the bright sun. He has the sprightliness of his half-goat nature. The *Homeric Hymn to Pan* called him:

Quick on the cliffs where scampering goats are seen.

As I watched the herds being rounded up and moved along, mostly by old women who used the ancient shepherd's crook as a very practical tool, I saw that real Arcadians do not, like Virgil's, lie in the shade and talk to the sheep (who mourn their master's unhappy love life as dolefully as the lachrymose mountains). Here is the way Virgil's herdsman puts his flock away for the night:

The Evening Star! Go, satyrs! Go home, goats.

Goats are as easily summoned to mind, and as easily dismissed, as imaginary satyrs.

Near the western base of Cyllene is another part of the map Milton's "Arcades" gave me: the river Ladon, which Pausanias called "the loveliest river in Greece." Its springs, held in awe by the Arcadians, lie just five kilometers north of the village of Kalivia. Water erupts from the ground with great force throughout Arcadia, fed by streams forced down hidden mountain clefts. Ladon's springs leap to get away from their source, clattering over rocks with a sound like the clunking of the sheep bells higher up the hill. Milton calls the river "sandy Ladon." Why? I checked it at various places downstream during my week here, and not a grain of sand did I see. Where did Milton get his adjective? Not from the land itself, of course, but from another poet, Ovid—who also never saw Arcadia.

Ovid seems to have wanted sand because the myth he knew called for oat reeds to be growing beside a river. Pan's emblematic Arcadian invention, his pipe, was taken from reeds on the margin of the Ladon. According to the *Metamorphoses*, the randy god had chased a nymph named Syrinx, famous for her song. To escape him, she plunged to her death in the Ladon. When reeds near the spot seemed to mourn her, he used them for a song of his own:

> For while he sighed, the wind wrought from the reeds
> A soft resisting music. He replied
> To this invention of an eerie sound:
> "Then I shall sing back on your own new terms!"
> He waxed together reeds of different lengths
> And gave his instrument the lost nymph's name.

Pan is also the patron of Arcadian bees, who lend him their wax so he can play a "honeyed" song. It is an unearthly kind of music, one that drives people mad, as the eighteenth century's glass harmonica was reported to do. Only by a god's miracle could a melody actually be played through limp oaten reeds—which seems to be the point of Pan's own performance. But Virgil took it for granted that any shepherd can do what Pan can do:

> Play, Tityrus, oaten musings about trees.

Other poets blindly followed this example. In his *Shepherd's Calendar*, Spenser talked of the herdsman's "oaten pipe." Shakespeare's song in *Love's Labour's Lost* has a stanza beginning: "When shepherds pipe on oaten straws…" Milton talked of the "pastoral reed with oaten stop" in *Comus*, and of "rural ditties" being "temper'd to the oaten flute" in *Lycidas*. In fact, in the last work, when he wished to move on to more serious poetry, he said: "But now my oat proceeds…" Pope had the same thing in mind when he wrote: "O let my Muse, her slender reed inspire." All this miraculous stuff came, supposedly, from the non-sandy Ladon.

Just under Cyllene's southern slope lies the Stymphalian marsh, which Hercules dammed and drained when he killed the man-eating Stymphalian birds. Backward Arcadia obviously had special need of his "civilizing" labors. Of his twelve famous tasks, Hercules performed the first six in Arcadia or on its borders. He slew the giant boar on Cyllene's brother mountain, Erýmanthos. He captured Diana's magic deer beside the river Ladon. He diverted the river Alpheus to clean the stables of Augeas, king of Elis. He killed the "arrow-proof" lion in Nemea and the many-headed hydra in Lerna—both towns on the eastern boundary of Arcadia. The Greeks' own picture of Arcadia is authentically reflected not in Virgil's lounging flute players but in the dread efforts the region summoned from this toughest of demigods.

The marsh at Stymphalus was typical of Arcadia's ancient problems. Mountainous as it is, Arcadia does have some valleys silted up with alluvial soil. But until modern times, flooding made them difficult to farm. Aridity is a problem for much of Greece, but Arcadia more often suffered from too much water. The *Homeric Hymn to Pan* called Arcadia "thick with rills"; the red clay of the valleys clogged natural fissures in the limestone underneath. When water was trapped in the huge bowls formed by the mountains, the Arcadians did not have the tools or technology to break through these rocky containers, or to keep and control the amount of water they needed. Today, a dam downstream of the Ladon has formed a beautiful lake, harnessing the river to produce electricity. The lake, elbowing its way in and around abrupt mountain angles, looks like a Scottish loch—but it was warm when I put my hand in it, and the red clay gave a bloody tint to its margins. I have little doubt that Ovid could have made more of *that*, in terms of myth, than of his nonexistent sand.

The Arcadian poets had their own hydraulic system, one that

gave them just the right touch of rain (or shade or sun) in just the
right places:

> Phyllis, arriving, brightens all our leaves,
> Zeus ripples his approval in glad showers.

Here Virgil launched what has been called the "where-e'er you
walk" convention, after some lines in Pope's *Pastorals*:

> Where-e'er you walk, cool gales shall fan the glade.
> Trees, where you sit, shall crowd into a shade.

Ben Jonson had already used the device in a pastoral play, *The
Sad Shepherd*:

> The world may find the Spring by following her.

For such poets, the whole of meteorology depends on the route
of a Phyllis or an Amaryllis. Nature, grand in other genres, in pastoral
is tiresomely nice—which is the last thing one could call Arcadia.

North Arcadia's westward mountain, Erýmanthos, the home of
Hercules' boar, has ancient ruins at its base, where three rivers meet;
but the most imposing spot I visited is on a peak just to the east,
one oriented toward Erýmanthos's cult sites. This is ancient Mount
Aphrodisium, reached via a single-track dirt road that zigzags up
from the modern village of Paos. A temple area was uncovered here
in 1967 beside a Greek Orthodox chapel of Saint Peter. Everywhere
in this place of holy mountains, pagans and Christians have sought
similar traffic with the gods on heights.

You feel cut off from the world below, intimidatingly intimate
with the endless space above. In three directions from Mount
Aphrodisium, you see serried peaks, ridges overlooking ridges. By
late afternoon, shadowed parts of nearby mountains seem to recede,
while brightly lit points beyond them spring forward in the liquid
air. Playing tricks with space. These mountains are heavy with per-
manence. Yet they also seem to shift about, in angles they create, to

block or open up vistas—to show, all at once, similar heights in differing atmospheres. The result is a psychological effect that might be called "mountain dissociation." The religious experience of these mountains is what is most essential to Arcadia and most absent from Arcadian poetry. This is the land of the sublime, which is always a bit scary, not of the beautiful, which tends to be sedate. The pastoral landscape is what the Romans called a *locus amoenus*, an "agreeable place" (we get "amenities" from *amoenus*). But Arcadia does not accommodate. It challenges. You are disoriented here on Mount Aphrodisium, the necessary preliminary to reorientation in the rituals that were once performed in such out-of-the-way and hard-to-reach places.

A gorge more accessible, and often walked, lies in the middle of Arcadia, where the river Lusius gouges its way through cliffs into which famous monasteries have been built, facing each other over the cut. I began at the New Monastery of the Philosophers—called "New" because you descend the gorge past the old monastery, now deserted, called the Hidden School. The New Monastery looked deserted as well. Its little church was closed, though water and Greek sweets were set out in the small residence's open parlor. It was a precipitous walk of twenty minutes down to the river, and a panting forty minutes back up. There is a little concrete mule bridge over the Lusius, and another forty minutes would have taken me up the opposite cliff, to the monastery of John the Forerunner. I was content to see the famous river where Zeus was bathed by his nurses—*Lusius* means "bathing"—after his birth on nearby Mount Lycaeus. The water bounces through large boulders here, then whitens back in a dead-end pool and lashes sideways toward an oblique escape—an appropriate cracking of the earth for the high god's baby bathtub.

When I climbed back streaming sweat at noon (bad choice of time), a monk had made an appearance at the Monastery of the Philosophers, and he brought out a fresh bottle of water from the refrigerator. The one man who lives here was in the nearby town of Dhimitsana getting supplies, so the monk had driven his van over the long twisting roads from John the Forerunner, the other, more popular monastery—though he was quick to tell me that the Philosophers' old site below was the historically most important building in the area. It had trained over a dozen patriarchs who served in Constantinople. Though the Forerunner monastery is larger and more picturesque than this one, it is seen to better advantage from here, since it is built into the cliffside like a honeycomb in a cleft. Looking from this side (especially with binoculars, everywhere helpful in this place of distant heights and depths), you see the sheer drop that enables the monks to live like the old stylite saints, suspended in air.

The ruins of ancient Gortys are nearby: acropolis high on a cliff, healing center (Asclepieion) below by the rush of the Lusius. When I wound my car down to that site, I met a camping group that had pitched its tent by the river's noise. The Alpheus, an even more historic river that winds its endless way through pastoral poems, lies just below. (It was put to earlier, rough use, remember, for cleaning the Augean stables.) Milton told this stream's best-known story in his learned shorthand. In his "Arcades," an Arcadian is greeted with these words:

> Of famous Arcady ye are, and sprung
> Of that renowned flood, so often sung,
> Divine Alpheus, who by secret sluice,
> Stole underseas to meet his Arethuse.

Ovid's *Metamorphoses*, Milton's source, told the tale more straightforwardly. It is another of those fleeing-nymph stories, combined with the now-you-see-it-now-you-don't nature of Arcadian rivers. The river god Alpheus chases Arethusa, who *becomes* a river to *escape* a river. A deep plunge actually takes her, shooting under the Mediterranean, all the way to Sicily. Before that, however, her flight on land gives us another Arcadian geography lesson from a man who never saw Arcadia. Arethusa is speaking:

> Orchomenus I sped by, Psophis, high
> Cyllene—through the clefts of Maenalus
> Past wintry Erýmanthos into Elis.

She avoids the Alpheus, you see. But we must cross it now, into the southwest corner of Arcadia, where the oldest and darkest shrines are, where beast gods linger from primordial times. An appropriate gorge offers itself for another walk, where the river Neda shapes a tunnel. Neda was the name of Zeus's nurse, who guarded him as a baby and as a reward became a river. (Women were hydrotropic in Arcadia.) The most famous site in this area is the preserved Doric temple of Apollo the Rescuer, called that because he saved the Arcadians from a famous plague. Pausanias says the Arcadians believe the temple was designed by Ictinus, who built the Parthenon in Athens. If so, it is an earlier yet powerful vision. Its power remains to this day, even under the huge protective tent that has been erected over it—a replacement for the scaffolding that previously put collars on the columns, tilted at perilous angles by earthquakes.

The inner cell of this temple has a highly unusual side door opening east. One guess is that it was meant to look toward Mount Lycaeus, where there was another shrine to Apollo the Rescuer. The main feature of Lycaeus was an altar on the very peak, where the secret rites of Wolf-Zeus were celebrated. By car, it is a long and nervous climb up the one-trace road. I began to worry, halfway up, that I would have to change a tire here (a sharp rock on just such a road had caused a blowout the day before), alone, on a tricky slope. But when I reached the top, where an artificial mound marks the site of the ancient altar, I saw a tanned man, fortyish, seated coolly in the hammering sun, watching bees go by. From time to time he would whip out a net, catch a bee, extract it with his finger, study it, and then let it go.

I observed this as I climbed the conical summit. The man told me that he was working. He came here often, and to all the other mountains of the area, since he was writing a definitive survey of the bees of the Peloponnese. The last such effort was made in the nineteenth century, and those data are now obsolete. How many species are there in the region? He was still counting, and thought the number might reach 1,500.

Bees are one thing that the poets got right: they are everywhere. Virgil tells of "shrubs murmurous with bees, inducing sleep." My entomologist loved Lycaeus best of all, since here he discovered a bee specimen thought not to exist outside the Caucasus: the *Megachile diabolica*. He caught me one and, turning her over delicately, showed me the purple pollen pulsing in her sac. "They like only this purple plant," he explained. He wished he could show me a male—"They are more gorgeous"—but the males don't like the very top of the mountain.

In all the years he had come here, he had never before seen an American on this mountain. When he said this, in a marked German accent, I realized that every visitor I had seen in Arcadia's rural area (which is most of it) had been German too—the campers at Gortys; a bicyclist who had underestimated the mountains' challenge; a young couple with a baby; an elderly married couple who were meticulously following in the footsteps of Pausanias.

Lycaeus, in Arcadia's southwest corner, offers a stunning panorama of the whole region. I looked north to my starting place, Cyllene. Off to the east was Maenalus, holding the other corner of the south. "Beautiful here," the beeman said, "though not so nice before." The cone we stood on has meters of built-up cinders and bones from hundreds of years of sacrifice. My companion

---

Pausanias, a Greek physician from Asia Minor, was one of history's early travel writers. He roved the mainland of Greece for ten or twenty years during and after the reign of Hadrian in the second century A.D. This was the golden age of the Roman Empire and the leisure to visit historic sites is revealed in part by Pausanias's detailed descriptions of many Greek cities, temples, and historic places. Pausanias is clearly describing sites for the pleasure and edification of his contemporaries. He would have no trouble understanding the concept behind modern day travel guides.
—Sean O'Reilly, "Footloose in Antiquity"

reached down to pick up a sliver of what looked like petrified honeycomb, and when he gave it to me, I put it in my pocket. It was the work of his bee friends. "Bone," he said. "Maybe animal. Maybe human." On that he was wrong, however. Archaeologists have made a careful search of the place, but no human bones have turned up. Though the ancient Greeks firmly believed that human sacrifice continued here throughout classical antiquity, modern scholars such as Walter Burkert think the myth of sacrifice was a "founding tale" to explain an annual rite that declared one person a "werewolf" for the next seven years, a victim of Wolf-Zeus but also sacred to him, obliged to live away from human sight until the end of the term and then be miraculously restored to the community. The secrecy of the rites, based on their primordial continuity with the past, made everyone from Plato down to Pausanias assume the worst of their celebrants. This was, after all, the corner of Arcadia most tenacious of its various beast gods—Demeter with a horse's head; Eurynome with a fish's tail; for that matter, Pan with his goat hoofs and horns. No wonder other Greeks called Arcadians "folk older than the moon" and treated them the way some American sophisticates treat people who hail from those parts of the Ozarks that still shelter snake handlers and glossolalists.

Pan had a temple (not yet found by modern archaeologists) on the side of Mount Lycaeus. But he was not so much Zeus's subordinate here as his partner. When the Arcadian League was formed in 370 B.C. to oppose Spartan pressures from the south, the newly minted coins showed Wolf-Zeus on one side and a dignified Pan, throned, on the other side. Pan's priest also presided every other year at the Lycaean Games, alternating with the priest of Zeus. Pausanias tells us that, after the Olympics, these games were the oldest in Greece. They were celebrated at a hippodrome on a flat place near the mountain's peak. I looked down on it with the beeman, who had parked his van there. It had been newly resurfaced in preparation for local games that were to be held there later in the summer. The billboards announcing this event, placed on the lower slopes, had a large Pan affixed to the top of the billboard, playing his pipe.

*

From the southwest corner I went east to the most populous part of Arcadia. Here is Megalopolis, an ancient city formed from the merger of half a hundred villages that needed protection from Sparta. Megalopolis is hardly an industrial center, but it is as ugly as one. There are Three Mile Island-style nuclear converters that announce, ominously, that the dammed waters of Ladon cannot meet all of Arcadia's power needs. In the ruins of a famous temple at Lycosura, shadowed by steam clouds from the converters, lie colossal statues of Persephone and Demeter, sculpted by Damophon in the second century B.C. The heads are plaster casts, since the originals were removed to the National Archaeological Museum in Athens.

North of Megalopolis is another "merged" town, Trípolis, the modern capital of Arcadia, with busy and noisy squares and the first large group of young Arcadians I had seen since I came here. I had gone to Magouliana, the hometown of a man I had met in Athens, because he told me the church contained a beautifully carved wooden icon-stand. But the church was locked, and I could not turn up a single person to help me get in.

When I recounted this on my return to Athens, the man from Magouliana told me, "Yes, they are all gone. There is no way of making a living there." Before my trip to Arcadia, he had praised his region's beauty with genuine emotion. Now I asked him if he would ever return. "I can't. There is no way." He was like the mercenaries Hermippus wrote about twenty-five hundred years ago, unable to feed themselves from Arcadia's beautiful but cruel mountain heights. The whole area is sparsely populated. The only people visible in most places are shepherds and goatherds at work. And the breathtaking grandeur of the country cannot distract one from its disheartening poverty. When I ate lunch in a Trípolis tavern, a woman off the street begged for the uneaten part of my meal.

This is pastoral "Arcady"? Pan was no Disney creature frisking about. He was majestic in his willfulness, slyness, and anger. One of his cult titles was Goatboy-Penetrator Pan—a title illustrated on a famous vase now in the Boston Museum of Fine Arts, where Pan swoops after a goatherd preceded by several feet of his own phallus.

I thought of this Pan, the equivocal patron and penetrator, at the most resonant site in east Arcadia, my last stop. Here on the plain of Mantinea, Arcadians had fought three famous battles of antiquity— in 385 B.C., 362 B.C., and 222 B.C. Despite Pan's protection, they lost the first and third. Pan was a famous patron of war, a god on whom even the Athenians called when they needed help on the battlefield. Not that he ever wore armor or wielded a spear. Pan was valuable because he spread his eponymous "panic" through the ranks of one's foes. Euripedes, in the play *Rhesus*, said this fear makes men "tremble under Pan's whip." Panic comes on the eve of battle, as soldiers hear night noises and eerie echoes.

Mantinea lies at the base of Mount Maenalus, whose pines were often filled with Pan's noises. If there is any place where he should have protected the Arcadians, it is here. But even those who prayed for his assistance might have felt uneasy if they remembered how he won his power over the echoes that cause panic. Rebuffed in his pursuit of a singing nymph named Echo, Pan stirred his goatherds to animal frenzy, and they tore her limb from limb. Even her separated limbs still hummed with her song from their various burial sites—whence the echo. Virgil as usual, prettified the weird noises heard from Mount Maenalus:

Maenalian flutings play upon my pipe.
The pines of Maenalus are musical
And whisper herdsmen's amorous complaints—
Or Pan's ache for his nymph now lost in reeds.

But in *The Way Things Are*, the skeptical Lucretius presented a different view of Pan the victimizer:

For those who live in fields hear Pan far off—
His goatface framed with pointed fronds of pine,
He feathers his slim reeds with close-fit lips
And fills the woods with his insistent syrinx.

Lucretius was mocking the way Pan holds the superstitious in thrall. But a very practical Roman author on military science,

Aeneas Tacticus, wrote a chapter of his book *On Sieges* to counter the efficacy of what he called "panic—a word invented in the Peloponnese, more particularly in Arcadia."

The classical ruins at Mantinea lie in a field next to a weird modern Orthodox church, which looks like a Red Grooms's version of the Venetian Gothic cathedral at Torcello. Mantinea's classical agora, with traces of lost temples, is just beyond a small ancient theater pocketed in a slope. The city, it appears, was very compact. But if you drive up the corkscrew road to an adjoining little peak, you can look down on the remains of what were once quite extensive walls, large enough to enclose far more than the population of ancient Mantinea would seem to justify. It is conjectured, plausibly, that they were meant to contain the Mantineans' real wealth—their flocks of goats and sheep—from enemies who would slaughter them.

The first defeat of the Mantineans came when the Spartans made a weapon of Arcadia's old enemy: water. They dammed the river Ophis and diverted its flow, in a seasonal spate, against the unbaked brick of the walls, which dissolved and fell. It is easy to imagine the panic of the penned-in herds, Pan's own goats spreading the disorientation of fear to their human companions. Pan was a dangerous friend.

Some trace of that menace lingers into later Arcadian visions, especially in the two Poussin paintings called *Et in Arcadia Ego*. That sentence has been mistranslated as "Even I have lived in Arcadia." (If that were an accurate translation, *et* would be in a different place.) In a 1936 essay, Erwin Panofsky proved that the line, inscribed on tombs, comes from an old tradition and is the voice of Death: "Even in Arcadia, I (Death) am present." One could fancy, at times, that the most truthful message would be, "*Especially* in Arcadia..."

Yet the harsh tales were hard to credit on the sweet June day, cooled by late-afternoon breezes, when I walked the Mantinean fields. Near the old agora a herder was taking her goats home. From where I stood (sweat made me leave my glasses in the car, so I can't say for sure) she seemed young—at least, she was wearing a long dress, not the trousers most other women wear when working the herds. She looked, in the sunny haze, like a lady-in-waiting playing shepherdess at Marie Antoinette's court.

More astonishing, the ancient theater was set up for a play, its tiers of grass supplied with wooden benches above the few remaining ancient seats of stone. The set was created by bundles of mown hay, and the play recently performed there (spray cans and other paraphernalia of scene-setting were strewn about) had included as a prop, a little hay wagon. The play must have been a pastoral one! The Arcadian poets win, after all. Their dream of "Arcady" can be entertained anywhere—even in the real Arcadia.

It is tempting to cherish this as my last, least expected memory of Arcadia. But back in Athens I took out of my pocket the sliver of bone the beeman had given me on Mount Maenalus, part of a sacrifice made to Wolf-Zeus in a place no respectable Greeks wanted to recognize. Which is the real Arcadia? Pan knows; but if you ask him, he just laughs.

Garry Wills is Adjunct Professor of History at Northwestern University and former Associate Professor of Classics at Johns Hopkins University. Among his recent books are Papal Sin: Structures of Deceit, Witches and Jesuits: Shakespeare's Macbeth, John Wayne's America, *and* Lincoln at Gettysburg, *which won the Pulitzer Prize.*

CAROLINE ALEXANDER

Climbing to the Gods

*Mount Olympus has a draw as
powerful as any peak.*

IT STANDS A SCANT 9,570 FEET ABOVE SEA LEVEL, A MERE THIRD
the height of Everest, a bump upon a topographical map of the
planet's surface. Yet while Everest has teased the imagination of the
Western world only since the mid-nineteenth century, Olympus
has cast its substantial shadow over Western mankind for at least the
past 2,800 years.

My first view of Mount Olympus was while driving on the
Salonika-to-Athens highway, a short distance from where it strad-
dles the Macedonia-Thessaly border, arising abruptly and seemingly
without surrounding foothills from the flat plain of the Thermaic
Gulf, a massif like a great wall cutting and deflecting the low, late-
afternoon light. Its slopes were shadowy with forest and, above the
tree line, its broad summit was streaked with snow, although this
was June. So much for Homer, who in the *Odyssey* describes
Olympus thus:

> Olympos, where the abode of the gods stands firm
> and unmoving
> forever, they say, and is not shaken with winds nor
> spattered

with rains, nor does snow pile ever there, but the
shining bright air
stretches cloudless away, and the white light
glances upon it.

The climate of Olympus is probably the most abruptly change-
able of any mountain in Greece, with prevailing high winds and
churning mists generated by moist air rising from the nearby gulf.
Its summit is routinely hidden by thick clouds, a feature that
undoubtedly helped develop the mountain's mythology. Since
what was actually there had been shrouded from mortal eyes for
centuries, the way was clear to indulge in fanciful speculation.

But now, as we turned off the main highway toward the small
town of Litóchoron, the most common point of departure for an
ascent of Olympus, there was not a wisp of cloud in sight. The
mountain's broad summit was almost disconcertingly apparent, its
whole great bulk and every peak and crease clearly etched in the
low light, its streaks of snow gleaming plainly. I had come to
Olympus because its very name is legend, because of its mythology,
but I now discovered nothing at all preternatural or even mysterious about the mountain before me. In fact from an imminent hiker's
point of view, it looked comfortingly welcoming and accessible.

Litóchoron is a pleasant resort town audaciously set on the low
flanks of the mountain, but otherwise typical of so many in Greece
with narrow streets and a small square that is populated in the
evening by the town's male inhabitants, who gather to close the day
with conversation. A paved road leads out of the town toward
Prionia, the trailhead of the most popular route up Olympus. Two
and a half miles along the road one comes to a guardhouse and the
entrance to the Olympus National Park, the first national park to be
established in Greece, in 1938, the core of which is some 10,000
acres. Here, I was given a brochure with useful information about
the park and a map that looked as if it had once depicted the mountain in careful 3-D, but had subsequently been squashed and all its
features blurred. Luckily, as I would soon discover, no map was necessary, either to Prionia or to the mountain trail beyond.

*

Lying some nine miles above the guardhouse (almost an hour's drive, given the tortuous winding of the road), Prionia consists of a rough wooden shelter that serves as a basic restaurant, run by a not-over-friendly German but set picturesquely above a stream that tumbles in from the mountain. Here one can park and leave one's car and fill canteens with water, simple food can be had at the restaurant, although since the proprietor's mood appears to be as fickle as the Olympian weather, it is safer to bring supplies from Litóchoron.

My mother was my driver on this trip. She and I had already covered a good deal of Greece, at a fairly brisk clip, and this ascent of Olympus was intended to be a break from the road, a chance for me to stretch my legs and for her to relax. Our plan was to part ways at Prionia. From there I would hike to the park's refuge, which I had been told by the park guard lay some two and a half hours ahead, to spend the night. She would return to a hotel back in Litóchoron.

"But you are not going up now?" The worried speakers were a young Swiss couple, somewhat plump and very sweaty, who had just returned from the Olympian heights to Prionia. "Remember, it gets dark earlier in the mountains." Due to circumstances too frustrating to relate, we had set out for Litóchoron many hours later than planned. I had counted on daylight until 10 P.M. It was now seven.

"It will be dark at nine," said the Swiss man, and looked pointedly at his watch.

"But it's only—what? Two hours up?" I said, swinging my day pack over my shoulder.

The couple politely raised their eyebrows. "I think it is more like three and a half hours," said the young man tentatively, reluctant to unsettle me completely.

"What do I do?" I said to my mother, as the couple plodded wearily away. I had read various accounts about how well Olympian trails were marked ("Many people get lost right at the outset," according to my guidebook). And then there had been the recent tragic events on Everest dramatically demonstrating that hubris on a mountain doesn't pay. This was only a short hike to be sure, a mere jaunt in the normal scheme of things—but then it was the home of the gods.

"Now," said my mother. "We have no other opportunity to do this." She was—and, indeed, still is—a successful racing swimmer, competitive by nature, one might say, a fact that occasionally gives a certain keen edge to her opinions. "You will just have to do it," she continued, squaring her shoulders. "Start walking and just go!"

"You can make it," she called after me, as I marched away toward the refuge into the gathering dusk.

In fact, had I not been racing against encroaching darkness, this would have seemed the ideal time to set out. The light was gold, filtering through the pine-and-beech forest. The air here was gentle and cool, while the Thessalian plain, only a few hours away, had been murderously hot. And, unsurprisingly at this late hour, there were no other people.

So far, the way was clear, marked less by a strict trail than by a narrow path. Bright wildflowers—violets, periwinkles, and buttercups—showed in the soft tussocks of grass beneath the trees. An occasional wind swept through. One has to travel widely in Greece to appreciate fully the richness of Olympus's forests and their protective shade. In the Argolis, for example, farther south, boulder-strewn hills glare so ferociously under the Aegean sun that the mere thought of climbing them makes one wilt. Elsewhere, much of the land that a casual traveler sees from the road, or from the most-frequented sites, is intensely, anciently domesticated, its forests long gone for timber, or firewood, or cultivation. The acres of silvery-leaved olive orchards, stunted and gnarled, are often the only relief for miles around. Yet here was towering shade, cool and occasionally pine scented. It would have been nice to linger, but dutifully, ever heedful of the night gods, I marched on.

The tree coverage soon changed, becoming stumpy pine. The forest opened, and I had views over the mountain's ravines and gullies. "Many-folded Olympus," Homer had called it, the kind of glib phrase, like "rosy-fingered dawn," that one assumes, before close examination, to be merely formulaic, poetic but empty. But with the dusky light manifestly trapped in the flank of the mountain's folds and creases, the epithet was revealed as dazzlingly apt.

The path crossed a more naked land, where trees appeared to have recently been felled by natural disaster—a high wind or storm, rather than the hand of man. Shortly before nine o'clock, just as the night had finally set in, albeit with the trail still unambiguously clear, I saw what appeared to be a building looming ahead. Puzzled, I wondered if it was a kind of halfway house. Closer, and its lighted windows showed that it was inhabited. Dripping with sweat, my pulse thumping hard, I clambered up stone steps to a paved court-yard and realized I had, in fact, arrived at the refuge.

"You are just in time for dinner," said the woman at the recep-tion desk. "We close the kitchen at nine." By the clock on the wall, it was a quarter to the hour; my determined pace had brought me here in less than two hours. Later, back in the United States, when I told a friend about how the Swiss couple at Prionia had inspired this unnecessarily speedy feat, he replied with a story about hiking in the Alps: "They have signs posted that tell you how many hours it takes to walk between each stage; and next to the hours it always says 'Swiss Time.' Apparently, Swiss time is a lot longer than anyone else's because they like to stop to take in the view."

The E-4 or European Long Distance Trail, a route devised to take hikers through the most scenic areas in Europe, from the Pyrenees to southern Greece, joins one of the routes on Olympus, insuring a steady stream of European hiking traffic. There are three refuges on the mountain (not including a shelter below Prionia), but at the time of my visit two were closed until the peak months of July and August. I had reserved a bed at Refuge A, Spilios Agapitos, which can reputedly accommodate some ninety people, but on that June evening there were fewer than twenty. And, as I discovered, it was not even necessary to have carried a sleeping bag. A supply of thick, soft blankets was in each room, and each bed had a pillow—with a clean pillowcase.

After a cold shower, I made my way to the cozy dining room, simply furnished with wooden tables and benches. The menu was basic (and reasonably priced), strongly favoring serious carbohydrates: thick Greek bean soup, pasta, chunks of bread and cheese. There were only three other groups of hikers present: some Englishmen, who had already made their ascent and kept watchfully to themselves; a group of determinedly hearty middle-aged Swiss men and women, dressed in high-waisted, suspender-held knee breeches, and a party of young Swiss mountain guides, who apparently spent all their leisure time climbing other mountains. They had come, as it turned out, less to scale the heights of Olympus than to hang glide off its summit.

"We have tandems," they told me enthusiastically over dinner. "We fly down in pairs." Their plan was to climb to the summit in the morning and then wait and see how the wind fared. One young man, lean and spare with a blond crew cut, explained tersely: "If the wind is strong, well, it can be difficult." Then he turned back to his dinner. I was both impressed and aghast at this image of nonchalantly stepping off the world's most legendary mountain. Wasn't this tempting fate? Hadn't they heard of Icarus? They grinned.

"Olympus is nice," said one of the women, smiling. "But it is just a mountain."

Before turning in, I went out for a farewell look at the stars. The sky was deep royal blue, the stars bright above the pine trees that surrounded the refuge. But in many ways the Swiss hang gliders were right: Olympus is just another mountain, and I had obtained this same bright view from any number of alpine villages throughout Greece. Olympus brought one no nearer to the heavens. Beautiful as its slopes were, its mystique nonetheless lay, I determined, in the view from below, the worm's-eye view, the view of earthbound mortal man looking to the heights.

The following day began abruptly at 6:30 A.M. with the start-up of the electrical generator. In the dining room, the tables were set for breakfast, with bread, jam, honey, pots of hot coffee and tea. I was unashamed of such luxury on a hiking trip. The Olympian gods had their cupbearers, so why not we?

From Refuge A to the mountain's true peaks is a walk of about three hours. Shortly above the refuge the tree line ceased, and the contours of Olympus were laid bared, rolling and gentle. The snow-fields, which seen from below appeared merely to streak the mountainside here and there, were now revealed as substantial features, great drifts of tenacious snow. In some years, I was told, paths can remain blocked through June.

The trail became more uncertain, stamped out now not on earth, but on pale, broken rock that slid and slipped beneath my feet. The climb became steeper, and although the day was still cool, I was conscious of the sun beating on me through the rarefied air. Again, the virtues of an off-season ascent were apparent: from Refuge A, there is only one sensible route to the summit, and to have to have shared this with a crowd of ninety people could only have made the going more difficult. As it was, I felt, again, as though I had the mountain to myself. Once on the actual rocky summit, I looked around; there was not another mortal in sight.

I sat awhile, enjoying the wind that had come up suddenly and wondering how it would affect the plans of the hang gliders. In one direction, I looked down onto the plain below, with its patchwork of multicolored fields and its one visible settlement. In the other, I looked into the heart of the mountain, with its sloping valleys of green felt, holding the last of winter's snow.

The hang gliders were coming up as I made my way down, carefully negotiating the loose scree underfoot. Their eyes were on the summit and their senses were attuned to each minute variation in the wind. We greeted each other as we passed. My mind was already on the wildflowers that lay in the pine shade of the forest below. I intended to dally there on the tussocky grass, to drink in the dappled shade.

Caroline Alexander is the author of five books, including The Endurance: Shackleton's Legendary Antarctic Expedition; One Dry Season: In the Footsteps of Mary Kingsley; *and* The Way to Xanadu. *Her work has appeared in major magazines including* The New Yorker, Outside, Smithsonian, *and* National Geographic, *and she lives on a farm in New Hampshire.*

KATY KOONTZ

The Wedding that
Almost Wasn't

It takes the will of the gods—and plenty
of faith—to get married in Greece.

MOST BRIDES WORRY ABOUT THEIR GUEST LIST, THE BRIDESMAIDS'
fittings, and about whether they're doing the Right Thing. When I
got married, the anxiety options were slightly different. I worried
that the mayor would be out of town, that no one would speak
English, and whether the ceremony would be legal.

When Steven and I decided to wed, we also decided we didn't
want to go about this in the ordinary way. We just couldn't see
ourselves in a classic wedding scene, so we shelved that idea for
something totally (and literally) foreign. Our dream was to be married on the Greek island of Santorini—no attendants, no garter toss,
and no audience, but atmosphere to spare.

The setting is certainly dramatic, with white, cube-shaped houses
and blue-domed churches clustered like LEGOS as they cascade
down red lava cliffs that encircle the largest volcanic caldera in the
world. But even more significantly this was where we took our first
shared vacation. Although Steven got food poisoning then and I had
to take him to the hospital, the same man who suffered a shot in his
derriere because I told him the cheese pies on the corner were
delicious insisted that Santorini would be the only place for us to
say "I do."

Thus began eight months of American-style type-A-personality planning. Armed with four pages of instructions from the State Department, I made lists, wrote letters, and placed trans-Atlantic phone calls at 4 A.M. Steven had our birth certificates translated, and I signed up for two semesters of Greek classes at New York University.

By an incredible coincidence, the mayor of Oía—the tiny fishing village on the northern tip of Santorini where we wanted to hold the ceremony—turned out to be a close friend of my Greek teacher. With her help, we thought, this was turning out to be cake. Pure baklava.

Even our parents were game for the adventure. Mine were mute at first, as though we'd told them we were moving to Nicaragua. Steven's father took the news well but his mother broke out in hives. Once the initial shock wore off, they all wanted to come.

Yet as well as our plans were going, a certain refrain continued to haunt me. One of the first letters of advice from abroad we received ended with: "As with many things in Greece, life changes. So our advice to you is to be flexible with both your time and your patience…. Life can fall apart anywhere along the line!"

I was confident that we were doing all we could to prevent anything from falling apart anywhere along the line. But I also understood from firsthand experience that for all its charm, Greece is not a place where people write dates in ink on calendars.

When the time came, we whizzed through the formalities in the American Embassy in Athens (where we were asked to raise our right hands and swear that everything we had written on the application was true; I answered "yes" and Steven answered "thank you"), and we were off to Santorini.

Perhaps we should have paid more attention to the fact that our appointment with the mayor had been set for Friday the thirteenth. When we went to the mayor's office the next day for the license, she wasn't there. She wasn't even on the island. No one knew when she would return and she hadn't left us any messages. Further, the town secretary, Petros, was the only one in Oía who knew how to grant us a license, and he, too, was gone indefinitely.

Things were starting to fall apart at some very important places along the line.

The vice mayor offered to marry us but he not only didn't speak English, he didn't know the procedure. The ceremony would have been about as legal as one officiated by Aristotle Onassis (alive or not).

For three days, we sweated it out until the mayor returned. She promised to marry us with or without Petros, but she admitted that she didn't know the legal requirements any more than the vice mayor. By the morning that was originally supposed to be our wedding day, she had finally heard from the all-powerful Petros. He was arriving the following day and if we came back at noon for the license, our wedding could be that evening.

We awoke the next day still not convinced we'd be husband and wife by sundown. At noon, we were in what passed for a line with about eight Greeks who also needed the popular Petros. He was so busy that the mayor suggested we return in an hour, but I wasn't letting this man out of my sight.

Good thing. Five minutes later, Petros burst out of his office carrying a small bag and headed for the door. "I think he's leaving," Steven told me in the same tone usually reserved for "I think I've been shot."

I turned to the mayor with an expression of incredulous horror, blurting out, "Is he really leaving?" She nodded, seemingly unconcerned, and replied with a wave of dismissal, "He's crazy." Crazy or not, the only man who could ensure we would be legally married by the end of the day had just quit.

I sprinted after Petros as he climbed into his car and threw myself on the about-to-be-closed door, pleading. He ignored me, putting the key in the ignition. I wondered if I would have to resort to jumping on the hood as Steven ran to get a friend to translate.

Petros, we found out, was infuriated because the mayor supposedly wouldn't allow him time to eat his yogurt (the contents of the aforementioned bag). He kept saying he'd quit and the mayor would marry us—we didn't need him. I kept insisting that without him, our marriage would not be official.

So there we were, one fuming and famished Greek, two frantic Americans, and a sympathetic interpreter on a piece of Greek paradise that was quickly becoming a living Hades.

Since logic was getting us nowhere, I did some fast thinking. I imagined what a Greek woman faced with the same insane situation would do, and thus staged a hysterical crying fit, flinging about phrases such as "halfway around the world," "eight months of planning," "everything ruined," and throwing in an agonized "gave us your word" as the kicker.

The plan worked. Reluctantly, and after being assured he could eat all the yogurt he wanted, Petros returned. I'd charged out of that office a ballistic missile. But I returned a bride.

The rest of the story is a fairy tale. Later that day, a violinist and a bouzouki player led the two of us and our parents through the narrow, winding marble streets of Oía. We kept one eye on the breathtaking scenery and another on our path (which was covered with donkey droppings).

When we got to city hall, the mayor and the license were both exactly where they were supposed to be, and no one could think of any reason why we should not be united in holy matrimony.

After the ceremony, there was spirited Greek dancing before we were led back through the streets as tourists and locals alike applauded and threw rice. In disbelief, we clutched our two marriage certificates (his and hers) as we climbed into a taxi and headed for a restaurant built into the cliffs overlooking the caldera.

Before dinner we stood on the terrace and sipped champagne, watching the sunset and catching our breath. Had this been worth all the emotional effort? No question, we agreed. But the next time we decide to change our lives drastically—by, say, having a baby—this couple is staying home.

Freelance writer Katy Koontz and her husband Steven Friedlander live in Knoxville, Tennessee, with their daughter Samantha (age seven). When they returned to Greece two years ago to celebrate their tenth anniversary, Sam in tow, they discovered that wedding consultants had become a thriving business on Santorini.

DON MEREDITH

One of the Twelve

*If you pay attention, you can
see the ages colliding.*

THIS HOUSE IN LÍNDOS BELONGS TO FRIENDS OF FRIENDS. COZY
and fundamental, it was built in 1620, the year our Pilgrim Fathers
set their buckled shoes on Plymouth Rock. The Greek sea captain
who put it up probably wasn't following the exploits of those dour
Puritans. He was more interested in a few storm-proof rooms to
bunk down in during the Aegean winters.

Líndos is on an island, of course. Islands are almost compulsory
in Greece. This island is Rhodes, one of a dozen that comprise the
Dodecanese—"The Twelve." Actually there are fourteen islands in
the group, but a forgetful cartographer skipped a couple when he
named the archipelago a few centuries back. Shaped like an obsid
ian arrowhead, roughly forty-five miles by twenty, Rhodes is the
largest. And of all Greek islands, except for tiny Kastellorizo, farthest
from the Greek mainland. On an autumn afternoon, from a dusty
olive grove high on the Psinthos Hills, I see the mountains of
Turkey only a score of miles across the Aegean.

An hour's drive down the island's rugged east coast from the city
of Rhodes is Líndos where, in a tangle of cobbled alleys, my sea
captain's house is one of a hundred or so. Scattered along the road
to Líndos are pastel resorts featuring long, torrid walks to mobbed

beaches, and toy swimming pools like green vitamin pills. For history buffs there's an overwhelming selection of modern Greek ruins—forever unfinished buildings of shabby concrete erupting in festive explosions of rebar like rusty fireworks. Beyond Archángelos, however, civilization fades to silvery groves, sea views, and shaggy goats cropping clumps of wild thyme. At the island's midriff the two-lane road passes over a wind-swept ridge, then cuts between bony metamorphic crags. Below, on a nearly landlocked bay that spreads blue and green as a peacock's tail, lies white-washed Líndos. Over it the acropolis soars, sheer cliffs crowned by a medieval tonsure of Crusader walls and the Doric columns of the Temple of Athena Líndia—the Pillars of Kleoboulos.

I arrived on the eve of the Little Summer of St. Demetrius, the last two limpid weeks of October when tourists fade and the weather, so the story goes, is splendid. In his book about Rhodes, *Reflections on a Marine Venus,* Lawrence Durrell chose the Saint's Little Summer for a jaunt through the Dodecanese "...counting on its last fine days to enable me to travel as far as Leros and back on equable seas." Clearly St. Demetrius hadn't read the English author, for on the 18th a Homeric tempest rolled in—thunder and lightning, wind and lashing rain. Five days and nights I hunkered in my sea captain's house while lightning crackled in the courtyard and rain swam down the walls. When the wind dropped at last and the sky turned a scrubbed Grecian blue, I stepped out to assess the damage. It was extensive: lanes were rivers, houses inundated, roads buried beneath Alps of mud or scoured into nonexistence. Near Archángelos a mountain had collapsed onto a car packed with English picnickers. Germans, hiking gaunt ridges to scrutinize the storm, were struck by lightning. Huddled sensibly in snug houses, Greeks went unscathed. When it was over, after endless shouting and arm waving, they set to work and quickly cleaned up. By noon of the 24th, two days before his feast day, St. Demetrius was again in ascendancy.

Tough, brash, and proud, Greeks are survivors. At the hub of the Balkans, they have to be. Nowhere is this more true than on Rhodes, the Eastern Mediterranean strategic stepping stone between Asia

Minor and Europe. From the Minoans of 1800 B.C. to the British occupying forces at the end of World War II, a dozen powers have ruled the island, Romans, Turks, and Germans among them. Phoenicians and Cretans colonized it in prehistoric times, and later the Dorians settled three major sites, Ialyssos, Kameris, and the capital Líndos. In 408 B.C. these prosperous and culturally advanced cities elected to build Rhodes, a new capital on the northern tip of the island. But Líndos kept its autonomy and, with its superb natural harbor, remained strategically and commercially important.

Two thousand years of civilization are sandwiched into Líndos like the ingredients in a historical Dagwood. Along cobbled streets just wide enough for a pair of donkeys to pass, arched doorways open into courtyards paved in sea-pebble mosaics. Here the deep, white-washed walls of four- and five hundred year old houses, some dating from the Age of the Knights of St. John, float in the resonant shade of hibiscus, bougainvillea, oleander, and geraniums.

On my evening walk beneath the shadowy arbor of Acropolis Street, I look in at the Church of Panaghia, the Virgin Mary. Built in the fourteenth century in the shape of a cross, it shoulders the tiled swelling of an octagonal dome. In a candle-lit interior fragrant with incense, women kneel before a seventeenth-century altar screen as a bearded priest in stovepipe hat and cassock shuffles from the vestry to say Mass. Smoky walls, painted in the Byzantine style, depict the lives of Christ and the Virgin Mary. Beneath layers of lacquer and candle grease is a curious zoomorphic portrait of St. Christopher resembling a jackal. A story goes that St. Christopher was so handsome women wouldn't leave him alone. Racked by temptation he asked God to make him less beautiful. God answered his prayer by turning him into an animal. A curious Christian twist on the fairy tale of *Beauty and the Beast*.

From the church I stroll to Eleftherias Square where I sit among stray cats under the great plane tree, listening to a spring-fed fountain spill into an ancient basin of carved stone. Around the tree's whitewashed trunk children scramble at hide-and-seek while mustachioed men in sweaters and caps gather on benches to gossip above the darkening harbor.

On the village's eastern rim lies St. Paul's Bay, a basin of sapphire water nearly penned in by rugged limestone walls. From a rocky beach at the bottom of a steep path I take my morning swim. The water is cool and translucent. Fish dart over pale stones while deep green swells slide through a narrow passage in the cliff's face that allows small fishing boats to escape to the open sea. Legend says the Apostle Paul landed in this tiny harbor to evangelize the island. He was being transported to Rome to stand trial when a storm nearly sank his ship. By a miracle the ship's crew found this small port and avoided catastrophe. On a rock shelf across the bay the Chapel of the Apostles, gleaming white, honors the saint's visit.

With few tourists to tote to the acropolis, Manoli Meletzis's donkeys grow sleek and lazy. Big dun-colored brutes sporting padded saddles and brass stirrups, they look bored as they loaf around the shaded enclosure on the street to the post office. To renew the beast's interest in life, Manoli volunteers an especially roguish-looking animal to give me a trip to the acropolis. Riding was never my passion. Donkey and I size each other up and conclude it isn't a match.

Like Switzerland's Matterhorn soaring above the spick-and-span streets of Zermatt, the acropolis of Líndos is always present—looming above my courtyard, rising across the blue expanse of Líndos Harbor, reflected in the quiet waters of St. Paul's Bay. I've waited for the perfect moment to savor the ascent. On a morning when wind and passing rain have scrubbed the sky clean, I follow a lane up the village's northern slope. It's just after daybreak. Even Manoli's donkey isn't here to divert me. Where the lane becomes a path, lilac, cyclamen, and crocuses big as teacups blossom among the stones. Goats bleat, and I hear the distant chuffing of a fishing boat. The path rounds a spur of rock, then mounts to the top.

This naturally fortified crag has a long history. Excavations begun by Danish archaeologists in 1902 have unearthed everything from 5,000-year-old Neolithic tools to a plaque inscribed by a priest of the Temple of Athena in 99 B.C. listing visiting dignitaries: Helen of Troy, Alexander the Great, the King of Persia. A temple stood on the site as early as 1500 B.C., but the existing ruins span just 2,000 years, from a sixth-century B.C. stairway to the fifteenth-century A.D. ramparts of the Knights of St. John.

The Order of the Knights of St. John, a quasi-religious, quasi-military association, was among the Crusader forces that stormed into Jerusalem in the sweltering July of 1099. Their Tenancy lasted 192 years, until 1291 when a Muslim army turned them out. The Knights retreated to the island of Cyprus, fortified their position, and took stock. To protect their western flank and keep lines of communication open to Europe, they needed Rhodes. They laid siege in 1307, and in the summer of 1309 captured the island from the Emperor of Constantinople. The Knights ruled the island for over 200 years, building the citadel at Rhodes, one of the finest and best preserved medieval fortifications in existence.

> For while the Rhodians believed they were going to the death, they gained the victory over the thousands of Turks who were besieging the city of Rhodes. I think the signs will remain until the day of the Last Judgment.
>
> —Pietro Casola,
> circa 1494

The crenelated wall at the top of the path is the Knights' legacy to the acropolis at Líndos. There's also the Commandery of the Knights and the medieval stairway that leads up to it. But the first step brings a feeling of historical schizophrenia so common here. For hewn into the cliffside is a Greek trireme, a stunning bas relief carved in the Hellenistic period, a large and lifelike impression of a second-century B.C. ship of war.

Beyond the vaulted rooms of the Knights' Commandery is the stairway of the Doric Stoa, the third-century B.C. portico with its colonnades partially restored. Its purpose was to monumentalize the entrance to the Temple Sanctuary. The Stoa and the dramatic stairway and colonnades of the earlier fourth-century B.C. Propylaea led the worshipers of ancient Greece to the culmination of their pilgrimage. Six hundred feet above the azure Aegean, poised majestically on a narrow wedge of rock, hangs the Temple of Athena Líndia—today a half-dozen slender, lion-colored columns and a fragment of a handsomely carved lintel.

From the cliff top the blue basin of St. Paul's Bay lies to the east, on the west Líndos Harbor and the village with its intricate, cobbled streets and blazing whitewashed houses. Below, in Eleftherias Square, the stone bench circles the plane tree, mountain water spills from the cliffside fountain, and tables and chairs catch the sun. The bells of the Church of Panaghia resound. Hundreds of feet below the temple a toy boat rides the translucent sea while a fisherman sets out his lines.

I'm content to loaf on a chunk of tumbled marble and admire the ancient stones. Athena was one of those anthropomorphic gods peculiar to the Greeks—an immortal being who could descend to earth to intervene in human affairs. One of the Twelve Olympians. Goddess of Wisdom, protectress of households and cities, patroness of arts and crafts, guardian of Greek heroes. Deep beneath my marble perch, hollowed into the cliffside above the sea, is a cave where rituals were performed before the Age of Bronze.

The temple was begun in the sixth century B.C. by Kleoboulos of Líndos. A tyrant who rose to power, historians say, by "illegitimate means." He was also a philosopher and poet. Nothing of his teaching endures although he was listed among the "Seven Wise Men of Antiquity." It is known he believed in educating women; his wife and daughter became his students. Only one poem remains, an epitaph of Gordius, King of Phrygia. The epitaph, and the architectural poetry of the Temple of Athena Líndia—six slender columns suspended like a dream against a sea and sky blue as delftware: Kleoboulos's pillars, pure and enduring as music.

Don Meredith's writing has appeared in numerous publications, including Poets & Writers Magazine, Texas Review, *and on* Salon.com. *He lives on the island of Lamu, off the northern coast of Kenya, in a house named after the dozens of ibis birds that wing their way overhead each morning.*

Slumming the Pink Palace

At Greece's #1 party hostel, the ouzo flows,
the crockery flies, and the unspoken laws
of romantic expediency run the show.

BY THE TIME VALENTINA AND I HAVE FINISHED OFF OUR CARAFE OF white wine in the little back-alley taverna, I can only conclude that our night in Corfu Town has been perfect. Tourist brochure perfect.

Fortunately, I have just the plan to keep things from getting overly quaint and predictable. "Let's stay at the Pink Palace tomorrow," I say.

Valentina raises her eyebrows. "Sounds romantic."

"It isn't," I tell her.

I first met Valentina in Innsbruck (where she goes to university) and we've been traveling together ever since. Though our love affair is just over one week old, it has already consisted of several canonical romantic experiences: hiking together through the mist in the Italian Alps, walking the canals of Venice at sunset, taking the night train down the Adriatic coast to Brindisi. This morning we sat together on the lifeboat-deck of a ship that took us down the Albanian coastline to Corfu—a Greek Ionian resort island that features historical Venetian fortresses, Byzantine churches, British palaces, and a French-styled esplanade in its colonial Old Town district. We strolled the narrow streets this evening until we found a tiny family-run restaurant that gave us a sumptuous introduction to moussaka and *yemista* and *choriatiki*.

Unfortunately, I'm beginning to fear that our experiences have been too easy—that our moments of romance have been pleasant without being distinctive. Since I don't want all these blissful moments to mix together into generic memories, I've decided to throw a wild card into the equation.

"What's special about staying at the Pink Palace?" Valentina asks me.

"Well that's just it. All I know about the Pink Palace is rumor and reputation. I've heard that it's kind of an ultimate party hostel for college-age travelers, but it has a mixed reputation. Depending on who you talk to, the place is either party paradise or Sodom and Gomorrah revisited."

"And why does that make you want to stay there? You're not in college and I don't much care for partying. Plus we're traveling together, and this sounds like the kind of place where single people go to meet other single people."

"And that's exactly why I think it'd be an adventure."

Valentina, who (as an Italian) was raised with much less an appreciation for irony than I, is not convinced. "Adventure? Inside a youth hostel?"

"Not an adventure adventure; kind of an un-adventure. Going to a place where we don't really fit in and seeing what happens. It's called 'slumming.' It's a very American pastime."

"This is how Americans entertain themselves?"

Since I don't have the time to explain the ironic middle-class appeal of, say, square dancing or gangsta rap or monster truck rallies, I decide to keep things simple. "Yes," I say. "This is how Americans entertain themselves."

Curious by nature, Valentina relents. The next morning, we take a local bus across the island to the picturesque beach town of Ágios Gordios and check into a room at the legendary Pink Palace.

Of all the hundreds of youth hostels on the European backpacker circuit, only a handful—Balmer's Interlaken, for example, or Bob's Youth Hostel in Amsterdam—have legendary reputations. Corfu's

Pink Palace has found its way into this elite rank through a combination of leisure-resort amenities (three-course dinners, a Jacuzzi, jet-ski rentals), and an ouzo-soaked party atmosphere. The resulting ambience garners mixed opinions: The Let's Go guidebook compares it to a "laid-back frat party"; independent student-travel websites call it the "number one party hostel in Europe"; travel writer Jeff Greenwald once called it "a knock-off Club Med for horny twenty-year-olds."

Valentina and I arrive at Ágios Gordios at midday and head down to the trademark pink-hued buildings. From a distance, the Pink Palace complex has a kind of neoclassical elegance—but up close, the place is all function: cement-and-asphalt simplicity, party-resistant by design. Supposedly, the complex can handle 1,000 budget revelers at a time.

I get my first and most vivid lesson in the social dynamics of the Pink Palace when I leave Valentina at poolside and go to fetch a spare key from the reception building.

When I enter the lobby, there is only one soul working the desk—and he is currently initiating a batch of new guests by distributing shots of pink-tinted ouzo. All of the new travelers clutch their cardboard Pink Palace "passports," and one of them has already donned a t-shirt advertising the "Ten Biggest Lies at the Pink Palace" ("I just want to kiss you…you can keep your clothes on," reads no. 8).

There's one other traveler waiting at the desk—a tall, sunburned British girl—so I ask her if any other receptionists are on duty.

"Calm down, big guy!" she says. "You're on vacation, now." She looks me over and shoots me a jesting grin. "Let me guess, you're from America."

"That's right," I say.

"I could tell because you talk like a cowboy. You can always tell Americans from their accents. That, and they always talk so loud. And they never know anything about the country they're in."

"I've heard of that reputation," I say. "But I'm actually learning to read Greek while I'm here."

The British girl gives me a playfully skeptical look and holds up a wrinkled drachma note. "What does this say right here?" she demands, pointing at one of the Greek-lettered slogans.

"It's easier than it looks to read Greek," I say, taking the money from her. "Look. The T, A, Z, E, and O in this phrase are all just like in English, but for example the triangle is a "D" sound, and the lambda here is like an "L." So this reads 'Trapeza tees Ellados.'"

"Wow! You could be my Greek teacher then, right? What does 'Trapeze...so and so' mean?"

"I'm not sure."

She shoots me an exaggerated look of suspicion. "How can you not be sure what it means if you can read Greek?"

"I just know the Greek letters. Once you learn the letters, then you can read things phonetically; it doesn't mean you can understand them."

The girl giggles and socks me in the shoulder. "You dummy! You don't really read Greek, just the letters."

For some reason, I can't understand why she's getting so worked up about this. "Knowing the letters can help you figure things out," I tell her. "For example, 'Trapeza tees Ellados' probably means 'Bank of Greece.' You know, Ellados, Hellenic. Greece."

> "*Yamas*," the brown-haired woman said to us as she held up a shot glass of ouzo, tinted pink. "*Yamas* means cheers in Greek," she explained. "It's the only word you'll need to know while you're here at the Pink Palace."
>
> She was right. Days of volleyball, sunbathing, and hot-tubbing—punctuated with shots of ouzo—gave way to nights of drinking, dancing, flirting, and groping among hundreds of well-tanned travelers from all corners of the world. Plates were cracked over heads, hangovers hung over, international hormones surged—and it wasn't even high season! After three days we left to explore more remote locales. The Pink Palace had been fun, but we had yet to see anything remotely Greek, except the ever-present bottle of pink ouzo.
>
> —Tara Austen Weaver, "Three Days at the Pink Palace"

"Well, perhaps I'll believe you then. I thought you were just, you know, taking the piss out of me. You don't meet many intelligent Yanks in Europe, you know."

"Well, I wouldn't credit my 'Yank' initiative as much as my Italian girlfriend. It was her idea to practice our basic Greek on the ferry in from Brindisi yesterday."

At my mention of the word "girlfriend," the girl's face goes red and she puts her hand to her mouth. There is a beat before I realize what this means. The British girl was never really interested in my intelligence or my Greek skills. This whole time she thought I'd been flirting with her.

Fortunately, our awkward moment is broken by the reception clerk, and soon I'm headed back down to the pool area with a new key. I arrive to discover Valentina sitting by the Jacuzzi with a couple of English guys.

"'Valentina,'" one of them says to her. "That's a great name. That's a beautiful name. You don't find girls named Valentina in England." As he's saying this, Valentina notices me walking up and gestures to me. "This is the traveling friend I was telling you guys about," she says to her new companions.

The English fellows stare at me blankly. Obviously, they'd assumed that Valentina's "traveling friend" was female.

"Howdy," I say to them. "Where are you all from?"

Neither of the English guys takes another look at Valentina. After thirty seconds of pleasantries, they both excuse themselves.

Within four hours of our initial arrival at Ágios Gordios—after a lull midday session of sunbathing and bodysurfing and hanging out at the Jacuzzi—Valentina and I finally conclude that we have ceased to exist in this corner of Greece.

There is almost an element of farce to this whole scenario. Whenever Valentina or I individually walk down to the beach or out to sit on the dining patio, each of us is able to strike up perfectly charming conversations with our fellow travelers. Whenever we go anywhere together, however, we're treated like chaperones.

Admittedly, our fellow travelers are not being rude. Rather, they are simply abiding by the laws of romantic expediency, and—as an

obvious couple—we don't register much of a blip on the Pink
Palace radar. Perched like ghosts on the balcony outside our room,
Valentina and I watch our single peers frolic in the Jacuzzi and on
the volleyball court below.

As the day nears its end, the poolside activity begins to pick up.
The sun-reddened Brits and Canadians and South Africans who
spent the afternoon nursing their hangovers are now whooping it
up over beers in the Jacuzzi, and an energetic gaggle of Americans
have just returned from cliff diving to start up a volleyball game
that integrates ouzo shots and kissing.

"This is a rather strange place," Valentina tells me.

"Do you wish we hadn't come?"

"No, it's nice here. Everything is quite pleasant. I just feel older
than I am."

In a sense, we are indeed older than our peers, but this has nothing to do with calendar years. At the Pink Palace, youth consists of
possibility: the possibility for loud camaraderie and drunken
epiphany; the possibility of sex, and the dance of ego and entendre
that comes with it. Though we've enjoyed the beach and the setting here, Valentina and I can relate to our single neighbors only as
objective outsiders, as scientists. To run down and join the ouzo-
volleyball game or frolic in the Jacuzzi wouldn't change our status
in the least.

From my perch on the balcony—listening to the Jacuzzi folks
quote lines from *Reservoir Dogs* and talk about how drunk they were
last night—I resist the dull instinct to pass them off as a bunch of
half-witted meatheads. John Steinbeck once wrote that the nature
of parties has yet to be perfectly studied—but I'll posit that it's
impossible to truly study party culture. As with love or the
Kingdom of Heaven, parties were never meant to be analyzed. By
definition, the moment one begins to analyze a party is the moment
one ceases to become part of it.

Beyond this, whenever I assess a party I'm not a part of, I invariably gravitate toward a single (and, I suspect, true) conclusion: that,
as with lawn-darts or pinochle, partying is just one of many creative
ways to pass the time on planet earth.

"What do you want to do tonight?" Valentina asks me.

"Well," I reply, "I think they put on a Greek cultural show in the Pink Palace nightclub after dinner."

"Oh my God," says Valentina.

The weekly Pink Palace Greek cultural show takes place in the Pink Palace Palladium nightclub, a cavernous indoor space that features mirrored columns, semidisposable plastic tables, and a 100-foot bar. Some 200 Pink Palace guests mill around the bar in the moments before the Greek dancing starts, and there is a hint of excitement in the air. Most everyone (including Valentina and me) clutches a beer, and the pink ouzo is flowing faster than ever. Tables full of sunburned boys swill beers and peer over at tables full of sunburned girls. Solo travelers line the bar like sock-hop wallflowers. Sitting with Valentina at the end of the bar, I entertain myself by eavesdropping on my neighbors.

"How about that guy?" says the girl on my right.

"What guy?" her friend replies. "That guy. The Greek-looking guy." She nods over at a muscular, dark-eyed local fellow who's been skulking and pouting his way past the wallflowers since dinner ended.

"Oh Jesus. That guy is a scumbag, honey—with a capital S."

"Yeah, but I'm on vacation!"

As the two girls giggle over this, a deeply suntanned blond guy in a floral-print shirt walks up to me with an exaggerated air of nonchalance. "You gonna hit dat tonight, dog?" he says, barely making eye contact.

"Am I gonna what?" I say.

The blond guy makes a casual nod at Valentina. "I'm just askin' if you gonna hit dat, 'cause if you ain't, then I'm all over it."

For a moment, I'm not sure if I should flash a gang sign or laugh out loud. Instead, I decide to clarify. "Yes," I say, trying to strike a balance between cordiality and sarcasm. "I'm gonna hit dat."

Mr. Hit-Dat gives me a knowing grin. "It's cool, yo," he says before sifting off into the crowd.

Before long, the cultural show begins: 200 Pink Palace revelers are suddenly caught up in a swirl of dancing and clapping, of mildly humiliating audience participation and gleefully smashed performance crockery. Plate shards fly, ouzo bottles empty, and—every so often—sunburned strangers lock lips.

Standing at the fringes with Valentina, I can't help but marvel at the marketing genius behind this booze-soaked corner of Corfu. Some people travel the world for spiritual reasons; others travel to shop exotic markets or take interesting photos. But a great many people, most of them young, want nothing more than to drink and flirt and make noise on a warm beach far away from home. The Pink Palace caters to this need with brilliant efficiency.

For a moment, I imagine an international Pink Palace Party-Travel Empire: a pink-hued fleet of planes and buses and boats and camel-caravans connecting youth reports styled on the party theme of any given culture. Pink rattan huts on the Andaman Sea featuring rice whiskey, Thai dance, and kick-boxing; pink desert pueblos in Baja featuring tequila, hat dances, and bull-fighting; pink onion-dome towers in St. Petersburg featuring vodka, Cossack dancing, and ice hockey.

Valentina nudges me out of my reverie before the Greek dancing reaches its climax. "Let's go down to the beach," she says to me.

We make our way downhill to the sand, past the now-quiet poolside buildings. By the time we make it to the beach, we can barely hear the shouts of partiers from the Palladium nightclub. We walk to a smooth stretch of sand and huddle together against the breeze.

The black Ionian bubbles and foams in the darkness beyond our feet; above, the hazy belt-strap of the Milky Way arches its way across the sky, nearly touching the horizon. A stray dog pads past, stopping momentarily to growl at the surf. Devoid of partiers, the beach is empty, peaceful. Valentina and I have the entire Pink Palace beachfront to ourselves. We move a little closer together and stare up at the sky.

After twenty or so minutes, Valentina breaks the silence. "You were wrong," she says.

"About what?"

"About the Pink Palace."

"How was I wrong about the Pink Palace?"

Valentina looks over at me with just the hint of a smile. "You said it wasn't romantic."

I grin back at Valentina, and we move still closer together in the sand—the premarketed, pink-tinged roar of Greek bacchanalia just barely audible from up the hill.

Rolf Potts writes travel articles for several print and on-line magazines. He is a frequent contributor to Salon.com, *where his articles won him a slot in* The Best American Travel Writing 2000 *anthology.*

ALAN LINN

The Apocalyptic Island

Look out for 666.

ONCE IN A GREAT WHILE, THE GOOD PEOPLE OF PATMOS GAZE
across the Aegean toward a light flickering over the stony slopes of
Mount Kerkettos on nearby Samos. Scientists say that the eerie
light show is static electricity, but pious Patmians know better. They
cross themselves and run to tell the neighbors that they've seen
another sign from the island's most famous citizen, who was ban-
ished to this speck of Greece just off the coast of Asia Minor almost
1,900 years ago. According to tradition, he took refuge in one of
Patmos's many caves, where he prayed and fasted. Eventually, he
heard "a voice as of a trumpet," which said, "I am Alpha and Omega,
the First and the Last, and what you see, write in a book...."

The book is still selling well. It has been described as one of
the most lurid and least understood works ever written—the Book
of Revelation, or the Apocalypse, the last book of the Bible. The
author, most scholars agree, is Saint John the Divine, the apostle
who was sentenced to "wild and desolate" Patmos for defying
Roman edict to worship the emperor as God. His eloquent, horrific
visions of the earth's final cataclysm—satanic beasts, stars falling
from the heavens, the blood-bath at Armageddon—have haunted
Western thought for centuries.

Anyone with a sense of the theater will applaud God's choice of Patmos, one of the northernmost islands in the Dodecanese, as the place to plot the end of the world. Rearing volcanic ramparts and plunging, dark-shadowed chasms jar against terraced green hills and flowered meadows that burn under the stinging Aegean sun with a van Gogh-like luminosity.

Climb the mountainside behind Skála, Patmos's port and biggest town, for a view of the entire island stretched out like an immense relief map adrift in the surrounding sea. It looks as if a giant with a taste for rousing topography had squeezed your normal Mediterranean island into a much handier size. Patmos gives you three islets for the price of one—pocket-size massifs that are joined by low isthmuses at Skála, in the midsection, and at aptly named Diakofti ("cut apart"), near the unpopulated southern end. You can circumnavigate Patmos in a *bezini*, or caïque, ride from nearly one end to the other on a moped, or crisscross it on foot, as I did, and still not believe that it's scarcely seven miles long and, at one point, narrower than the average Frisbee toss.

For me, just one other Greek isle compares—mysterious Phraxos, which exists only in *The Magus,* the John Fowles novel about an eccentric rich old Greek who spares no expense in creating vast outdoor illusions to amaze and manipulate a series of visitors.

Patmos is up to the same tricks. For example, near the little resort of Grikou, a few miles south of Skála, a pristine beach curves sensuously along a protected bay. The beach is flat and featureless except for Kalikatsou ("cormorant"), a boulder plunked down smack in the middle that's five or six stories high and riddled with caves like an enormous, gray Swiss cheese. It's akin to seeing one of Salvador Dalí's melting watches draped across the landscape.

From the tiny, whitewashed chapel atop Mount Prophitis Ilias, which at 883 feet is the island's highest point, you can look north toward the Shangri-la-befitting Monastery of Saint John on the second-highest point (800 feet), and you'll swear on a stack of Revelations that you're looking up. Even photos confirm the illusion.

It's little wonder that Patmos has been considered sacred almost since the first settlers arrived about 4,000 years ago from Asia

Minor, less than 100 miles to the east. Oddly, the early Patmians set the precedent of blessing the second-highest point on the island, choosing it for their temple to Artemis, goddess of the hunt.

About A.D. 95, when Saint John is thought to have been exiled here, Patmos was under the heel of imperial Rome; it became part of the Christianized Byzantine Empire in the fourth century. Both old and new gods forsook the island between the seventh and tenth centuries when the terrible swift sword of Islam, in the form of Arab pirates, swept over the Dodecanese with that peculiar kind of cruelty one religion reserves for another.

Patmos remained deserted and barren until 1088, when a Greek Orthodox monk, who believed in solid masonry as well as in God, began building the fortified Monastery of Saint John on the site of the pagan temple. Settlers gradually returned and constructed the delightfully hodgepodge, white cubical houses of Hora, the town that still huddles like a pile of scattered dice against the monastery's protective walls.

The island flirted briefly with glory during the late 1800s when its inhabitants owned one of the richest merchant fleets in the Mediterranean. This fleet was indirectly responsible for a new invasion. In the 1970s several of the world's megarich, such as relatives of the Aga Khan, discovered the beauty and cheap real estate of what was basically a forgotten island. They gussied up many of the sea merchants' old mansions and, along with new port facilities, helped put Patmos on the tourist map.

By God's grace, Patmos so far has escaped the stampede that nearly ruined other Greek islands. The main reasons are its lack of an airport and the monks' insistence that it remain largely a holy precinct. Signs everywhere remind you to "Respect Our Traditions," which translates as "Keep Your Clothes On." No nude bathing, no shorts or revealing shirts in churches, and none of the orgiastic nightlife that characterizes Mykonos and Santorini.

My arrival on Patmos was appropriately Fowlesian. As the Piraeus ferry hove groaning and creaking into the outstretched arms of the fjord-shaped harbor around midnight, clouds parted exactly on cue and revealed a full, bloodred moon.

I decided to follow in Saint John's footsteps, physically if not spiritually, the next morning as I sipped an industrial-strength espresso beneath the sun-bright awning of the Sagittarius coffee shop on Skála's busy waterfront. *Yayas* (grandmothers) dressed in black from head to toe waddled after fleeing toddlers. A bewhiskered, hungover fisherman sitting nearby lazily beat his lunch, an octopus he'd just jerked from the water, against the cement quay to tenderize it. In the background, like a cacophonous Greek chorus, caïque captains chattered as they assembled their color-drenched flotilla, caulking and painting their commercial little hearts out. Every summer morning, these spiffed-up boats nose in at the quay beside a chalkboard listing which of Patmos's handful of beaches each vessel is going to and how much the ride costs (a few dollars).

Theologos (a favorite name here), my waiter, directed me to the 400-year-old cobblestone road (a resurfacing of a much more ancient thoroughfare) behind town that leads up through a scented pine forest to Saint John's cave and the Monastery of Saint John. On the outskirts, I passed an ominous graffito freshly daubed in red on a crumbling stone wall, *Ohi sto 666*—"Look out for 666"—John's numerical code for the Prince of Darkness.

The Monastery of the Apocalypse, containing the tiny Chapel of Saint Anne, was built in 1090 to enclose the entrance of the holy grotto where Saint John is said to have had his awful reveries. I watched a lone woman kneel and attach a *tama* to the icon of John, which shows him with a sword coming from his mouth, as good a depiction of his literary style as any. The faithful, who believe the icon can perform miracles, use *tamata*,

> The three-pronged crevice in the Monastery of the Apocalypse is said to represent the Trinity: God as Father, Son, and Holy Spirit. The monks of the monastery often ask visitors to consider which side of this crevice they count themselves, the side of Christ or the Antichrist of the Apocalypse.
>
> —Brian Alexander, "Thoughts on the Apocalypse"

small metal likenesses of people, body parts, houses, even cars and boats, to direct the benefaction. Before rising, the woman reverently kissed the silver plaques placed where John rested his head and hands. Above her, the rough gray rock of the cave ceiling, with the strange, three-pronged crevice from which the Word came, looked like a violent thundercloud about to burst.

The fifteenth-century Convent of the Annunciation west of Hora has a happier air. The friendly nuns gladly show visitors the Chapel of Saint Lucas with its 379-year-old tapestry and even older icons, one by Damaskinos, a pupil of Titian. Another convent, Zoodochos Pigi (Source of Life), virtually in the shadow of the Monastery of Saint John, has many sixteenth to eighteenth-century icons and an exquisite, carved Patmian iconostasis.

Wherever you wander on the island, you may hear the quavering quarter tones of a Byzantine priest chanting in some unseen church or smell the heady burst of incense on the changing wind. Patmos has more than fifty churches, several convents and monasteries, and countless small shrines. Most of the larger places of worship permit visitors, and you can peek into many churches simply by asking around for the caretaker. If it's Sunday or the appropriate patron saint's holiday, the church will be packed with worshipers and, if the saint is important enough, richly robed priests, cantors, and processions bearing icons.

One sun-bruised afternoon as I entered the courtyard of the Monastery of Saint John, a black-robed giant with a flowing white beard and matching ponytail hanging below his stovepipe monk's hat appeared from the labyrinth of corridors. Papa Pavlos (Father Paul) took personal pride in showing me and several other meandering tourists the monastery's treasures. Saint John's, which owns much of Patmos, is one of the richest and most influential monasteries in Greece; its 900th anniversary in 1988 was attended by hundreds of Christian leaders from around the world.

Papa Pavlos explained, by means of quaint English and ingenious pantomime, the seventeenth-century frescoes in the narthex of the main church, which depict miracles attributed to Saint John, such as his turning an evil magus into stone. We wandered through the cool, candle-blackened Chapel of the Blessed Cristodoulos, where the earthly remains of the monastery's founder lie, and the Chapel of the Virgin, built in part with stones from Artemis's temple. In the museum, we saw a king's ransom in gold and jewels donated by the czars, the monks' eleventh-century deed to the island signed by Byzantine Emperor Alexius I Comnenus, a sixth-century Gospel of Saint Mark, and other rare manuscripts.

I had a sinner's interest in what Papa Pavlos thought about predictions that the Apocalypse was nigh. Each time I visited, I discreetly asked him, but he would just rub his temples and say that such questions made him dizzy.

In the end, the best way to absorb Patmos is to simply ramble all over for as many days as you can spare. You must sit in the searing sun amid the unexcavated ruins of the ancient acropolis at Kastelli and listen to distant sheep bells and the shepherd's shrill whistle. Or, some afternoon when the Aegean spreads its gauze against the sky, glance up to see the Monastery of Saint John floating like a halo above its rocky perch. Favorite beaches on the island include those at Grikou, Lambi, Kato Kampos, Melloi, remote Psili Amos, and Agriolivado, where caïques departing in the evaporating mist look as if they're climbing into the sky.

Every evening, I would return to Skála, dusty and road-weary. Late one afternoon, an apocalyptic red sun magnified the town below. Out on the bay, lamp fishermen were readying small motorless boats, known as *gri-gri* (ducklings) because they're pulled in a line behind a mother ship.

The whole island seemed to glow, but this was no tourist postcard. A chilling wind and high waves tossed the *gri-gri* dangerously. The oarsmen (one per boat) looked much too old for the ordeal they were about to face—risking their lives at sea after dark to earn a living.

I saw the boats again a few hours later from the deck of the Piraeus ferry as it slid swiftly past their fishing grounds a mile or so offshore. The men had ignited the blindingly bright lights they use to attract fish. It was a scene straight out of Saint John's writings. That night, until they disappeared from view, I watched fallen stars bobbing in the waters off Patmos.

★

Alan Linn is a freelance writer based in Homes Beach on Florida's gulf coast.

PART THREE

GOING YOUR OWN WAY

TOM JOYCE

The Ravens and the Virgin

A pilgrim recounts his quest for
understanding on Mount Athos.

IN THE NORTHERN GREEK PROVINCE OF MACEDONIA, PROTRUDING like a bone spur from the last finger of Chalkidikí, Ágion Óros, the holy mountain, rises above the Aegean in the primrose mist of a September evening. According to Christian legend, this narrow peninsula was sanctified by the Blessed Virgin Mary, who took refuge here one dark and stormy night. As a result, all females—human or animal—are prohibited from approaching within 500 meters of the rugged shoreline, ostensibly in deference to the Virgin's legacy. Were I a woman, this absurd irony would really piss me off. But since I was born into the "privileged" gender, I feel compelled to follow in the shimmering wake of the Virgin's veil, and act as Her excluded sisters' eyes.

Might this be called *gynaecomorphism*, I wonder?

"Look, look, there is Saint Athos." Kostas, my effusive Salonican cab driver, nudges me out of a groggy half-sleep. The lavender wedge of granite seems to levitate above the smooth obsidian sea, an icon from another eon—a time when Zeus and his brother Poseidon ruled the land and water in this corner of the world, oblivious to the imminent *Christos* who would eventually displace their kind forever.

I was never to learn why Kostas insisted on referring to the sanctuary of Byzantine Orthodox Christianity as "Saint." As far as I know, Athos has always been a mountain—and an impressive one at that. It rises to a sharp peak 6,668 feet above the Singitic Gulf, perilously steep on its northern face, more forgiving on the southern exposure, according to the Austrian topo map I've been studying. Then again, Athos seems very much like the Orthodox Christian God, Himself: lofty, imposing, and stern—yet approachable, if one is willing to follow the designated course.

Earlier that morning I stood on the 9,568 feet summit of Mýtikas, highest peak of the Olympus massif—from whence a legendary cohort of brooding, squabbling deities once determined the fate of humankind. But I found no trace of the old gods' splendor or excess remaining on the peak Homer had called *Pantheon*—only a book (courtesy of the Greek Alpine Club) recording the hubris of men who climb holy mountains, and the garbage they leave behind to mark their brief moment of rarefied glory.

But I have no intention of climbing Mount Athos. I approach it with head bowed, as a pilgrim—all the more odd because I am neither Orthodox nor Christian, rather something of a heretic. And that I've gotten this far in my attempt to penetrate the final bastion of Byzantine conservatism seems…well, "miraculous" is the word that comes to mind.

Mount Athos is not a tourist destination. For the past millennium, it has been the most important place of pilgrimage for all sects of Eastern Orthodox Christianity, where male Greeks, Russians, Serbs, Bulgarians, and Romanians, have found monastic refuge from the Ottoman fire of Islam, Balkan belligerence, and the postwar geopolitical volatility of Eastern Europe.

The mountain is situated at the southern tip of Aktí, a long, narrow peninsula to the east of Thessaloníki—or "Salonica," as the Greeks call it—approachable only by boat from the nearby resort town of Ouranópolis. A *diamonetherion*, special permission from the Greek Church, is needed to enter the semiautonomous republic of Orthodox monks, and that is obtainable only after one has presented a letter of recommendation from one's own embassy to the

Ministry of Political Affairs for Macedonia, and paid an entrance fee of 7,000 drachmas. Access is rigidly controlled, and once there, the peripatetic pilgrim is required to move from monastery to monastery, sleeping in dormitories, and eating the simple fare consistent with a monk's Spartan lifestyle. Officially, visitors may stay for only four days, but during that time they are given the opportunity to participate in liturgical services largely unchanged for fifteen hundred years.

I decided I had to see this Byzantine relic for myself, but that turned out to be not so easily accomplished. After a series of late night calls to Greece, I finally tracked down the bureaucrat in charge of issuing permits to Mount Athos, and explained to her my interest in pilgrimage. "Are you Orthodox?" Ms. Plesa inquired. My negative response was met with icy finality. "It is impossible," she replied.

But I was not easily put off. Through a friend, I contacted the head of the Greek Orthodox Diocese of San Francisco. "I'll fax your request to the Patriarch of Constantinople," Bishop Antony assured me. Although I found it curious that he referred to Istanbul by its pre-Islamic name, I was elated to have penetrated the sectarian barrier. But when September came, and I had received no reply, the bishop's secretary set me straight. "The Patriarch has a lot on his agenda," she admonished. "It could take months."

Undaunted, I flew to Thessaloníki, arriving on the evening of September 11th, tired, unshaven, and ready to submit myself to a higher authority—even Ms. Plesa, if necessary. I knew only that I had been "called" here—by whatever internal beacon is responsible for such certainty in the face of an overwhelmingly discouraging reality.

When I noticed a man attired in the black raiment of an Orthodox priest directly behind me in the airport taxi queue, things got interesting. The monk was slender, almost delicate, beneath his austere robes; he wore a long, silver beard, round spectacles, and pillbox hat reminiscent of a medieval scholar. There was tranquillity to his demeanor, but a sparkle in his eyes that belied the sartorial solemnity.

"Father, do you speak English?"

His incisive eyes assessed my interest. "Yes."

"I'm trying to get to Mount Athos," I continued quickly. "Perhaps you know something about it?"

A pause, and then he replied, "I live there."

Bingo.

"Mind if we share a cab?" I asked, trying not to sound overly anxious.

On the way into Salonica I made small talk with the priest. "So, what do you do on Mount Athos?"

"I'm a monk," he replied, his soft voice measured and patient, but tinted with a hint of amusement. "I don't *do* anything."

"Of course, I meant besides your duties as a priest?"

"I write a little," the monk admitted. "Mostly poetry."

"I've been very interested in places considered 'sacred,'" I told him. "I don't know if they are sacred because people *think* they are, or whether there is something inherently powerful that exists in these places. But my personal experience has led me to believe that some palpable energy can be experienced at these sites."

"What sort of energy would that be?" He went along with me.

"Well…," I groped, "I guess you'd have to call it 'divine nature.'"

The priest raised an eyebrow; his lips pursed into a restrained smile beneath the silver strands of his mustache. "In that case, all places are sacred."

"I suppose you're right," I admitted, attempting nonetheless to salvage my theory. "But some places seem to be more sacred than others. I've been told Mount Athos is one of those places."

The priest looked straight ahead—a penetrating stare that passed through the driver, the windscreen, the approaching city, all the way across the Palm of Chalkidikí to his monastic home which I had yet to see. "That may be so," he said with an abbreviated nod, the lights of Thessaloníki reflecting in his glasses. "I think you must go there."

He handed me an envelope bearing his name and address:

HIEROMONK SYMEON, SKELLI TIMIOU STAVROU, MT. ATHOS, GREECE.

On the envelope he scrawled a telephone number. "If you have difficulty, I'll be at this number in Salonica until Sunday morning."

The cab turned a corner, and stopped in front of a town house. Father Symeon politely declined my offer to pay, told the driver something in Greek, and handed him 3,000 drachmas. "Good luck," he said, then slipped out of the cab.

When we arrived at my hotel ten minutes later, the driver refused money. "It is all settled, " he said flatly, without even a hint of curiosity. "The priest paid for you."

By 8:30 the next morning I was walking along the quay where fishermen were hauling in their morning catch from the Gulf of Thessaloníki. At nine, I rang the bell of the American consulate on Nikis Avenue, where I was given my rubber-stamped "letter of recommendation" by the USA's official representative. Precisely at ten, I climbed the steps to the faux classical edifice of the Ministry of Macedonia and Thrace at Platia Dioikitiriou.

I found Ms. Plesa's office at the end of a long marble corridor on the second floor. A humorless woman with short dark hair and the naturally suspicious demeanor of a bureaucrat, Ms. Plesa held court behind a cluttered desk, back-lit by casement windows which didn't quite open onto an eighteen-inch balcony. Just outside her door, an uncomfortable wooden bench kept her callers at bay until she was ready to hear their tedious requests. I waited while she took her time stamping permits for a couple of Greek nationals before entering her office with what I hoped was an ingratiating smile.

"It's a pleasure to finally meet you, Ms. Plesa. We spoke on the phone several weeks ago…from San Francisco…perhaps you remember?" She didn't, of course.

Reaching into my folder, I produced the letter written in Greek by Bishop Anthony, which, for all I knew, denounced me as a dangerous lunatic. The Patriarch, I assured her, would be faxing a response to her office. As Ms. Plesa scrutinized the letter through her bifocals, I mentioned offhandedly that my "dear friend," Father Symeon, was expecting me at his hermitage on Mount Athos with all possible speed. To clinch the deal, I presented her with my letter of recommendation from the U.S. Consulate, then sat back and waited for her to stamp my permit as perfunctorily as she had the Greeks who preceded me.

"Have you a reservation?" Ms. Plesa asked, setting my documentation aside as if it were just another batch of wood pulp destined to take up space in her filing cabinets.

"A reservation for what?"

"To stay on Mount Athos, you must have a reservation. Please understand that I am only able to issue ten permits each day to foreign nationals, and all available permits have been issued through October the 29th. If you do not already have a reservation," she paused momentarily to satisfy her sense of dramatic tension, "what am I to do?"

I must have looked pathetic, mouth open, dazed from hitting the bureaucratic wall. What a fool I had been to waste my time and money on such a long shot. Just as I was promising myself never again to listen to those stupid "inner voices," an outer voice shattered the silence.

"*Parakalo, Frau Plesa?*" The gentleman in the doorway was dressed in expensive outdoor clothing, flanked by two strapping young men in shorts and hiking boots. "Perhaps I can be of some help," he switched to perfect English for my benefit. "I have reservations for myself and my three sons to go to Mount Athos this Sunday."

"And you are?" Ms. Plesa asked, consulting her database.

"Gerhard Jaeger, from Wuppertal."

Frowning, Ms. Plesa tapped her keyboard, scrolling through the list, and finally nodded. "Yes, you and your sons have reservations, Herr Jaeger. But how does this help the American?" she asked, inclining her head sideways toward me without making eye contact.

Herr Jaeger smiled. "Well, one of my sons was unable to make the journey, and so I have an extra reservation, you see, which I will be quite happy to transfer to this gentleman."

Rather than jumping onto her desk and hooting like a Lakers fan, I managed to contain my reaction to stupidly grinning at Herr Jaeger as if he had materialized like a *deus ex machina*. Finally, I turned to see Ms. Plesa staring at me in disbelief over her bifocals, as if I were surrounded by an angelic glow.

"You are a very lucky man," she remarked dryly.

On the upper deck of the ferry the next morning, the Jaegers and I watch the final trucks on-loading, then settle into fiberglass seats beneath sun tarps.

The Northern European pilgrims are obvious in their sturdy hiking boots and rucksacks stuffed to the gunwales. They study maps, read books on Byzantine history, and take photos of everything. The Greeks, in exquisite contrast, rarely have cameras, are usually dressed in street clothing and shoes, and carry only a small athletic bag—more than likely filled with food and cigarettes.

And then there are the "Ravens" the black mantled monks, bearded, robed, and hook nosed—who pace the decks with disdainful expressions. I feel about them as I did those Sisters of Perpetual Corporeal Punishment to whom I was entrusted for an education. Will Christians never learn how ominous their spiritual representatives appear to children? Buddhist monks aren't scary; they look like Mr. Clean in saffron pajamas.

Then I spot him by the railing, talking with a group of the Europeans, very un-ravenlike despite the identical robes and silver cross, the antithesis of austerity when his intelligent face lights up in lively conversation.

"Father Symeon." He recognizes me as I approach, and nods in approval.

"Congratulations," he replies, sea breeze rippling his silver beard as the intense sunlight illuminates his eyes. "Apparently you are meant to go to Mount Athos."

When I introduce him to the Jaegers, Father Symeon slips effortlessly into German. Later, I hear him speaking fluent Spanish with another group.

"What are your plans?" Father Symeon asks.

"The angels are in charge," I reply with a shrug.

He smiles. "Well, if the angels decree it, come visit me at the hermitage near Stavronikita. I'll be there all day tomorrow."

Our ferry lumbers into the port at Dáfni, and there is a mad rush to find the bus that will take us up the steep road to Karyaí, administrative capitol of Mount Athos and seat of the Ierá Synaxis (Holy Council). Dust wafts in through open windows as we are jostled along Aktí's central ridge to Karyaí.

Gerhard, Tilman, Philipp, and I sit down to Greek salad, lemon chicken, *tsatsiki*, and liters of Amstel beer in the raucous taverna. "Eat well," Herr Jaeger admonishes. "We don't know when we will see food again."

Gerhard has been four times to Mount Athos, and seems to harbor a good-natured disdain for the austere regimentation of the Orthodox community. "They keep Byzantine time, you know. The daily cycle begins at sunset, which changes every day. They have evening vespers and compline (the last prayer at night), then, depending on where you are, the monks rise at perhaps one or two in the morning, pray in their cells for a few hours, then gather for a meal before the liturgy. This begins at four-thirty, maybe five o'clock, and lasts until seven-thirty or eight. Then they might have coffee, go off to do some chores, and return to eat their midday meal—often with wine—at nine or ten. The problem is that you must be there when the food is served, or you will miss out. There is no set schedule; everything revolves around the prayers."

After the meal, we hoist our rucksacks and hit the dusty road. On our way through Karyaí, we pass the Protaton, probably the most important church on Mount Athos. Gerhard has a word with the gatekeeper, and we are admitted to the dark sanctuary. "This is great fortune," Herr Jaeger informs me in a whisper. "The Protaton is rarely open to the public."

As my eyes adjust to the dim light, I am greeted by a cosmological pantheon of saints and bishops, lovingly painted into the once-wet plaster of the dome and adjacent vaults above me. The anonymous frescoes, Gerhard explains with great reverence, are the oldest on Mount Athos, dating from the fourteenth century. A filigreed brass chandelier hangs from the center of the dome, and silver censers draped from its circular superstructure glitter in the scant midday light leaking through the stained-glass windows. I move closer to inspect the hand-carved iconostasis, where the penumbrated faces of Jesus and Mary peek from their shimmering raiment of silver and gold. Beeswax candles dimly light our journey back in time, accompanied by an austere parade representing a heavenly hierarchy of the Christ-nature.

In the eighth and ninth centuries, any depiction of Jesus and the saints came under attack by iconoclasts of the period who decried the making and use of any religious images as "idolatry," an idea exhumed from the ancient Mosaic *Torah*. It is somewhat ironic that the most vocal and effective champions of iconographic veneration were women—the Byzantine empresses Irene and Theodora. But it was John of Damascus who upbraided the iconoclasts most eloquently: "Nothing is to be despised that God has made."

We spend the afternoon burrowing beneath a green canopy, negotiating rocky goat paths through wormholes in the dense underbrush. Transported into a gnomic world of stone cottages and cambered bridges, we would emerge occasionally from the vaulted green trail into a breathtaking vista of blue-roofed chapels and sea-framed fortresses jutting from the upper lip of weathered promontories.

It is past six by the time we arrive at the imposing medieval fortress aptly called *Pantokratoros*—"The Almighty Christ." With its crenellated siege tower and fortified stone walls, Pantokratoros seems to have been designed more for the purpose of repelling Ottoman Turkish invaders than bringing peace to its contemplative monastic residents. But to the Byzantine mind, these were not mutually exclusive endeavors.

By the ninth century, monasteries formed a formidable rampart of defense around medieval villages. While Loyola's Jesuits positioned themselves as the "Army of Jesus" in Western Europe, they appeared wimps beside their brethren of the Eastern Church. The tough intransigence of Orthodoxy is most colorfully exemplified in the story from Crete. Rather than surrender his charge to an Ottoman assault in 1866, the Abbot of Arkadi blew up his monastery—along with all 943 inhabitants—as Turks stormed the walls.

"The word *orthodox* means 'right-believing,'" Gerhard explains to us. "And some of the monasteries take this very seriously, allowing only Orthodox Christians to eat with the monks and participate in the liturgy. There is one," he chuckles, "Esfigmenou—which has a sign posted at its entrance: 'Orthodoxy or Death.'"

"I think we can skip that one," Tilman replies.

We climb a steep path to the outer walls of Pantokratoros, entering into a cobblestone courtyard through massive wooden gates completely wrapped in iron straps and studded with spike heads as big as baseballs. Within, the walls rise in a series of open loggias surrounding the red-painted chapel. Eventually, we are met by a silver-bearded *archontaris*—the guest master—who dutifully bids us rest on a stone bench, and brings thin tumblers of water with the traditional *loukoumi*—cubes of gummy glucose dusted with powdered sugar, sometimes called "Turkish Delight" by those insensitive to the history of this region. I reckon it to be the Greek equivalent of a Power Bar.

We are shown to our room—a dormitory with steel-framed bunks, semiclean linens, and casement windows so weathered that glass falls out when I attempt to open one.

As the Jaegers rest, I explore beyond the gates. Below the walls, a sheltered inlet from the sea provides a wharf for contract fishermen to land their daily catch. The small, weathered boats are docked and tied in for the evening. A solitary caretaker totes bundles of wood into a stone cottage on the quay.

"Don't stray too far," Gerhard has warned me. "If you miss the meal, you will go hungry tonight." Mindful of his caution, I climb a sloping rock that overlooks the lapis sea. At its crest, an ornate iron cross has been implanted into the weathered stone, casting an oxidized blessing over the breakers below. To the south, the marble buttress of Mount Athos looms over the Aegean, glowing golden in the oblique western light, while its lush green flanks fall precipitously into eastern shadow. Between the mountain and myself, capping another coastal promontory, the battlements of Stavronikita monastery receive a final kiss from the retreating sun.

When I return the Jaegers are waiting in the courtyard outside the chapel; within, antiphonal voices reverberate off the stained-glass windows and stone walls.

"It goes on forever," sighs Tilman, pacing back and forth over the rough cobbles. "This bowing and singing and kissing of icons and chanting. When will they get hungry?"

"They are hungry for something other than food," Gerhard reminds his son, checking the time on his Tag Heuer chronometer. My surrogate father is a multidimensional Teuton, combining the punctilious precision of Albert Speer and the mystical musings of Thomas Mann. Although he finds the trappings of Orthodoxy positively rococo compared with the lean logic of Lutheranism, Gerhard seems to hold a very soft spot in his heart for the monks of Mount Athos. Not merely a goodwill ambassador for his own Protestant tradition, Herr Jaeger's textile company in Wuppertal also donates material for candle wicks to the monastic hermits.

I wander into the outer chamber at the back of the church and stand stupidly for a few minutes, until a tall monk bids me join the assembly. Within the curtained nave, I find one of the creaking wooden chairs that surround the circular chapel vacant, and slip into its uncomfortably elongated frame, as Ravens in their flowing black veils circulate to pay homage to the icons. It is a very different pageant than the Latin mass, yet certain features exhume memories from my childhood—especially the one Greek invocation still used by the Roman Church: *Kyrie eleison* (Lord, have mercy).

When the evening vespers have ended, the Jaegers and I join the silent queue into a cavernous refectory for supper. We remain standing behind the long row of trestle tables as the abbot, accompanied by a group of well-heeled Athenian civilians, enters the hall, nods to the rabble, and proceeds to the head table. The prayers never cease; one monk stands at a lectern, reading swiftly as the assembly digs into the cold fish stew, coarse bread, and fragrant chunks of feta.

"Eat fast," Gerhard whispers. Not more than fifteen minutes later, the abbot rises and the silent meal comes to an abrupt halt. The praying Raven at the lectern never misses a beat, continues his litany as the abbot's VIP entourage files out of the refectory. Finished or not, dinner is over.

"You said they had wine with meals," Philipp remarks when we have filed out beyond the walls to a wooden bench overlooking the sea.

"Sometimes not," Herr Jaeger answers. "Life here is always an adventure, *ja?*" He reaches into the cargo pockets of his trousers, producing tiny bottles of ouzo—one for each of us. "To help you sleep," Gerhard explains with a tight grin.

Sipping the clear anisette liqueur, I watch the last light of day paint the arrowhead of Athos a dusty rose. The deep hue of night-fall saturates the landscape like ink, until there are only variations of this rhapsody in blue. Gerhard gazes in peaceful satisfaction at the slowly blurring line between sea and deep space. He is at last reunited with his hirsute hierophants, unspoiled natural wonders, and incalculable artistic treasures of his sacred place, accompanied by his strapping sons, while his woman waits like Penelope on a distant shore. All is as it should be in Herr Jaeger's world of precise delineation.

"Tomorrow we shall walk north to Vatopaidiou," Gerhard glances toward me as if reading my thoughts. "And you?"

"South," I reply with a nod toward the black keep of Stavronikita. As much as I enjoy their company, I feel compelled to proceed on this pilgrimage alone.

"Ah, yes," Gerhard replies with understanding. "The hermit. Well, we must each go our own way, yes?"

I toast his wisdom with the best of my German and the last of my ouzo, "*Das ist wahr, Herr Vater.*"

At 4 A.M., we ignore the rhythmic clacking of the wooden se-mantron calling the monks to liturgical service, and when we finally roll out of our bunks at 6:30, there is no breakfast to be found. The Jaegers, somewhat disgruntled, decide to make an early start.

"Perhaps we will see you on the boat," says Tilman. Gerhard offers his firm hand, and I bid my surrogate family farewell at the gates, then go back in search of sustenance.

In the kitchen, a Greek pilgrim is heating a fresh pot of coffee over a butane stove, and seems happy to share it with me. We find a few biscuits left over from the VIP breakfast to which we hadn't been invited, then savor our scrounged feast in silence on a rickety balcony overlooking the blue Aegean. Accompanied by the taste of sweet coffee and smell of the sea, I greet the morning sun with rare pleasure.

Shortly before eleven, I walk along the aqueduct that has carried water since the fifteenth century to Stavronikita, last of the fortress monasteries to be built on Mount Athos. Dropping my rucksack by the ornate marble fountain from which pilgrims once drank, I eat the ritual *loukoumi*. The *archontaris* speaks no English, but seems to understand that I am ravenously hungry. He disappears and returns with a young Asian monk dressed in civilian clothing.

"I'm Gregory," says the black-bearded newcomer in a mellifluous accent, taking my hand warmly. "We'll be having our meal in the workshop up the path." The old refectory within the monastery walls is undergoing major renovation, he explains, motioning to the huge construction crane peering over the battlement walls like a mechanical dragon. Gregory is an Indonesian novitiate monk. He escorts me into a broad workshop where axes, picks, and plowshares are stacked against the fieldstone walls. But in the center of the long room sits a rough-hewn trestle table laden with a feast that brings tears to my eyes: hot lentil soup, fresh bread, feta, and olives—the most beautiful, marinated black olives on which I've ever laid eyes. We sit, give thanks to the Lord, the gardener, and the cook, then silently, reverently, stuff our faces.

With food in my belly and a bed in the castle keep for the night, I stow my rucksack and hike up the dusty road toward the peninsular crest. Fifteen-hundred meters along, I approach the ruins of an old chapel, its tile roof caved in, broken walls overgrown with trees and strangled by vines. The wisp of a sensation draws me down into more of a rabbit's warren than a path, descending through a maze of roots and underbrush to a hole in the base of the chapel wall.

Inside, sunlight streams through the cobwebs and splintered boards of the nave's rotted floor. Turning around, the breath catches in my throat. Within a dark grotto beneath the chapel, a catacomb is filled with a stack of human skulls and bones—the remains of all the good abbots who cared for this little church throughout the centuries. Each was exhumed from his grave and stored here in eternal congress with his predecessors and successors. I pay my respects and leave quickly.

Farther up the road I spot a tiny red marker nailed to a tree, hand-lettered in both Cyrillic and Greek characters: TIMIOU STAVROU—"The Glory of the Cross." Descending once again into a verdant tunnel, I follow the goat path that drops into a gully, encounters a stream, then rises for a couple hundred meters, emerging into a clearing. There, I am greeted by a stone house, simple in form yet elegantly constructed, with tiled roof and bougainvillea covered walnut beams forming a pergola over a flagstone patio.

The *Hieromonk* walks out from under the dappled shade of his patio, wearing a lightweight black robe, open at the neck and belted around the waist. His long brown hair is drawn back into a ponytail; his silver beard ruffles sensuously in the afternoon breeze as he steps forward to take my hand.

Patra Symeon welcomes me into his home with characteristically restrained warmth. The small house is light, open, and aesthetically planned, with built-in cabinetry, full glass doors opening onto a veranda with walnut decking, and a spectacular view of the holy mountain in the distance. His living room is filled with textiles and primitive sculpture, framed black-and-white photography, and gilded icons. His desk is artfully strewn with work in progress, poetry written in his own hand competing for space with volumes of Rilke, García Lorca, and Li Po. He bids me sit on the shaded veranda, then brings coffee in fine china accompanied by a small blue glass on a silver tray.

"Ouzo?" I ask.

"Raki," the priest corrects, referring to the clear alcohol distilled from the remains of the wine press. Far from being a renunciate, this is a hermit who has embraced as much of life as his arms can encircle.

"Some of your art and rugs looks Incan," I venture.

"I'm Peruvian," he replies with a deferential nod.

That explains his proficiency in Spanish. "Is there a large Greek Orthodox community in Peru?"

"No." Symeon explains, "My family is Roman Catholic. Like many, I found its attempts at modernism spiritually unsatisfying. So, in my early twenties, I traveled to India to study Advaita Vedanta and Mahayana. Ironically, those traditions seemed so foreign to me. While I could embrace them intellectually, I never felt that they...," he grasps the phrase from somewhere in his past, "...*belonged* to me.

"Then, during the 1970s, I spent some time in New York, where I met a Greek monk with whom I deeply connected. After several months of discussion with him, I was surprised to find I had at last found a home in Orthodoxy. I studied the Greek language and eventually took vows as a priest. The choice to live as a monk—to remain celibate—was made after I came here to Mount Athos thirteen years ago.

"In the fifteenth century, many of the monasteries here abandoned strict community rule, allowing monks to possess personal property," he explains, anticipating my curiosity. "So, when my father died and left an inheritance, I found myself in a position to build this place as my hermitage."

> Our people have followed the path that Alexander laid down for them in the pre-Christian world and Constantine in the fulfilled world—of becoming gods. This is a part of our Orthodox theology, not like your "salvation," which puts a piece of virtue in a bank and gets back divine grace as interest. To understand us, you must understand the concept of theosis. Our church teaches that the goal of each Christian is deification—Saint Athanasius wrote that Christ says to us, "In my kingdom, I shall be God with you as gods."
>
> —Patricia Storace, *Dinner with Persephone*

This is a hermit after my own heart. As the afternoon lingers, Father Symeon serves fresh-baked bread, *spanikopeta* brought from Salonika, and Boutari wine from Crete. Any minute I'm expecting him to break out the Cuban cigars. Hospitality is regarded as an integral part of a monk's vocation, selfless giving considered to be the soul of *philanthropia*—active love for humankind—and the very core of Christian tradition.

After lunch, Father Symeon escorts me to his chapel. A heavy wooden door opens into a cool white room with cove windows slit by vertical panes of glass. On a tiny altar, a covered chalice, silver censer, and incense urn are neatly arranged, accompanied by a Greek Bible on a sculpted wooden lectern. Aside from a single chair and a rug on the plank floor, the room is decorated only with icons of the Christ, the archangel Michael, the Virgin and Child, and my host's tenth-century namesake, Saint Symeon.

Called the "New Theologian" of the Studium in Constantinople, Symeon dedicated his life to the pursuit of *hesychia*—a stillness, or silence of the heart—incorporating inner attentiveness, control of the breath, and the invocation "Lord Jesus Christ, Son of God, have mercy on me." Through this discipline, the *hesychasts* of Mount Athos were reputed to have attained visions of divine light and union with God.

I spend some time alone in Father Symeon's chapel, sitting in the cool white silence, digesting the sensory feast of the past forty-eight hours. When I return to the veranda, I ask him the question on which I've been chewing.

"You are obviously an educated man, Father. You've traveled extensively; you've studied various spiritual traditions firsthand, and yet you've embraced Orthodoxy—which seems to me so much more conservative than you. Why?"

Symeon looks thoughtfully up to the roof of the veranda, "I think it is closest to the source. It was not in Rome, but here, in the Greek-speaking world, that Christian communities of the first century flourished. It was the tradition common to both East and West for a thousand years. While the Latin Church placed more and more power in the hands of its pope and bishops, Orthodoxy affirmed that the guardian of truth is the entire people of God. So, while it may appear more conservative, the Eastern Church has a long tradition of democracy—in the Greek sense of the word."

"What tipped the scales for you?"

Father Symeon looks puzzled, then amused, then thoughtful. "I think it was the 'Contraries,'" he replies after some time. "It is a concept you will find in all religion, but there is something about the way this is articulated in Orthodoxy that enabled me to comprehend its significance for the first time in my life:

"We are born on Earth victims of the Contraries: life/death, pleasure/pain, heat/cold, desire/frustration, freedom/bondage, and so on. This is what Christians call 'original sin'—the state of perfectly balanced dichotomy, a prison from which we cannot escape. We can only overcome this condition through the salvation of Christ, who 'tips the scales,' as you say. Because, through the 'Son' we are able to return to the 'Father'—to live with God; to *become* God."

The mountain reflects the golden glow of afternoon sun, and Father Symeon turns into the light; his glasses seem to blaze like the polished shields of Constantine's army at Milvian Bridge.

"When I finally grasped this truth," Father Symeon

———✦———

According to Church legend, Constantine the Great had a dream before his battle with Maxentius at Mivian Bridge: *In Hoc Signo Vinces* he saw inscribed on a great cross in the sky— "By this sign you will conquer." Constantine ordered his men to emblazon their battle shields with *Chi Rho*, the first letters of *Christos*, and his subsequent victory eliminated any opposition to the Imperial throne. Thus Christianity, once an obscure Jewish heresy kept alive in small Hellenistic communities, was transformed into a universal Roman orthodoxy.

The *Chi Rho* monogram was found to have been inscribed on the tomb of Pompey long before the birth of Jesus. And Constantine was a practitioner of *Sol Invictus* [Invincible Sun], a Syrian religion whose festival of *Natalis Invictus* was celebrated on December 25th, and the Persian Cult of Mithras, which stressed immortality of the soul and resurrection. Thus, Jesus rose from his tomb, and his day of worship was moved from the Jewish Sabbath to the "venerable day of the Sun."

—Tom Joyce

concludes, "I knew I had at last come home. *This* is what belongs to me."

In the tradition of Orthodox monasticism, the *geron* is a charismatic "elder," a spiritual guide: look below the surface and you will find that the substance of all things is identical, he admonishes. Beneath the veneer of your belief, truth is only and always *truth*. It is an astonishingly simple cognition that slaps one into wakefulness.

As I sit here with this mystical monk, in sight of the holy mountain, exhuming in reverie a long-forgotten history lesson, I finally understand why I've been compelled to come here. I arrived at this *geron's* hermitage carrying the baggage of my childhood rebellion against my parents' faith; I leave now with empty hands.

The morning sun never penetrates a gathering gloom. Ominous clouds billow in from the west—just the direction I'm heading—and my destination is eight hours by foot, across the mountainous spine of the peninsula.

Near the pump house by the main road, I encounter Nikos, a former Athenian policeman, with whom I spent some time talking the night before. More accurately, he talked; I listened.

Nikos is a man who punches the air when he speaks, fending off his personal demons with evangelical zeal. After relating the story of watching his partner die in his arms from gunshot wounds, Nikos concluded, "It all comes down to this: I understood I was only living to die. There was no hope. But here…" his intense blue eyes surveyed the medieval cloister around us and the muscles of his jaw relaxed. "Here, there is something more."

Like myself, Nikos has avoided the morning liturgy. And, like so many who receive spiritual vocation, he struggles constantly with his convictions. The big man smokes a cigarette as he paces across the path like a panther, greeting me with a hungry grin that furrows his square jaw. "*Yasou. Kali mera.* You are going today?"

"To Simonos Petras."

"A long walk, my friend. You may get wet."

We both ponder the dark clouds gathering above the ridge and the wind sweeping leaves from the undulating walnut over our heads. "Are you staying?" I ask him.

Nikos shrugs and drags on his cigarette. "I must finish some business in Athens. Perhaps after, I will return for good."

"Can you really spend your life here, Nikos? Without women?"

He grins painfully and shakes his long sandy hair. "Only if Christ gives me strength."

Shouldering my rucksack, I extend a hand to him. "Then perhaps I'll see you here on my next visit."

Nikos takes my hand and nearly crushes it. "Remember, my friend, you never come to Mount Athos just to 'visit.' There is a reason, eh? *Adio.*"

For the next hour I follow a rutted, overgrown path down the eastern coast, emerging onto the rock-strewn shoreline, littered with the jettisoned debris from ferry traffic, and finally rounding a surf-beaten point to the harbor at Iviron, one of the first monasteries to be constructed on the peninsula. Its grim ochre walls house medieval manuscripts and artifacts from ten centuries of monastic life on Mount Athos.

I join a group of Greek Army officers escorted by an Australian monk through the eclectic chapel combining salvaged second-century Corinthian columns with fourteenth-century geometric Turkish frescoes. Our guide brings us reverently to the most important icon on Mount Athos—a Madonna and Child whose faces appear black amidst their glittering golden surround, until a flashlight illuminates their delicate Byzantine features. So precious is this icon, according to the Aussie Raven, it is believed that Iviron would be destroyed if the treasure were ever to leave Mount Athos. The ground beneath our feet, he explains, is the very location of the Virgin's landfall.

According to legend, the Mother of Jesus was on route from Anatolia to Cyprus, where Lazarus had become bishop of the local community of disciples. But an unforeseen storm blew in from the south, carrying her craft northward to the mountainous Aktí peninsula. Finding a sheltered harbor, the crew put ashore near an old temple of Apollo. The captain bade Mary take refuge within the heathen structure, but as she entered, its columns shook and the temple fell into rubble around her. The storm suddenly subsided, and the sun god's statue proclaimed itself false before the Mother of the true "Son of God."

This typically Greek myth illustrates how the old gods of Olympus had been dramatically supplanted by the Christos, and that Mary, the Blessed Virgin Mother, had usurped the long-held mantle of Demeter, the Earth Mother.

But legends seldom tell the whole story. As Christianity spread throughout the Levant and Europe, the sacred sites and ancient temples built to honor the Goddess in her myriad forms—Isis, Inanna, Ishtar, Asherah, Astarte, Artemis, etc.—were obliterated, left to die a slow death of neglect, or replaced with chapels dedicated to Mary—by *men*. It was my privileged gender who made war on the Goddess, who desecrated Her holy ground, who enforced the rule of a stern patriarchal God with a foul temper and fiery sword, who paid obsequious homage to the Virgin with one breath and denounced her sisters as contemptuous harlots with the next. But why?

Because it was a woman who got us all evicted from Eden, was it not? A woman, and a serpent—ancient symbol of the Goddess—the same serpent we find pictured in Christian iconography beneath Saint Michael's angelic boot.

The sky threatens, but delivers only sporadic drizzle as I ascend a broad trail toward the ridge. By 4:30 I am straddling Aktí's pine forested spine. Ágion Óros looms in the angry clouds to the south, while sun-dappled green hills descend gently to Xerxes's Canal in the distant north. Wind blows fiercely from the west where the land drops away precipitously into the slate-blue gulf. I drain the last drops from my water bottle, shoulder my rucksack, and begin the steep, single-track descent toward food and shelter for the night.

Like some vestige of Bram Stoker's imagination, Simonos Petras squats on a sheer granite promontory a thousand feet above the sea, a nest more befitting raptors than ravens. The Monastery of St. Peter seems to grow organically from the surrounding upthrust of rock, each of its seven stories surrounded by a narrow wooden balcony clinging precariously to the stone by claws of steel cable, its slate-roofed towers breaking the monolithic profile of the surrounding quadrangle.

Wind from the southwest blows so fiercely that I must lean forty-five degrees into it approaching the monastery. Already six o'clock, the evening vespers are under way. A stern, gray-bearded *archontaris* shows me to a wooden perch at the back of the chapel, and I wait patiently for the call to refectory.

When the bell tolls, I savor the cabbage stew and black bread as if it were an entrée from Lutèce. A grizzled Englishman seated beside me stuffs an apple and wedges of bread into his pockets before the meal has ended. "Might fancy this later," he whispers sideways. A few days of deprivation can really test a pilgrim's mettle. I wonder how we would behave after forty days in the desert?

Following dinner, I join Nicholas who turns out to be a grizzled Oxford don specializing in Byzantine art and history—and a collection of Euro-pilgrims in the newly constructed dormitory. Like college students, we sit up chatting about our respective adventures as pilgrims, but when the topic turns to an intellectual joust on the finer points of Orthodox sacred cannon, I find myself at a distinct loss.

When Nicholas breaks for a cigarette, I join him on the breezy wooden balcony leading to the loo. A west wind rattles the floorboards, and bullets of rain resound on the roof above our heads. Beyond the railing, a black abyss drops into the sea a thousand feet below us, where irresistible waves crash against immovable rocks.

"When I was young, and forced to be a church-going Catholic," I tell the don, "I used to wonder why all these different people calling themselves 'Christian' held such great contempt for each other. My great aunt finally explained that the 'dirty Protestants' ruined the Lord's Prayer with an extra line at the end, and refused to recognize Mary's virginity, so I could understand why you'd want to burn *them* at the stake. But all she seemed to know about the Eastern Orthodox Church was that they'd once had some vague beef with the pope."

Nicholas emits a slow, rolling laugh, and his belly shakes over the top of his boxer shorts. "Needless to say, we 'dirty Protestants' got a slightly different story," he replies in an exceedingly proper Oxfordian accent, "but I can give you the textbook explanation of how Rome and Constantinople came to blows, if you like."

It seems that, in contrast to the itinerant Nazarene rabbi, the early church fathers had way too much time on their hands. They spent their days in endless argument over questions such as: Is God, the "Father," *identical in being* to Christ, the "Son?" And how can the "Divine Triad" (Father, Son, and Holy Spirit) have three distinct realities, yet only a *single substance*? Debate surrounding these questions was so intense that, in 325 C.E., the Emperor Constantine convened a synod of bishops from the Greek provinces, Roman legates, and representatives from the ecclesia of Alexandria and Antioch at the seaside town of Nicaea.

This "ecumenical" council began by censuring Arius, a very popular Alexandrian priest whose alleged heresy was his belief that Christ proceeded from the sovereign "will" of the Father, rather than sharing His "identity." Next, the bishops drafted a creed and canon (declaring that the Holy Trinity is "one in essence"), exiled two of their colleagues who refused to sign it, and finally petitioned the Emperor for a church tax exemption—ostensibly to help the poor. Constantine, relieved that the august windbags had come to some agreement, happily granted their request, declared himself a "bishop of external things," and eventually received baptism on his deathbed—by one of the bishops who had agreed with Arius. A smart emperor always hedges his bets.

But the Nicene Council and Creed did not end theological controversy by a long shot. Not only was the semantic hair-splitting over the precise nature of Christ a major concern of six subsequent councils; the nature of the Virgin Mary became an issue as well. Cyril of Alexandria, at the Council of Ephesus in 421, declared her to be *Theotokos*, the "Godbearer," precipitating a whole series of complicated outrages, denunciations, and schisms. Oddly, throughout all of this, no one ever questioned Mary's "virginity."

In 863, Photius, Patriarch of Constantinople, had a blowout with Nicolas I, Pope of Rome, severely damaging relations between East and West. Around 1054, Cardinal Humbert traveled East as a papal legate to patch things up with Patriarch Michael Cerularius. Instead of smoothing ruffled feathers, they succeeded in rubbing each other the wrong way, finally exchanging mutual *anathema*—excommunication not formally revoked for over 900 years.

The cause of these disagreements had both a theological and political component. The Latin Church had inserted *Filioque* into the original Nicene Creed, making it read that the Holy Spirit "proceeds from the Father *and* the Son." The Eastern bishops felt this addition devalued the Holy Spirit by stressing unity over the diversity of divine essence. They also had major trouble with Rome's prohibition against married men entering the priesthood, their use of unleavened bread in the Eucharist, and, worst of all, their insistence on papal infallibility. Orthodox Christians saw the church as councilor in nature, Roman Catholics as monarchical, and there was no room for compromise.

"Add to these tensions the European sack of Constantinople during the Fourth Crusade, in the early thirteenth century, and a final antipapal breach at the Church of Antioch in 1724, when rival patriarchs were elected, and you have a nutshell history of bad blood between Eastern and Western Christians," Nicholas concluded.

"Who would have guessed?" I said. "But that said, what could Eastern Orthodoxy possibly offer to an intellectual English Protestant scholar?"

"Mystery, dear fellow," the don replies with a supercilious cluck, and lights another Dunhill. "Since Luther nailed his theses to the door, Christians have been trying to intellectualize something which is, by its very nature, a *mystery*. The core of all Christian liturgy is the Eucharistic consecration: *epiclesis*—an invocation of the Holy Spirit, in the East, or *transubstantiation*—changing bread and wine into Christ's body and blood, in the West. This is an alchemical process; don't you see? It transforms the act of having Passover supper with your fishing mates into a mystical communion. After the Protestant Reformation, this ritual was eroded over the centuries in a misguided attempt to make religion more 'relevant' to an increasingly educated populace. Even the Latin Church began to succumb to social pressure with the ecumenical movement

of the 1960s. But the net result of this intellectual political correct-
ness was a demystification of the very heart and soul of the religion.

"Eastern Orthodoxy, on the other hand, never eviscerated the
mystery of the Christos; they guarded it, and cherished the paradox
of the Virgin Mother." Nicholas coughs harshly, then crushes his
cigarette on the wooden railing. "Just look around you, lad." He
gestures to nothing in particular with myopic eyes, breathing in
the humid sea air and smiling peacefully. "Here…the mystery still lives."

At 5 A.M., it is a mystery to me why any sentient being should be awake. We dress in silence as hungry ghosts howl in the dark and rattle the dormitory windows. Outside, the clouds lurking in the shroud of night spit the threat of rain as we climb the cobbled ramp into Simonos Petras's stone belly. Torches light our passage into the courtyard where a choral of resonant voices within the chapel invokes the

---

It is no accident that all of Jesus's teaching was recorded in Greek, but a divine mystery. He only says one Aramaic phrase in all the gospels, and that is an expression of anguish, of betrayal. The Jews say they were chosen by Jehovah, but it is we who were chosen by Christ. Christ is incarnated in Greek.

—Patricia Storace, *Dinner with Persephone*

---

dawn. Inside the church, I watch in somnambulant wonder as an
ancient ritual unfolds in glittering, candlelit austerity. An angry
wind batters the dome above our heads like Satan seeking shelter,
but the Prince of Darkness is held at bay by a black-robed angelic
army singing "*Kyrie eleison.*" Once more, as it has been done each
day for fifteen centuries, the alchemical transformation of bread and
wine into spiritual sustenance is celebrated as a reaffirmation of
divine redemption through the personage of a Galilean carpenter.

On Mount Athos, the mystery is alive and well.

By eleven that morning, I await the boat at Dáfni, sipping
Elinikafes as Greek pilgrims purchase overpriced icons from the

wharfside trinket shop. It seems that even in austerity there is room for commercialism.

On the quay, I spot Nikos with his battered athletic bag, now apparently depleted of cigarettes. He bums one from another pilgrim then nods to me. "I must go back to arrange things with my girlfriend," he explains, squinting into the sun that has finally broken through the cumulus. "Perhaps I will return here after Christmas. I don't know. I am always fighting with the devil."

"Why not surrender?" I suggest.

"We *must* fight," Nikos maintains, his intense eyes flashing. "Always! The devil is strong in us. Drinking, drugs, sex—we are weak." There is such pain in his face; the scars from Nikos's personal war cut canyons through his tight jaw, but it is only in the deepest recesses of those blue eyes that his self-loathing can be detected. "To fight is the only way. Otherwise, we are like the dead."

When the boat docks at noon, we ripe and ragtag pilgrims board, but the Jaegers are nowhere in sight. The sun and wind have blown the threatening clouds somewhere in the direction of Turkey. Lapis sky melts into indigo sea as our prow cuts the water toward Ouranópolis. I stand alone at the white enameled railing, feeling the sun and wind caress my stubbled face and cool my sweat-drenched clothes.

With great fondness, I recall that afternoon with the Peruvian Hieromonk at Timiou Stavrou, the sharp afternoon light streaming into his pristine little chapel—somehow more beautiful, more honest, more sacred in its simple aesthetic austerity than all the frescoes in the dim, decorous recesses of the Protaton. Although I cannot count myself a believer, that afternoon with Patra Symeon brought me closer to the Christos than ever before. I suppose that is the real purpose of pilgrimage—the "becoming"—movement toward the promise of being. Otherwise, there is no reward you can display on your chest like a spiritual Medal of Honor. The process is all there is, any "realization" overshadowed by a compulsion to continue the journey.

My ruminations are interrupted when the boat docks at Konstamonitou to pick up some stragglers—my weary "family" from Wuppertal.

"Yesterday was most difficult," Tilman groans after they have dropped their gear on the sun deck. "We crossed the entire peninsula from Vatopaidiou. Somewhere at the crest, the road goes away and there is nothing but a rabbit tunnel through the bush."

Philipp, looking like an Armani model with his boyish beard and tousled black hair, laughs laconically. "You should have seen Father crawling on his hands and knees through the bush. He was a sorry sight."

Herr Jaeger's trousers are torn at the knees, and his beautiful handmade leather boots are scarred with deep gouges from the brutal trail. But there is contentment in his sunburned face, and peace in his tired eyes. He drinks in the sight of his strapping sons with paternal pleasure. "Four days of honoring the Virgin Mary is enough," he sighs. "Philipp is very anxious to see his girlfriend, and, oddly enough, I am feeling the same about my wife."

When we break simultaneously into spasms of laughter, Gerhard comes close to blushing, but seamlessly segues from embarrassment into aphorism. "Time with men is good, *ja*? But we need the balance of women in life." He closes his eyes, clasps my shoulder, and grins into the west wind. "This is all the wisdom your old father has to give you. "

I think of the woman I'll be meeting at the airport in Athens tomorrow evening, and how much she would have loved to see this place. I find myself becoming angry on her behalf, and for all women who have been told they are not worthy to walk in the Virgin's garden. It is nothing less than women's punishment for being so desirable to men, for our unfathomable need to possess them, and inevitable guilt for having succumbed to those "baser instincts"—all the obsessive stuff from which great epics are made.

On the starboard deck, Nikos stands alone with his demons, perpetually torn between the prohibition of ravens and the temptation of serpents. He is staring out to sea like Odysseus caught between Scylla and Charybdis, fighting, like so many of us, that archetypal war of Contraries.

Kyrie eleison.

★

Tom Joyce is a writer, photographer, and graphic designer who lives in the San Francisco area. He is currently working on a documentary film project called The Heritic's Pilgrimage.

LAURIE GOUGH

★ ★ ★

Naxos Nights

*A traveler from the cold north discovers
the heat of her soul.*

NO SINGLE INCIDENT IN MY LIFE HAS BEEN SO STRANGE, SO HARD
to grasp, so totally lacking in feasible explanation. It's the weirdest
thing that's ever happened to me and it happened on a Greek island.
I came to Naxos by mistake, but maybe there are no mistakes.
Maybe sometimes we're meant to be led here and there, to certain
places at certain times for reasons beyond our understanding, beyond
our will or the spell of the moon or the arrangement of the stars in
the sky. Maybe all the dark and eternal nameless things lurking
around us have their own purpose and vision for us. Who knows?

When I was twenty-three, I was traveling alone through Europe.
I'd been in the rain for two months in Britain and discovered I
didn't like being wet. I wanted to dry out and perhaps I wanted
more than that—an inner light, a deeper understanding of life's
complexities, a friend. With all those rainy days traveling alone, a fire
had been extinguished within me and I needed rekindling. One
morning I woke up soggy. I was on a beach in Scotland at the time
so soggy was to be expected, but I was also shivering and miserable.
I decided to escape to Greece as fast as possible.

Three days later I was on a midnight flight to Athens. At six in
the morning, dragging my sleepless, jet-lagged body around the

port of Piraeus, I came to a clapboard sign of a ferry schedule for various Greek islands. I was still dripping wet psychologically and dead tired, but I wanted things: a beach, the sun, a warm dry place to sleep, a Greek salad. I bought a ticket for the island of Paros because the ferry was leaving in ten minutes. Arbitrary, yes, but I was young and still arranged my life that way. Six hours later we pulled into the Paros harbor. From the wooden bench on the boat where I'd been napping, I looked up to see a jammed crowd of passengers swarming the exit doors. Since I was groggy and exhausted, I decided to stay on the bench a few more minutes and let the crowd disappear. When I looked up again, in what seemed just a few minutes, I was appalled to see the boat pulling away from the harbor, the passengers all gone, and me left alone on the boat. For the next two hours I worried we were sailing back to Athens, and I was too embarrassed to ask the men who worked on the ferry about it.

Fortunately, in two hours we arrived at another island. I got off the boat on the island of Naxos and walked with my backpack along the dock where I was immediately swarmed by a sea of short, round, middle-aged women in polyester black dresses and black socks who wanted me to stay at their guest houses and sleep on their roofs. Assuming the roles of foreign eccentric aunts, they took my arms and patted my hands, trying to pull me into their lives, their doughy bodies.

I didn't go to the houses of any of those women. In the recesses of my drowsy mind I remembered I needed a beach, and sleep. Leaving the busy little port town behind, I headed south along the beach, walking for a long time through scatterings of bodies lying on the white sand, topless French women playing frisbee, nut-brown boys throwing balls, incoming waves and tavernas off to the side. A pure Aegean light fell on my head like a bleached curtain draping from the sky. It was a lean and haunting landscape, savagely dry, yet the light was uncannily clear with a blue sky big enough to crack open the world, had the world been a giant egg. The crowds thinned as I walked farther along the beach and music from the tavernas faded in the distance. Finally, I spotted something under the shade of an olive grove—a small bamboo wind shelter that someone must have constructed and recently abandoned. Perfect. I'd found the place to drop down and sleep. And, although I didn't know it at the time, I'd found the place that would become my home for over a month.

I had forgotten about that light. I had forgotten the numberless evenings I'd sat on the same terrace, alone or with friends, watching it change, wrapped in that expanse of rose gold light. That night, with the heavy labor of cleaning over at last, I could feel something inside begin to loosen, that chronic knot I never knew I had until I came to Greece, and it disappeared. This night on the terrace I could feel it loosen, thread by thread, so that it seemed as if I had just swollen up by taking in some of what was around me, and what was around me had taken in some of me—a kind of psychic orgasm, where there was no separation, no barrier between figure and ground. As if the universe had been trying to tell me something: that in reality there were no barriers, no barriers at all and most of all no barriers to light, no more to learn about.

—Nancy Raeburn, *Mykonos*

I slept the rest of that day in the bamboo wind shelter under the olive grove and when I woke up it was dark and all the people were gone. A night wind danced across my face and shooting stars crashed across the sky. I ran along the beach, delirious, exalted, and finally dry.

My days on the beach took on their own rhythm. In the morning, rose rays of sunrise from behind a dark mountain would wake me, and if they didn't, the island's omnipresent roosters would. The sea would be calm at dawn and I'd go for a swim before the day's beach crowd arrived. Walking back to my bamboo shelter I'd say hello and chat with the smiling waiter, Nikos, at the nearby taverna as he set out his chairs for the day's customers. Nikos was handsome in the way many Greek men are handsome, which has more to do with the way they look at you than how they themselves look. Nikos was good at looking rather than good-looking, which was almost the same thing in the end. When the sun got too high I'd escape its burning rays and read books in the shade of my olive grove. I'm a redhead—an absolute curse in a desert like Greece. The waves would gather momentum as the day passed and at some point every afternoon they would be at their fullest. That's when the old men would appear. From seemingly out of nowhere, a gathering of weathered, mahogany Greek men with sunken chests and black bathing shorts would converge to stand on the shore and survey the sea. The Aegean in dark-blue spasms would be reaching its zenith there in the afternoon light and, from my olive grove, I'd watch it also. The old men would enter the sea together, simultaneously turn to face the shore, and hunch over with their knees slightly bent, skinny arms outstretched, waiting. They'd look over their shoulders at the ocean beyond, ready to jump up and join it at precisely the right moment. They always knew when that was. I would join them and always laughed when riding the waves, but I never saw those men crack a smile. I decided that when I was eighty I would take the waves that seriously also. After that many years of life on earth, what could be more important than playing in the waves?

Sometimes I'd walk into town to explore, buy fruit and bottled water, and watch old men argue politics over their Turkish coffee served in tiny cups. The coffee was sweet and strong and one-third full of gooey sediment. At sunset the men would turn their chairs to face the sun as it melted the day into the sea. They'd sigh and drink their ouzo or citron or *kitro*—a specialty of Naxos lemon liqueur—and stop talking until the sky drained of color. Parish priests with stovepipe hats, long robes, and beards would stroll the narrow alleys with their hands behind their backs looking exactly like movie extras. Old women in black would watch me as I passed, ask me about snow occasionally. I'd wander through the maze of whitewashed houses, the stark lines of white and blue, and stumble back home over the rocky land of dry absolutes in a heady daze. Nothing is murky in Greece, nor hazy, nor humid, nor dewy. Lush doesn't live there. Greece is a rock garden of shrubs and laurel, juniper and cypress, thyme and oregano. Wildflowers spin colors

that surge out of a pure clarity and in this clarity the forms of things
are finer. Greece shimmers from afar, is hardy in the distance, and
chill beneath your bones. In the dry heat of this arid place, donkeys
sound-off at all hours, as if agitated. They'd wake me even in the
dead of night.

One evening at sunset a man on a moped zipped by as I was
walking along the beach. He came to a stop in the sand ahead and
turned to ask my name. I'd seen him before at the taverna, throwing his head back to laugh when Nikos the waiter told jokes. The
man on the moped offered me a ride down the beach and I took
it. Naxos has one entire uninterrupted beach and in twenty minutes
or so we came to his village, a cluster of houses and an outdoor
restaurant overlooking the sea. The man let me off, smiled without
speaking and disappeared. I went to the restaurant for dinner and
chatted with some tourists. We didn't say anything significant.
Mostly we watched the sky, which by then was bloodred cracked
apart with silver shots of whisky. Shortly after I found a bus that
took me back to the town of Naxos.

By the time I finally arrived at the olive grove it was dark except
for the light of the moon heaving itself full over the mountain. I
came to my bamboo wind shelter and found it creaking in the
wind, desolate, as it was the day I arrived, abandoned by its inhabi-
tant. My backpack and the little home I'd made with my sleeping
bag and pillows were gone, taken. For approximately three seconds
I felt a panic spread through me, which didn't seem healthy, so I
looked at the moon and seeing that dependable milky rock hover-
ing up there like the planet's eccentric uncle made me smile, and I
remembered that in the great scheme of the universe, this kind of
thing didn't matter. I had my money, traveler's cheques, and passport
with me and could buy the few things I needed. My backpack had
been too heavy anyway, and traveling light would be a relief, a new
challenge, something to write home about in postcards. Sitting on
the sand I thought of the stolen things I would miss: my journal, my
camera, some foreign change, a pair of Levis, my toothbrush, my
shoes. My shoes!

I fell asleep surprisingly quickly under the full moon that night.

Luckily the thieves hadn't stolen the floor of the wind shelter—the bamboo mats—and I was comfortable and warm, but an hour or so later a group of hysterical German women came and woke me. They'd been staying at a campground down the beach and they too had been victims of an annoying petty crime. Standing with them was a quiet, tall Dutch man with a blond beard and thick glasses. His belongings had been stolen also, even an expensive camera was gone, but I noticed that, unlike the women, he wasn't the least perturbed by it. In fact he was calm, even amused, and I felt an instant affinity for this unusual man. In the midst of the German panic, three Scottish backpackers came along and asked if this was a safe place to camp. I laughed, which seemed to irritate the German women, while Martin, the Dutch man, said it was safe except for the occasional theft in the area, but really quite peaceful during the day. The German women went off to search for clues down the beach. Martin and I lay back on the sand and watched the stars swirl over the wine-dark sea as we discussed the lapses

At lunch on my final day in Naxos, I ask the waiter where he's from. He replies shyly, "Lésvos." I ask about Sappho, which starts him talking, and I feel as if one of the Greek statues I've seen in the museum has come to life, a figure from an earlier time, eyes the color of the Aegean. And farseeing.

When he isn't serving others, he visits my tiny table, as grateful to talk about ideas and poetry as I am. When I get up to leave, he shakes my hand respectfully, saying, "My soul has been sore and empty for some time and needed filling." He speaks from the heart. Then he quotes Oscar Wilde, who spoke of "the quality of certain memorable moments." His big, rough farmer's hand shakes mine, and he says, "I get nostalgic for these talks I've had with people where for a few moments we've met, really touched."

That encounter was perhaps the greatest gift for me, the culmination of my stay in Greece.

—Lily Iona MacKenzie,
"The Island of Ariadne"

and betrayals of the modern world. We should have been helping in the search, but what was the point? Our possessions gone, we felt free in a funny way. We didn't care. We were two whimsical souls colliding in the land of Homer. Half an hour later, the German women came running back, exhilarated and out of breath. "We found everything! Our things! Come!" It was true. Over a sand dune not far away, most of our belongings, including my backpack, were piled together like a happy heap of children hiding in the dark. My backpack had been slashed with a knife and anything of value, like my camera, was gone, but my journal was there and so were most of my clothes, even my toothbrush. It felt like Christmas. I found my sleeping bag and tent in another sand dune and since I hadn't used the tent since Britain anyway, I gave it to Martin because his had been taken. Somehow losing everything and so unexpectedly finding it again had given us a new perspective on what we valued. One of the German women gave me a book. A festive night! The best part of the thievery was that in the semi-crisis of getting our stuff ripped off, I'd met the strange, fair-haired Dutch man and he made me laugh.

Martin and I spent the next two days together talking continuously. Just being with him filled me with an excitement and a calm, deep knowledge. There are people with whom you feel mute and around them you forget you have a head and a heart full of ideas and wonder, poetry and longing, and there are those who can reach straight into your chest and pull songs and stars out of your heart. Martin wasn't quite like that—I didn't sing around him—but he was close, and he was the best friend I'd made in months of traveling. Traveling is so temporary, so peculiar to the nature of the human psyche, that you forget you need friends. When you find one, you remember the miracle of another person and you remember yourself. Talking to Martin made me feel I was availing myself to whatever was extraordinary in the world. He had a special interest in the spirit world, also in plants and modern history. He was a storyteller too, with stories of his long journey through India and Tibet, stories of love, betrayal, auto accidents. I told stories also, most of mine involving medical mishaps in Third World countries.

On the third day Martin left to catch a plane. I walked him to the ferry. He limped because he'd stepped on a sea urchin. He was sunburned. I waved good-bye from the dock to the Dutch man with gawky glasses and violet eyes underneath, and I wondered if I'd ever see him again.

As the days passed, I found it increasingly difficult to leave my wind shelter. I had the moon, sun, stars, my books, the old men in the waves. Why would I leave? I'd seen enough of the world and I liked where I was. Perhaps the more you stay in a place, the more it grows on you, the way some people do. I'd wake at dawn thinking today should be the day to go to another island, go back to the mainland or to another country. But then I'd go for a swim and read a little, take a walk, jump through the waves. The sun would sneak across the sky making its way towards its great dip into the sea and I'd still be there like a lotus eater, lazy some would say, if they didn't know better. One day I decided to take an excursion away from my beach, maybe try to leave it for good. I wasn't prepared to leave Naxos yet. I'd just see more of it. I took a bus to the other side of the island and was gone for four days. It felt like forever.

The bus driver could have gotten us killed several times as he rampaged around hairpin curves into the mountains. From the window, I watched the dramatic patchwork of Naxos, its gardens, vineyards, citrus orchards, villages, and Venetian watchtowers. Farmers plowed with donkeys in the fields. Children played barefoot along the roads. The people of the island may have had only a scruffy flock of goats or a small grape orchard, a rowboat to search the night waters for fish or a taverna with three tables, but they weren't poor. Life brought them regular random encounters with friends and relatives each day, not just occasional carefully selected lunches with them. Their lives were rich, plentiful, and cheerful.

I stayed at a fishing village called Apollon on the roof of a house of one of the women in black. In Greece, a woman puts on a black dress when a loved one dies and she wears a black dress the rest of her life. That's devotion. That also cuts down on clothing expenses. Some women also rent out rooms to tourists and, if the rooms are full, they rent the roof. That's a good head for business. By that time

I was so accustomed to sleeping outside, I chose the roof over an inside room. The woman in black gave me a fine example of a tsk tsk—something people the world over do with their teeth and tongue when they disapprove of you—and she said something in Greek, which was Greek to me, and gave me an extra blanket. For hours I watched the stars and thought of our dark ancestral past far away, the stars where we originated in some distant long forgotten explosion. Under the weight of the stars I could hardly bear the full force of the universe, the randomness, the chaos, the chance of it all. What is one to do with a life when eternity surrounds us?

One could return to a wind shelter under an olive grove. That was one option.

So I returned. And that's when the strange thing happened, the one for which there is no logical explanation. On the first night back from my excursion I had fallen into a deep sleep in my wind shelter when I had the distinct and uncomfortable feeling that something was moving towards me along the beach and I should wake up to chase it away. I tried with all my might to wake up but my eyes felt glued shut and I couldn't open them. The thing was approaching fast, faster every second it seemed, and it was determined, perhaps running, and I knew it was looking for me. Although I couldn't fathom what it was, it felt horribly dangerous and I knew it was imperative I wake up to protect myself. Yet waking was impossible. My body and eyes were paralyzed. Like a great black shadow the thing was coming across the sand and still my body was comatose. Then I could feel it close by and, I knew suddenly, this dark and unknown thing was with me in the olive grove. My heart seemed to bang out of my chest, loud enough to hear. I forced myself to climb up through layers and layers of a deep sleep, the sleep of centuries it felt like, and at last I broke out of it and woke, or so I thought. Pulling myself up on my elbows, I saw what the thing was: a tiny woman in black, no more than four feet tall, and very old. She lay down beside me, curled her body against mine, and shivered. Whatever she was, she was very cold and wanted inside. I knew instinctively she didn't mean inside my sleeping bag. She wanted inside me. No, I said, you can't come in. I live here. She pulled herself closer and her long, damp silver hair fell like sorrow, like misery, like an ancient sad longing. She needed a home, a warm body to live in, a place with a fire. Her face was that of a crone and I could feel her wrinkled icy skin on my cheek. Even her breath was the frigid night air of winter. Her eyes seemed bottomless at first, empty, like black holes, but buried deep inside were two brilliant stars for eyes, blazing stars light years away. Again and again I told her No, which seemed to make her unbearably sad. Please let me in, she pleaded. No, you can't. This is my body, this is me! For a moment an uncanny intimacy hung there between us as we stared at each other across the distance of two worlds. Her eyes shone so brightly they burned my own, burned straight through to my inner core. No, I told her again firmly. No. With that, she was gone. She raised herself up and drifted off down the beach, still shivering and still wanting a home. She left as she had come, with the night breeze.

The incident itself I could easily have dismissed as a weird dream, and did in fact do so the next morning when I woke to the call of the roosters, shaking my head at the previous night's dark madness. Although the dream had been unusually vivid, perceptible and oddly lucid, it had to be a dream nonetheless. A four-foot-tall woman in black trying to pry her way into my body? How rude. Crazy. What happened later that day, however, made me wonder how far dreams travel into the waking world.

That afternoon, the taverna near my wind shelter where I always ate lunch was closed, the tables, chairs, and the owner, Nikos, nowhere in sight. Strange, I thought, since I had never seen it closed in all the weeks I'd been there. Perhaps Nikos was taking a holiday. I decided to walk down the beach to the campground restaurant instead. By chance, my table happened to be next to some back-packers who were discussing where they would travel after Greece. As I ate my fruit salad I listened to their conversation, which fortunately was in English since they were of several nationalities. The conversation took a twist when a German woman began to tell the others about a strange dream she'd had the night before.

"It was horrible, a nightmare. I dreamt a little woman came floating along the beach. She was kind of like the women here in Greece, the ones who wear the black, but she was tiny. She was cold. It was terrible, terrible. Such a clear dream."

My spoon fell from my hand and I felt a sudden constriction around my heart. Had I heard her right? Was this too a dream? "Excuse me," I said to the German woman, "I couldn't help overhearing you. What did the woman want?" The German woman looked over at me, startled, almost familiar. Her face was pale.

"To get inside me."

In a land where myth and reality swirl around each other in a luminous haze, lessons clear and absolute can be found after all. I said nothing is murky in Greece but I was wrong. A woman came to me on the mist. She crossed over from the other side and sent me a gift. In all my life I have never known such a moment as when those haunting eyes from eternity stared into mine. Although she may not have intended to, she gave me a message: a human life is an extraordinary treasure. She wanted to feel life, maybe feel it again as she once had, and she wanted it desperately. I was alive, breathing, warm, strong, with a fire and light inside me she ached for. When I pushed her away, proclaiming my life as my own, never had I felt the life inside me so intensely.

I left on the ferry the next day. I didn't need to stay in Naxos anymore. I needed to see the rest of the world. To stay in my wind shelter and live amidst the lure and myth of Greece would be to believe in magic and fate, superstition and dark mysteries. I had this world to explore first, the one with cities and rivers, foreign faces and Woody Allen movies. From the boat I watched the island shrink on the horizon, getting smaller and smaller like a puddle evaporating in the sun.

Yet I knew then as I still know now, that from the shore where the sand dunes begin, the olive grove grows old, and from the bed where we sleep, the shadows of secret things lurk, forbidden, timeless, and forever calling our name.

✳

Laurie Gough's work has appeared in numerous travel literature anthologies, national newspapers and magazines, and Salon.com. Kite Strings of the Southern Cross, *silver medal winner of the* ForeWord *Magazine Travel Book of the Year, is her first book. She lives in Ontario, Canada.*

ROBERT PEIRCE

A Breathtaking View

A poor student finds a way to learn Greek.

THE BEST WAY TO LEARN A LANGUAGE, THEY SAY, IS TO GO TO THE country where they speak it. This sounded fine to me when, as a college student in 1948, I was given the chance to spend the summer in Greece. I have trouble with languages. I knew that I would never learn Greek from a grammar book but looked forward to acquiring it effortlessly through osmosis. I was imagining the words being somehow out there circulating in the atmosphere, and that after sufficient exposure, I would start speaking and understanding Greek.

I was wrong (you knew that). One of the problems was that the people with whom I spent the summer spoke nothing but English. I was a summer school student at the somewhat ponderously named American School of Classical Studies in Athens and was surrounded most of the time by Americans. Our mentors were classical archaeologists of the old school, many of whom had not themselves bothered to learn modern Greek, and tended to think that nothing of much importance had happened in Greece since the Battle of Actium in the first century B.C. "These people (the modern Greeks) are not Greeks!" one of them told me, somewhat indignantly. "They're Albanians!".

202

But I can't blame it all on my companions. Poor language students, I now know, remain poor language students no matter what they do or where they are. There is no magic way.

Yet I tried. I thought that, for starters, I would concentrate on "hello." I watched and listened carefully as Greeks met and greeted one another. They tended to shake hands and say something that sounded like "kaleemayross." But when I did the same, the people I greeted either looked at me blankly as though I had not said anything at all or smiled in a way that suggested something more than polite cordiality.

I sensed I was doing it wrong, and asked a friend who knew both languages. "The Greeks," he explained, "are saying '*kalimera*,' which breaks down as '*kali*' (good) plus '*imera*' (day). But the word *you* are using is '*meros*,' which means toilet. You are wishing them a 'good toilet.'"

That convinced me I had better have a tutor, so I hired Kostas. He was the brother-in-law of the school's cook and a man of many troubles. I am sure that he knew his own language well; the problem was that he didn't speak English. I, on the other hand, didn't speak German, his second language. It somehow seemed more important to him that I learn German than Greek, and if there was any didactic character at all to our weekly meetings, it was focused on him learning English and me German. We tended to leave Greek out of it. The reward for Kostas, in these sessions, was a chance to make a few drachmas, smoke some American cigarettes, and talk to himself in two languages about his troubles. It took me a while to realize that there was no reward at all for me, at which point I wished Kostas a good toilet and terminated the lessons.

Yet somehow, all those words floating around out there in the atmosphere had filtered deeper into my brain than I knew. It just

> Surely to have seen Athens gives a man what Swift calls Invisible Precedence over his fellows.
> —Sir Edward Marsh

needed the proper occasion for them to come out. This came one day near the end of summer on the upper slopes of Mt. Párnis.

Mt. Párnis sits immediately north of Athens, and, at around 4,600 feet, is the biggest mountain in the vicinity. All summer long I had been looking at it, and at some point decided I was going to climb it. Because it was there. And because, I assumed, there would be a wonderful view of Athens and its surroundings from its top. (In those days, there was no smog.)

You are thinking of ropes and pitons, but the real climbing problem here was getting to the mountain and past the police who guarded its approach. The place to start, I learned, was Acharnaí, the home of Aristophanes and the subject of his earliest comedy. By the time I found my way there, it was already midmorning.

I headed for the track that seemed to be leading up Mt. Párnis, but here was confronted by three armed policemen.

"Blublublublublublublub!" they screamed at me.

"I don't understand Greek," I responded with what I hoped was a pleasantly cooperative look. "I am an American. A student."

"Blublublublub!" they countered, and marched me to the police station.

There I remained for the next four hours. For a while, people came and went, shouting at me in Greek. Then there was a long interval during which, I assume, they were looking for a translator. Finally, a heavily mustached man named Nikos arrived to begin the interrogation.

"This area is forbidden," he announced, grimly. "What are you doing here?"

"I want to climb Mt. Párnis," I told him.

"*Climb* it?" repeated Nikos, incredulous. The idea seemed not only preposterous but a little sinister.

"What for, *climb* it?"

"Because it's there," I explained.

He had other questions, many other questions. Who was I? Why had I come to Greece? Did I have any connections with the Communist party? etc., etc. After a while, the focus of interest turned to the guerrillas lurking above us on Mt. Párnis. These were wicked people, Nikos told me, but the legitimate Greek government of which he was a representative had them on the run.

In 1948, you may remember, Greece was still in the throes of civil war. At the end of World War II, a coalition of partisans under Communist leadership had helped drive the occupying Germans out of Greece. The British, followed by the Americans, supported the anti-Communist forces in the struggle for power that followed. By 1948, the Communists had been pushed out of Athens but were continuing their resistance elsewhere. This was mainly in the north of Greece, but they were also making trouble in a number of pockets all over Greece, including the surroundings of Athens. It was not always an organized effort. ("There've always been bandits in the more inaccessible parts of Greece," the old hands told me at the School, "but now they call themselves Communists.")

As a college student who had read a few articles, I felt I knew a little more about the struggle than most. It was cynical self-interest that was dictating America's aid to the non-Communists, and cynical self-interest that allowed the latter to accept it. The threat of *andartes*, as the rebels were called, had been deliberately magnified to justify the large amounts of American money and support that were coming to government forces in the conflict. I, for one, was not worried about guerrillas on Mt. Párnis.

The interrogation session went on, with long interruptions while some other authority was consulted, presumably by phone. After a while, coffee was served, then a small lunch. By early afternoon, Nikos and I were sharing a bit of ouzo. We were no longer concerned about my motives in wanting to climb Mt. Párnis nor the evils of Communism and the particular menace of its bloodthirsty representatives lurking above us. We were drinking to the glory of Greece's past and the greatness of America. Nikos spoke with emotion about his wife, his two small children, and his chickens.

Somewhere along the line, Nikos or his unseen superiors decided it was all right for me to go. He shook my hand warmly, and I made my way unsteadily out the door and up to the guard post. This time I was greeted with warm smiles. The guards shouted jovially as they waved me on my way.

It was now late and I knew that I had to move fast. I half ran and half walked, full of joy at my unexpected release, and dizzied by ouzo.

An hour or two later, there were unmistakable signs that the afternoon light was about to fade. I accepted the fact that I would never be able to reach the ultimate summit. But ahead of me was a lesser pinnacle—a top but not the very top. It was a respectable goal and it would do. I aimed for that. Head down, I charged for its highest point.

It was hard work, and about 100 feet from my destination, I stopped to catch my breath. I glanced up. Two men with guns were standing near the summit, their backs to me.

Honesty compels me to admit that my first reaction was to look around for a place to hide. But these were open slopes, covered with dry grass and slabs of limestone. No trees. No large boulders. Retreat was not an option. The nearest cover was far below. I had been lucky so far but if I now turned to retreat, they would surely notice me. I preferred not to be shot in the back.

So it was not courage but calculation that made me decide to advance boldly on the enemy. I marched up the hill and shouted "Hi!" They wheeled around and trained their guns on me. I kept climbing, with what, once more, I hoped would be looked upon as an attitude of pleasant cooperation.

"Nice afternoon!" I exclaimed jovially, giving them my best version of a good-natured American cowboy smile.

They glared at me silently. I came a little closer. One of them raised his gun and seemed to be taking aim. "Stop!" he said.

I stopped.

I know very little about firearms but could tell that these rifles were ancient. The men too looked as if they may have seen better days. They were dark and bewhiskered, with shabby clothes full of patches. It was not hard to imagine them living under rocks.

"I am American," I said. "A student."

They accepted this information without comment.

"At the American School of Classical Studies in Athens," I added helpfully. "It's a school." I pointed in the general direction of Athens. "American. I'm a student."

They did not seem interested. "What do you want?" asked the man who seemed about to blow my brains out.

"The view. I came to see the view."

Without dropping their guns, the two men held a consultation. I waited.

"Where did you come from?" one of them finally asked.

This was not the time to talk about the police station. "From America. I mean, I walked. Walked up the hill. I came on a bus. From the American School of Classical Studies. Took the bus and walked up the hill. American."

It was when for the second time I pronounced the full name of the school in all its cumbersome American glory that I first realized I had not only been talking to them all along in Greek but understanding every word they addressed to me. It must have momentarily crossed my mind that I didn't *know* Greek, but this was not a time to be worrying about that.

Now they were talking again to each other. They looked over to the place I had regarded as the summit, a little knoll just beyond them that dropped off into space on the far side, then went on with their discussion. I supposed they might be trying to decide how they would dispose of the body. They had never taken their guns off me.

At length they concluded the conversation and addressed me. "We are hunters," one of them declared. "We come here to hunt."

"A *good* place to hunt!" I squealed enthusiastically, nodding my head up and down as I looked around at the barren slope. But they did not seem to care about my opinion.

"You came to look at the view?" demanded the guy whose gun was aimed at my head. I nodded even more vigorously.

"Then look at the view!" Both rifles were raised.

I marched over to the little knoll and looked. It may have been one of the most breathtaking views in two continents, but I saw nothing. One shot, I was thinking, and that will be it. No need to dispose of the body. I will be way down there somewhere. I continued to stand there waiting. How long does it take for someone to look at a view? I could not decide, but my friends knew, exactly.

"Enough view!" shouted one of the hunters. "Go on back!"

I turned around and saw that they were pointing the way back down the hill. Still nodding compulsively, I started the descent.

But how should I say it: I prefer not to be shot in the back. A short way down, I turned around.

They were still standing there, their guns trained on me. I waved and shouted, "Thank you! It was beautiful!"

They did not wave back and probably did not hear me add in a softer voice, "Good toilet!" as I turned and continued down the slope to safety.

After a lifetime of doing other things in other places (primarily editing publications at the Portland Art Museum) Robert Peirce returned to Greece in the early 1980s to take a small group on an informal tour, and has been leading such groups off and on ever since. He still does not know how to speak Greek.

LAWRENCE DAVEY

The Marble Island

On Paros an expatriate learns about Greece
the old-fashioned way—through work.

SHORTLY AFTER OUR RETURN FROM ATHENS, I FOUND WORK WITH
Vasilli, the mason, and this work would last at least off and on until
the end of our stay.

Vasilli was the archetypical Greek stone mason, born and bred on
the marble island. He had worked so long and intently at his trade
that I could see he had begun to evolve right into his medium,
taking on many of the characteristics of the stone he worked with.
Now in his late middle ages, he looked not unlike a block of marble himself, hard and clear, with well-worn hands always half-
clenched as if grasping on to yet another chunk of stone. He was a
cheery fellow and knew what he was doing which made him the
perfect man to work for.

It was hard work, heavy work—carrying rock, mixing cement,
and carrying more rock, mixing more cement—all for about 3,000
drachmas a day. This was the perfect job for a man in my circumstances. It was imperative that I work, not only for the money,
which was needed, but to get an understanding of where I was. I
don't know that there could be another way. Had I just visited during the high season, enjoyed the beaches, the party atmosphere, the
fine sunny weather, clearly I would have absorbed a distorted view

of Greece, not only of modern Greece, but of the all important earlier eras here.

Living in Greece, I soon discovered, is a struggle. Even in the golden age of Athens, this was never a land of plenty. Well, there were plenty of some things, plenty of sun, plenty of clear air, plenty of wine, figs, olives, and plenty of wind, not much rain, not much soil, stunted forests, a near-empty sea. Plenty of wars. Above all, plenty of ideas. And plenty of hard work. People have been working hard here for thousands of years.

Vasilli, I knew, had been working hard all his life. He must have been, judging from both his appearance and his modest success. I was signing on for a while, for his bigger jobs when he needed an extra hand. The first job was to lay marble floors and patios in two new houses, mansion-villas I would call them, almost identical to each other, but reversed as if staring at each other sideways through a great mirror, shoulder to shoulder just down the road from the village with the new *dexamenie*. Most of the work I found seemed to lie on that stretch of road along the island's western coast, from Paroikia to Aliki.

The marble, for which Paros was famous all through history, comes from the mountain quarries at Marathi and was cut into rectangular slabs of three or four different sizes. Many island homes had floors of gray marble but here we were laying the more costly white stone, tricky, almost translucent material. One could see a little way into it, which made it appear mysterious and magical. Neither Vasilli nor I could have afforded such stuff. One of these elegant houses was being built for a Swiss banker, and the other, its inverse identical twin, was for his friend, or accountant, or business confidant. Some sort of arcane and questionable tax arrangement, I suppose, but I couldn't much concern myself with that as I had cement to mix, slabs to haul, concrete floors to level, and my Greek was needing improvement.

This was obvious to the patient Vasilli, but he hired me anyway, and it wasn't long before I learned to adjust to his thinking and bring him a hammer when he wanted a hammer and a level when he wanted a level, not the other way round like on the first couple of days.

We were a crew of four. Besides Vasilli, there was Marcos, his son, and another man, also Marcos, old Marcos. That Vasilli's son was a Marcos led me to wonder if there weren't some Latin genes in his family; there have been Venetians stranded on these islands for some centuries now. Whatever their roots, they were all skilled experts in this business of marble masonry, and I was able to learn something of the trade as time passed

The Greeks, for some reason, had much difficulty pronouncing the name "Larry"; it never seemed to come out right. With "Lawrence" they fared no better, and since I've never had a nickname, at least not one I was at all inclined to resurrect, I became "Lorenzo," one more stranded Venetian mason.

No English was spoken at the job site, so my Greek inched forward. After a while, during our midday break, while we sat sheltered from the wind alongside the new house, facing the sunny hillside, all rock and cactus, I could even join the conversation, though with mixed results. Their interests in America were several; foremost among these was the subject of cars. This was of particular interest to young Marcos. What kind of cars could be had in America? Well, I pointed out, I once had an Opal, just like Vasilli drove. An Opal? No, they didn't want to hear about Opals, weren't there some other cars I could talk about? Big cars? Fast cars? Well, yes, I said, there were big, fast cars; probably the biggest, fastest cars in the world. Most people from Maine, I added, are pretty conservative on the road. We mostly drive Subarus, Toyotas, Escorts; there are not a lot of '57 Thunderbirds, Plymouths, Impalas, and Mustangs around any more. There are speed limits, not to mention pot holes, frost heaves, sharp turns. It is not like the Bonneville salt flats and the world famous California freeways. Marcos's eyes lit up. The Bonneville salt flats! California freeways! Yes. This is what they were waiting to hear. How fast can you drive on the salt flats, they wanted to know. In my limited Greek, I endeavored to explain that I knew very little about that, most of our driving at home was on errands, to work, to school, to the grocery store, to the gas station, but it was too late. We were on the subject of land speed records. Marcos grabbed an imaginary steering wheel, stepped on the gas, and began accelerating. I guess he was on the salt flats. Vasilli and old Marcos also took hold of wheels and began racing, swerving to avoid slower vehicles in the way. I had no choice but to do the same. Either this or be left behind while the others roared out of sight. In a minute, all four of us were sitting on rocks wildly steering nonexistent wheels, making loud roaring noises. We screeched and raced all through our lunch break.

My own old Saab which I had managed to push into the barn just before we left home, I didn't have a chance to talk about. A good thing, too. We could all have ended up pushing cars on a later lunch break.

Occasionally I did get to talk about New England. I talked about Maine, blessed with so much snow and trees. I mentioned that one special tree that was no blessing at all, the one that came crashing through my roof in the "big storm," which was how I translated "hurricane," and I told them how long it took me to set things right. I spoke in Greek. During this story, they all showed incredulous expressions, finally breaking out in laughter. Either I was being misunderstood once again, and was telling a hilarious tale, or these three shared a perverse sense of humor.

"I don't think they believed my story," I complained to Spiro that same night while we were out for one last futile stab at the fishing. This was just before he hauled his boat out of the water for the winter at Santa Maria, around the other side of the northern tip of the island, past Náousa.

"How tall did you say the tree was?" he wanted to know.

"One hundred feet. Maybe about thirty meters," I answered. "Big."

"Yes, that is a big tree...maybe they think you are exaggerating. Thirty meters may be bigger than any tree in Greece. What else did you tell them? What did you say?"

I repeated as best I could what I had told Vasilli, explaining in English what I had hoped to say in Greek.

"I see," Spiro said when I was through. "I see the problem. You have told them that a big animal, a giant animal came by and pushed the tree, a tree thirty meters high, over, and it crashed through your roof!" Now Spiro began to laugh. "Why should they believe that? I don't even believe that myself!" he added. "They are going to start thinking you are crazy. It is not good to have such a reputation, not on an island."

I could see I was not quite ready to tell long tales in Greece although this is a land of epics. The next day I was tempted to put the story right to Vasilli and the others, but I declined, recognizing that I could easily dig a deeper hole. Best to let it all lie as it was.

Shanghaied by romantic notions of travel and the sea, Lawrence Davey has earned his way as a fisherman, oil field diver, and tug boat hand. He now writes documentary films in Cambridge, Massachusetts and often can be found in the state of Maine.

EMILY HIESTAND

The Crones

A search for a hair dryer leads to the
discovery of Greek traditions.

ATHENS IS A JUMBLED CITY, WHOSE MERCHANDIZING STYLE HAS A
strain of the Middle Eastern bazaar: sandals, rugs, tables of books,
pyramids of food, inexplicable carts of steaming-hot, charred corn
peddled in ninety-degree heat, and racks of clothes take up the
slender sidewalks, on which few Athenians walk anyway, most
preferring the streets, where they weave among traffic, screaming
destinations into the windows of taxis with fares, hoping to piggy-
back—a custom that sounds energy-efficient and is only horrible,
adding to the hustle, making another bit of city life a predator/prey
suspense. Like New York, Athens overstimulates and disorients.
Overstimulated and disoriented, returning from the appliance store
with a Black & Decker world-wattage blow-dryer in hand, we see
the tiny shop in whose window is this beguiling display: two
skulls—one human, one cow—a basket of tall dried herbs, two
candles in the shape of roses, a hefty stack of beeswax and votive
candles, a rack of paperback books with illustrations of women and
devils licked by flames, and a book on aerobic yoga. We go right in.
The shop is cool, dim, eight feet wide, maybe fifteen feet deep, with
one long wall lined from top to bottom in dark mahogany drawers,
the other wall composed of open shelves stocked with candles,

incense, and books. Three women tend the βοτανα (*vo tahnah*), women for whom the word *crone* originated. Ancient they are, stooped, wrinkled, and gnarled, survivor women far beyond the temporal concerns of the young or the middle-aged, or the merely old. All three crones turn ever so slightly to take us in as we enter and then continue what they were doing, which is weighing and measuring amounts of dried and powdered plants into small brown paper bags. Along the back wall are five chairs on which are seated three silent customers. The preparations proceed at a deliberate pace; the crones collect substances from drawers, crush them in a mortar, funnel them into bags, occasionally ask one of the customers a question. The latter, two men and one pale, thin woman, answer in a few, almost inaudible words. The crones look terrifically angry.

Beeswax candles smell like bees and honey, and are the color of honey; they are thin and pliant and sold in banded bundles of one dozen. When I pick up two bundles, the crones give me a hard look, turning slowly in concert to glare uncannily like the three deadpan musicians of Sid Caesar's enigmatic Nairobi Trio. Of the whole dried plants stacked loose in large boxes on the floor, some are rec- ognizable—branches of bay leaves (also called daphne), long wands of oregano, bunches of thyme—and some are unfamiliar. One unknown, labeled only as "mountain tea," is sweet and heady with a tincture of fennel. I select some of these plants to buy, gently pry- ing the stems and leaves from the heap. The crones glare. Bracing myself, I take the herbs up to the crones to be wrapped. Store pack- aging in Greece is a cultural study in miniature: either the goods are dropped into the thinnest, cheapest possible poly-plastic bag, or they are hand-wrapped, carefully, in a strong paper, often one printed with a floral pattern. If a store hand wraps, even a purchase of five postcards is wrapped as though it were a gift, the paper's ends folded into a triangle and secured with a small square of tape. When one crone finishes compounding her remedy, she takes the candles and herbs from my hands and begins to roll them in heavy pink-brown butcher's paper, making a big bundle flared like a bunch of lilies from a florist.

Bumping so immediately into the βοτανα, I assume that there

are many herbal medicine shops in the city. Later, when I mention the βοτανα to a native Athenian who teaches urban planning and architecture at the Polytechnic, she is quite interested. Could I tell her how to get there? She knows of no such shops. I'm surprised the shop is as rare as all that, but it is no surprise that herbalists have become scarce. Plant lore emerges from intimacy with the land and, like great basketball teams, relies on a large, predictable pool of youth who are capable of assuming, perhaps improving, the practice with each generation.

Like traditional healers in all parts of the globe, the βοτανα crones curate a vestige of a Paleolithic moral order in which the Earth was alive, figured as a goddess who made the land fertile, received the dead, and caused life to be renewed. Her two great emblems were the serpent and the tree, and in the Mediterranean world her name was Gaia. That something of Gaia lives on, and fiercely, in the βοτανα crones is beyond question. Perhaps the balmy air, light, and waters of southern Christendom have been more tolerant of the *pagani*. Yet everywhere now the survival is slender; while the likes of Henry David Thoreau and John Muir were artic-ulate witnesses of the natural miraculous, such talk has been care-fully abandoned by environmentalists as they make their case to a pragmatic, materialist society. As the twentieth century closes, we have no common, respected vocabulary to name and cultivate the experience of an innately valuable Earth. As this being is not recog-nized by our prevailing worldview, it is difficult to shape language with which to honor and defend it. Even much of ardent environ-mental talk reduces the planet to a storehouse of raw materials for human use and assumes that value is determined by human needs. We are urged to care about rain forests because they supply sources of medicine for us, because they help keep the Earth's climate con-genial for us—though, paradoxically, when the Earth's value is de-termined merely by changing utilitarian values, the planet and source of our well-being remains at risk of degradation.

Merely standing in this old shop among the crones' pungent plants, one can feel a residual infusion of an older, more intimate rapport with the land. From the drawers of powders, tawny stems, roots, and drying flower-heads rises a subtle, spicy, musty aroma. The quiet meditative mood of the room is a property that mute, generative plants reliably bring to human beings. Rousing myself, I realize that even if I were fluent in Greek, it might not be possible to tell the crones of the βοτανα why they are so moving to me. The very fact that they *are* is an index of the distance between our worlds. Between their furious glares as they sift powders, and my tentative smile is a space of some two thousand years of consciousness. It is our first day in Greece; my only Greek is "F. Harry Stow," a phonetic device for the Greek word for *thank you*. "F. Harry Stow," I say to the crones, who glare, press the flared package of herbs and candles into my hands, turn their stooped collective back, and abruptly Katherine and I are out of the gum-sweet, dark shop, into the gray light of downtown Athens. In hand, we have two lovely products of *physis*: a cone of fragrant, healing herbs which we plan to use along our journey, and a plastic travel blow-dryer, a high-tech artifact that may tame the Gorgon in our appearances.

Emily Hiestand also contributed "Lessons from the Taverna" in Part One. This story was excerpted from The Very Rich Hours: Travels in Orkney, Belize, the Everglades, and Greece.

On the Way Home

An isolated chapel provokes
a surprising christening.

THE GODDESS ATHENA, IN HOMER'S TALE, PLUCKED ODYSSEUS from his twenty years of travel and travail and dropped him on the shores of his home, "clear-shining" Ithaca. To its long-lost and disoriented king, the island "showed an unaccustomed face," but Athena nevertheless upheld the Olympian tradition of putting even the most favored mortals through their paces. Odysseus had to make his own way from the quiet Bay of Dexia over the island's "crags and precipices" to his palace.

Near sunset on my first day in Ithaca, I sympathized whole-heartedly with the plight of the legendary wanderer. I had arrived on the dawn ferry from neighboring Cephalonia, the island of my grandparents' birth, determined to squeeze in two days on the island of myth before leaving Greece for my own return home. In the afternoon's last light, the port town of Vathý glistened too invit-ingly to allow for a sensible nap, and soon the surrounding hills lured me upward. I drove my rented car along a contortionist of a road, the only kind that exists in narrow, rugged Ithaca (which Homer described as even "unfit for horses"), to reach the village of Perachori. There, a guidebook promised I could find a Venetian-era chapel adorned with Byzantine frescoes.

A farmer directed me onward, pointing across the ravine toward a small building on the opposite hillside. Startling white against the silvery green of an olive orchard, the Marulata chapel stood alone and isolated, halfway up the sheer slope. The road didn't go there, and my weary legs recommended I not, either. This pilgrimage could wait for morning. But suddenly the sun, in the hands of Apollo, tossed a spark of its dying flame onto Ithaca, illuminating the little chapel with the astonishing pink of a midsummer rose. I drove to the end of the road, got out, and hiked.

The path had been worn by goats, or by someone intent on discouraging visitors. It shot nearly straight up over jagged boulders. Tree branches and thorny bramble clawed at me with every step. Ithaca had called to the sailor Odysseus from across the sea, drawing him homeward, and so the chapel on the hillside summoned me through the fading light and my own fatigue.

When at last the path leveled, it set me among the familiar arms of olive trees. For a moment I drifted there, as breathless and ragged as the wayward king. To get my bearings, I looked back across the ravine. The hills, the village homes, and the becalmed Ionian Sea burned cinnamon-red with Apollo's rekindled fire. When I turned around again, the chapel had appeared—tiny and freshly white in the surrounding world of red.

A short wooden door groaned as it let me in. One step led into darkness, and the step beyond that into Byzantium. Slowly my eyes adjusted to cowrie blue, wine red, and the glitter of gold leaf in a dozen somber icons. Sunset rays struggled in through small, dusty windows, setting several colored-glass, hanging lanterns aglow with their own light. Two scents—the bite of holy incense and the sweet, sad exhale of a decaying building—twinned in a perfume that took me back to childhood. I sat beside my mother in the Greek Orthodox cathedral of Houston, a congregation of immigrants and new Americans. That church, the realm of black-robed men and judging eyes, could never know me. This one, only the smallest of chapels held to the hill in the embrace of an orchard, was just for me.

I knelt between two saints. Tall, five-hundred-year-old icons,

they guarded the altar with forlorn gazes, left alone and nearly forgotten in their hillside aerie. They had endured a decade of sun and
rain after earthquakes in 1953 brought down the chapel's roof, an
indignity that had muted their colors but not their brilliance.
Shimmering eyes, soft shoulders, and supplicant hands—the angels
of a love-smitten artist. On my knees, looking up, I became their
ardent admirer. I regretted not knowing their names.

Just as much, I regretted my self-imposed ignorance of their
home. A pint-sized version of my mother's Houston church, it had
been miniaturized for me (or so I felt), an Alice come through the
looking glass to a Mediterranean land of wonders. I wanted mean-
ings for icon, incense, altar, sacristy, for ancient words murmured
and chants sung in minor key.

I tried to pray. To be more than just a fan of those gathered angels—to be their charge and to ride on their wings out of life's
odysseys—would require true believing. Such faith promised the
comfort and confidence of my ancestors, of my mother. If I could
just bow my head, if I could close my eyes and give over, they would
have what they wanted and so would I. I could join the procession.

But all that came was an ache in my knees. A donkey's distant bray
stood in for psaltery. The room's damp darkness gathered in too close.
Still, through the gloom, I began to sense the simple beauty of
Byzantine line and color, of arched doorways and muted dyes. And
after a moment I realized that the saint on the far wall looked something like my great-aunt, and another one like my gay uncle. Hellenic
and familiar, their expressions seemed a little lost, as if after all those
centuries they felt no more sure of belonging in that room than I did.

My great-aunt beckoned to me from the wall. I rose and committed sacrilege, passing beyond the altar into the tiny vestry behind
the sentry icons—in my mother's church, a territory strictly forbidden to females.

She was a plump, particularly beatific saint. At her gold-slippered
feet I found a box of matches on a small round table dressed in lace.
I lit a row of tapers, one of the jewel-hued oil lanterns and finally,
hesitantly, a dish of incense on the sacristy. A vestige of guilt
tweaked at me. Who was I to impersonate a priest?

The sound of footsteps outside took the guilt and torqued it. Here must come the priest himself through the olive grove. I imagined his black robes winging around him, then his swoop into my nest, and the ensuing flurry of squawks and scoldings.

I looked for a place to hide. Lamplighter, incense-burner, trespasser of vestry, I'd be caught red-handed.

Maybe it was a passing shepherd. I listened anxiously for the flock's bells, but only footsteps persisted, louder and clearer, stopping at last outside the door. I drew a deep breath and braced myself between the two sentry saints at the altar, never having dreamed I'd need them so soon.

The short wooden door groaned open. Rosy sunset light silhouetted a figure.

"*Kali spera*," I ventured. "Good evening."

The response was emphatic and unmistakable. My visitor shrieked. She was a plump, middle-aged woman, and I had terrified her.

"Oh!" I shrieked back, for no logical reason except to reassure her.

Her hands fluttered above her head, her eyes wide. A big black dog appeared at her side, gold eyes glaring in at me. I realized that to them I must look like a ghost in the dim light, dressed in traveler's black, smudged and ragged after the arduous hike up.

"*Signomi*. Excuse me." I sputtered apologies in Greek.

The woman squinted at me. She took a step closer while her dog kept watch from the doorway. Then she smiled. "Where are you from?"

I came down off the altar. We met in the middle of the room, circled by saints. After hearing I'd come from the United States and that my grandparents came from Cephalonia, Ithaca's neighbor island, the woman asked, "Did you light the incense?"

I nodded.

Her eyes took me in. To her I was clearly something different— in October a postseason holdover on this vacationers' island, a Greek-speaking *Amerikanaki*. As she gazed at me, sorting me out, the light from lamp and candles seemed to center itself within her. The solace I'd found in that home of lonely angels gathered in her blossoming smile.

※

The decision to return to the village—to the past—was not that unusual, Niko said. People were slowly going back to the country ways. Life in the cities was becoming untenable. The old ways were harder, but there was health and poetry in them; they fed the soul. An example: elderly Ikaríans still walked great distances—if they tended goats they walked maybe thirty kilometers a day—and they were as strong as cypress trees. In the old days, people had walked all over the island. If their walks took more than a day, they spent the night in cells maintained by the island's priests; the cells still existed.

Ikaría was a place like no other, according to Niko. Had I noticed the singsong way in which the old people spoke? It was ancient Greek. As recently as this century an Ikarían community had still celebrated the rite of the wind, as they had in ancient times; the practice was stopped when a village priest threatened to excommunicate them.

—Katherine Kizilos,
The Olive Grove

"It's beautiful here, isn't it?" she murmured in the sweet, soft Greek of Ithacans. She moved away and took a plastic bottle from a table near the door, holding it up for me to see. "This oil is from my olive trees." She waved toward the orchard outside the chapel. "The caretaker usually performs these duties, but once in a while, when I come to see about my trees, I stop in to help."

I followed along as she filled the row of jewel-hued glass lamps, one for each saint. It became my task to wipe stray, fragrant drops of oil off the globes and chains.

"When I was a girl these frescoes were even lovelier." She crumpled her cheek and lifted one shoulder in the characteristic Greek shrug at fate's caprice. "The earthquakes of 1953 knocked the roof in. For ten years, until a wealthy woman here in Itháki paid to repair it, the saints were like sheep on the mountain or tourists on the beach—no roof over their heads."

When we came to the vestry she showed no hesitation, made not even so much as the sign of the cross for exculpation. She passed into that prohibited space as casually as if it were just another corner of her orchard.

The saints seemed happy for the company. We must have been a crowd for them—the two of us a congregation making our own ceremony, the liturgy of becoming friends.

After filling the last lamp, the woman and I blew out the flames and snuffed the incense. I whispered good-bye to the chapel while she latched the door behind us.

"Ah! Look!" She turned toward the world below our cliff-hanging aerie.

The sun had finally sunk into Homer's "wine-dark sea," leaving Ithaca a shaded, violet land aglitter with the lights of the port town, Vathý. The mournful horn of an outbound ferry, a donkey's insistent bray, and the raspy gossip of *zdizdika*, cicadas, blended in an evening choir.

"There is my home," said my new friend, pointing out the village of Perachori just below us. She slipped her hands into the pockets of her flowered house dress. Then she breathed in the warm, dry air, perfumed with wild thyme and the tang of the sea. "I could never leave here. My daughter wants me to live with her in Athens, but why would I?"

Something soft brushed my fingers. The black dog pushed his head into my hand.

The woman laughed. "He greets you just as Argus welcomed his master Odysseus home from his journey."

Scratching this Argus's ears, I thought about my own dear, deeply missed dog at home, while the woman chattered about her beloved "Loupi."

"You know my dog's name now," she noted, "but after all this time I don't know yours."

Petting Loupi with one hand, I offered the other. "Kathryn. Katerina."

"Ah!" She clutched at her heart. Her eyes brightened. Then her arms spread wide. "And *I* am Katerina!" She folded me into a hug, almost sobbing.

In that christening embrace, Katerina was my priest, ambassador of the chapel on the hillside, messenger of a true, boundless faith in the human heart. Her unrestrained joy in meeting a kindred soul showed me the "clear-shining Ithaca" of Homer's poem, and brought me home.

Katerina took my face in her olive-scented hands and kissed both my cheeks. It was for this moment, I realized, that my mother had named me.

Kathryn Makris is the author of seventeen novels for young readers and a "CBS-TV Schoolbreak Special" adapted from her Children's Choice Award winner Crosstown. *Currently she is at work on a book and a screenplay set in Greece's Ionian islands.*

* * *

Embracing the Fates

Luck comes in many forms.

EXHAUSTED AND ELATED AFTER THREE SUMPTUOUS WEEKS IN THE Greek Isles, I was ready to find the other Greece. Mykonos, Paros, Naxos, and Santorini embody all the famous visual stereotypes— winding, narrow cobbled lanes, white plaster walls, arched door- ways, red-tiled roofs, diminutive churches each capped with a wrought-iron cross—the famous sights which are a veritable three- dimensional travel brochure.

But while these weeks were infused with ouzo, retsina, tadziki, and baklava, the cultural flavors were overwhelmingly European. In fact, the brochures invariably picture these islands devoid of inhab- itants, in part because the crowds are rarely Greek. To me, the islands represented a timeless Greek veneer hosting unabashed tourism for the rest of the world.

I'd been drawn to the Greek Isles, along with an endless stream of tourist companions, by guidebooks rightfully extolling the his- toric beauty and economic bounty found here. Now it was time to embrace the Fates and indulge a personal odyssey in search of the cultural essence and less-traveled paths of this land.

My Homer was a simple pamphlet of maps from the visitor's bureau. I scanned the pages: no text, just blue for sea, white for land, with roads in red, and items of interest marked by little yellow boxed icons perched adjacent to the names of towns. One of these, Lefkada, on the coast of the Ionio Pelagos, boasted six of these boxes. In the map index, I looked up their significance: fishing boat supply station, prehistoric site, archaeological site, Byzantine site, medieval site, and a cave. The ones missing were indicators of hotels, golf courses, beach facilities, spa resorts, ski centers, or airports. Perfect.

In spite of due diligence, none of my current companions had ever been to or heard of this place, and it didn't merit mention in the guidebooks we were using. These credentials inspired optimism.

The following day, I boarded a crowded ferry back to Athens and along with hundreds of others on the top deck, waved farewell to the outdoor cafés, the t-shirt shops, and the festive flock of Germans, Italians, French, British, and others. After arriving in the port of Piraeus, a taxi took me to the appropriate bus station. Using the map as a guide (its drawings transcending language), I found a kind man whose beard was born of Zeus and body born of much lesser gods, who directed me to a dusty bus worthy of its own archaeological icon. Inside the bug-spattered windshield hung a stenciled sign: Lefkada. My backpack was casually tossed on top with the other bags, boxes, and contemporary relics. I sat near the front, and glancing down the rows of occupied seats, noticed I was the only foreigner.

Six hours and many stops later, the bus pulled into a large, dark, and empty square. The driver called out: Lefkada.

The bus purged its few remaining occupants, and their bags were deported from the roof. With a slow rumble, the vehicle departed. The others were met by family or friends, and quickly dispersed. Abandoned, I stood alone—lost and surrounded only by my own growing anxiety. A single streetlight hovered above the echo of the vacant bus. Across the square a bare lightbulb, dangling on a string, illuminated an outdoor café. It was closed. In dim shadow, a boy was putting chairs upside down on top of square wooden tables, then sweeping the concrete floor. The bristles of the broom made the only sound.

Homer writes of "The Fates," three very old goddesses who determine human destiny. In this ancient and lonely plaza, my imminent future was now in their venerable hands.

After an eternity of several minutes, a small black taxicab rolled into the square, approached me, and eased to a halt. The driver rolled down the window, and behind a massive mustache emerged a smiling face. In a verbal patchwork of Greek, Italian, and English, he asked if I needed a place to sleep.

What luck! I humbly thanked The Fates. He explained that the town did have one guest house, however the madam with the key, Philormina, was never there. But perhaps, he continued, we could find her drinking this time of night in Spiro's tavern.

My alternatives were few, so I happily tossed my backpack into his trunk, and we slowly drove along the narrow streets lined only with silence and dark doorways. We stopped near a set of hazy windows—a warm, yellow light outlined people within. We entered and inquired. My optimism sank when the bartender indicated that Philormina was not there. But, he said, pointing to a robust woman surrounded by empty beer bottles and laughing men, maybe Agatha would know where she could be found.

We approached the festive group, and the taxi driver asked Agatha if, by chance, she knew where we might find Philormina. "You are lucky tonight, my friend. She told me to meet her later at Plato's café. You just might find her there."

"You are lucky tonight," echoed the taxi driver, as we drove around a few more dark blocks, and came to another set of glowing windows. "I can see her from here."

We walked into the crowded room, and I immediately noticed one flaming red head above the rest. In high heels, black dress, and wrapped in rouge, it was Philormina. The taxi driver introduced me and I inquired about a room. "Well, my dear, you know it's quite late...but you are a lucky boy. I may have just one room left. But first, perhaps you would enjoy a drink with us?"

I agreed, then later learned that Philormina was born in Ireland, but raised on Crete. The daughter of a World War I general, she enjoyed luxurious living until a broken marriage had deposited her at her sister's doorstep in Lefkada. An archaeological monument worthy of her own icon, Philormina's scarlet locks remained the most vaulted vestige of her former architecture. And in keeping with methods of historic preservation, she was trussed and buttressed at every curve. Clear and colored stones set in gold dripped from her ears, her wrists, her neck, and glittered on her finely creased fingers. Amidst all the luster, like a lens magnifying time, the crystal stem of her delicately clasped wine glass focused my attention on the amplified lines of her palm.

After a few more rounds, she rummaged through her purse, light shimmering from her many rings, and extracted an ancient looking key. "Yes, you are the lucky one. Here's the key to the last room. Let's go have a look, shall we?"

The guest house was just around the corner. The taxi driver, who had waited patiently throughout the wine-laden conversation, removed my pack from the trunk. We entered the house, climbed up a flight of stairs, and Philormina inserted the key and opened the door. The room was lovely and clean. Fresh flowers stood in a vase on a desk, and a neatly folded towel rested on the bed.

She handed me the key along with modest instruction: $20 per night, bath down the hall, hot water day and night. I was elated, exhausted, and appreciative. I thanked her, thanked and paid the taxi driver, and after a shower, reflected on the amazing sequence of events that had led me to this comfortable pillow. The Fates had been kind.

The next day, I immersed myself in Greece—the Greece of which I'd read and dreamed. Tracing back along last night's fortuitous trail, I passed by the café on the square. The seats were now occupied by men in sport coats playing dominoes and sipping coffee. I meandered out of town on a small road that became a dirt path, and atop a small hill, sat beneath the remains of a windmill built of lichen-covered stones. A series of short whistles preceded a procession of goats flanked by a frisky dog. Soon, I met the seasoned goatherder who bid me hello with a broad smile wreathed by a trim gray beard and matching cap. I got up, we shook hands, and escorted by the goats and dog, we walked along the path eventually coming to rest in a grove of olive trees.

With their deep roots and outstretched limbs, the trees stood as sentinels of tradition. And in their company, I listened to the echoes of Homer's Greece.

Late that night I returned to my room, and as I climbed up the stairs, I was greeted by a young traveler. Just having taken a shower, he was wearing a smile, a towel, and little else. We introduced ourselves and spoke briefly of our travels. Judging by his accent, he must have been British. As we opened our respective doors and said good night, he turned to me and added with an appreciative sigh: "Most remarkable thing, really. I've only arrived tonight on the late bus from Athens, and, well, between this taxi driver and two strange and wonderful women, you just wouldn't believe how incredibly lucky I was to find this room!" I just smiled back, nodding my head in agreement—thoroughly bemused by the hospitality these three Fates had provided for us. In fact, I could hardly wait to meet tomorrow night's "lucky" guy.

Joel Simon's photo and writing assignments have taken him to all seven continents, including the North Pole, the Antarctic, and ninety-five countries in between. When not traveling, he's at home in Menlo Park, California, with his wife, Kim, their cat, Ichiban, and an itinerant possum named Rover.

JIM MOLNAR

Tongue–Tied and Bottoming Out

Sometimes you really need to know the language.

THE OLD GREEK, HIS HAIR THINNED TO A SALT–AND–PEPPER WISPI-ness, his stoic face roughened by a day or two's growth of whiskers, sat in a corner behind the counter.

An undershirt worn to gray hung on him loosely under a faded cotton shirt whose open, wrinkled collar pointed out wildly like wings.

It was eleven o'clock in the morning. A demitasse of raki sat next to his elbow on a café table.

The younger man was crisper, in a pressed white shirt stand-ing behind the glass counter whose shelves were stocked with brown bottles stoppered with eye droppers; an array of small, an-tiseptic-white cardboard boxes; and a stack of green-and-white lozenge tins.

I stood for a moment just inside the door of the pharmacy, on a side street in downtown Thessaloníki, the capital of Greek Macedonia. Shelves were lined with bottles, boxes, and bags labeled cryptically in an alphabet I'd practiced enough to pronounce but was far from understanding.

I walked the narrow length of the shop slowly, but with an obvious, painful desperation. It wasn't so much a walk, actually, or even a limp, as a kind of shuffle. As if I were wearing raw wool shorts, starched.

I'd been in Greece for a week already, mostly hiking between villages around Mount Parnassus to the south. My diet had been almost exclusively taverna food—*mezza*: olives, tomatoes, peppers, bread, and lots and lots of cheese. My body, obviously confused by the change in routine, was struggling to work out a balance between the pleasure I took in the place and the strain of new patterns of exercise and food.

The three Greek phrase books I carried to the pharmacist's counter might help. I'd found and practiced the words for "pain" and "medicine" and "please." But I couldn't get any more specific.

None of the books had the translation for hemorrhoids—the worse case I'd ever had.

The pharmacist tugged at his ear and looked at me blankly as I exhausted my Greek vocabulary. He shook his head and glanced back at Zorba—I'd already given the old guy that name—who still sat stoically at his café table. He'd pulled out a loop of worry beads and was calmly clicking his way around them.

I was the one who needed worry beads. I was on my way to Mount Athos, a peninsula that reached into the Aegean Sea to the east, to spend the next week hiking between medieval monasteries and hermits' caves. Days would be spent on ancient rock-cobbled trails, nights lit by candles and scented with incense. My diet would be monkish, mostly bread and fresh herbs, wine, and lots more constipating cheese.

I couldn't survive with the thorny pain that dogged every step, torturous, taking me close to tears. The only lubricant of any sort in my light day pack was sunscreen—hardly appropriate for a problem centered where the sun don't shine.

I found the word for "emergency" in one of the books. I thought of looking for the words "pit bull" and "buttocks" and "implanted"—a good descriptive metphor might help communication.

In the end, there was always English.

"Hemorrhoids!" I cried.

The pharmacist shrugged. Zorba sat stoically.

They waited calmly for my next move.

I knew pantomime would work—it had never failed me in my travels—but I also knew it would be embarrassing. I turned my back to them, bent over and pointed. Suddenly I realized how the gesture could be misinterpreted.

I whirled back quickly to face them and smiled sheepishly, waving my hands in the air as if I were erasing a blackboard. I made a little circle with my fingers, then expanded it and, making a few painful sounds, tried to signal swelling and throbbing. I held the circle behind me and marched in place, whimpering. The pharmacist nodded his head slightly, as if getting the idea. Zorba looked away quickly, grabbing his cup of raki and taking a sip.

They seemed to be waiting for more.

I took out my notebook.

I scribbled desperately, aware that my pictures looked more obscene than clinical.

When I finally held the tablet up for them to look at, the pharmacist was grinning and Zorba, no longer able to contain himself, broke into a laugh and slapped his knee. A little cloud of dust rose from his pants leg.

After I paid for the salve the chuckling pharmacist handed me and gratefully accepted some privacy out back for a first application, I returned to see Zorba standing at his table and waving to me.

I've passed the following information on to many hemorrhoids sufferers during the past sixty years, and it has always been effective. In a container small enough to carry in your pocket mix one-third Camphophenique and two-thirds olive oil (any good grade of oil will do) and apply to the affected area. If your hemorrhoids are internal, you may use an infant's ear syringe to apply; if external, a small cotton swab will suffice.

—Letter to the Editor from Carl Ransdell, *Seattle Times*

An excellent homeopathic remedy for hemorroids is *Aesculus Hippocastanum* in a 30c dose.

—James O'Reilly, "Homeopathic First Aid for Travelers"

"American," he said and motioned for me to approach. He pulled out a chair from against the wall and set it next to the table and pulled me over to sit.

The pharmacist went to a cupboard, pulled out another demitasse and poured it full of raki for me. He filled a small plate with figs and olives, slapped me on the back and invited me to eat.

For the next hour or so, we sat there drinking raki together, and talking about all kinds of things, from politics to our families to my trip to Mount Athos.... Well, actually we drew and pantomimed those things, pored through my phrase books and sang some songs.

By the way, the word "hemorrhoids" derives from the classical Greek *"haimorrhoides"*: roughly, flowing blood. My two friends in the pharmacy undoubtedly knew from the very beginning what I was asking for. But I know I—and I'm sure they—ultimately enjoyed the exercise in communication, and the story all three of us have been telling ever since.

When Jim Molnar sets his tail down between journeys, it's in the Pacific Northwest, where for fifteen years he was a travel writer, editor, and columnist with The Seattle Times. *He's won dozens of awards for reporting, writing, and editing, including three consecutive Lowell Thomas awards as best travel writer in North America. He currently works independently, writing fiction, nonfiction, essays, and travel stories; freelancing as a writing coach and editor; and teaching poetry writing to teens in juvenile detention.*

The Mad Priest of Lésvos

The island of Lésvos plays host to Greek drama.

HE HAD A ROSE JAMMED BEHIND HIS LEFT EAR AND HE CAME strutting into town like an old gunslinger. Even from a distance his blazing eyes and weathered face were distinct. He was a villager, over sixty, but still walked tight and firm, arms swinging at his sides like a fighter, or an actor playing the part. He came in a straight line, eyes forward, missing nothing.

"Who is that man?" I asked Nikos, a young sailor also from the village.

"That is Yorgos," he answered. "Crazy George. Too much sun. Too much Greece. Watch out! Now there is trouble!"

We sat at an oilcloth-covered table overlooking the blue Aegean. All around us the breeze whisked about the sounds of argument, conversation, and chaos. At nearby tables adults chatted and sipped ouzo while children chased each other on the beach. Ships dotted the horizon, and, closer to shore, two fishing boats, stragglers from the local fleet, came putting across the baby waves. Women hurried out of the cafés and went down to meet them.

George passed through the outlying tables of the terrace, then stopped, his chin thrust forward like an ancient dagger, his hands suddenly and dangerously at rest on his hips. He cocked his left leg toward the sea. Twenty feet in front of him young Vasilis, my employer, was transacting business with a vegetable vendor. George glared at them.

"Watch out! Big trouble now!" Nikos whispered excitedly.

For two full minutes George stood motionless, a bizarre statue in the center of bustling movement. He was dressed in khaki pants and shirt, and wore a tattered, yellow-and-white tablecloth around his neck as a kerchief; it fluttered in the breeze coming in off the sea. Then he began to move. Like a cannon swinging on its mount, his head slowly turned until his fiery eyes were looking, sizzling, directly into mine. He stomped toward our table.

"Look other places," Nikos warned in a rapid whisper. "Not see him. Not see him."

It was too late. He was already on top of us. He placed himself solidly in front of me and scanned adjoining tables, daring anyone to say a word. All heads looked away; not a man, woman, or child even peeked in our direction. But down at the shoreline the women and fishermen had turned around. If Greece is anything it is theater: the curtain goes up, the audience rushes in. They quickly left the boats and hurried up the beach.

George threw a glance at me and suddenly started shouting at Nikos. Heads swiveled around and the entire café turned their chairs to watch the show. Crazy George went on shouting. He seemed inexhaustible, a lunatic on a rampage. But all at once Nikos banged his fist on the table and launched into his own tirade. I grabbed our teetering beers and stopped them from spilling over.

At first Nikos seemed to be holding his own, but bit by bit he tired and George went on at top volume. Finally Nikos hunched his shoulders and grinned sheepishly. People at other tables threw him sympathetic nods and shrugs. A few waved. It had been a good performance.

"What the hell's going on?" I asked.

"Don't talk like that," Nikos told me. "Don't swear."

I stared at him. A Greek sailor warning someone not to swear? George kept on shouting. I had to yell to be heard.

"But what's the matter? What's he saying?"

Nikos leaned over the table. He spoke in an urgent whisper: "Yorgos want to know who you are."

I glanced up at George, hesitated, then suggested, cautiously, that Nikos should introduce us. Nikos nodded and started yelling again. George folded his arms across his chest and lifted his nose into the air, forcing Nikos to petition the underside of his scruffy chin. Around the café people chuckled, pointed and traded comments. George's unshaven face stayed impassive; the chin stuck out from the face and gray hairs stuck out from the chin, that was all. He neither blinked nor drew breath.

Finally the introduction seemed to end; at least Nikos stopped talking. George turned and looked at me. I had already decided that a handshake was out of the question. Instead I smiled and spoke in English.

"Hello, George," I said. "How are you?"

"Nevermind!" he roared, and shot off across the café.

He came to a skidding stop in front of another table and launched into a second attack. Nikos and I shifted our chairs in unison with everybody else. A large family from the upper village had been caught eating. With their mouths full, not one of them could defend the tribe. The patriarch tried to gulp down his food; he waved his arms, motioning George away.

But George flew into a rage which turned the scene at our table into a mere warm-up. He jumped backwards, pointing at the patriarch with one hand, the other thrust onto his hip, screaming, bellowing, calling upon everyone to watch and listen. He stomped and pounded circles around the table, wagging his finger at each family member.

"Who the hell is he?" I asked, keeping my eyes on the fireworks.

"Don't swear!" Nikos warned again. "He's a priest."

"A–?" I turned and looked at Nikos. "Are you sure? He doesn't seem like a…"

"Yes, yes. He priest from monastery. Anybody knows. Ask anybody."

The priest was at the far end of the café still letting out wounded-bear howls, still pointing at the family who had started eating again, trying to ignore him. All at once George stopped. He looked over the entire café, at each and every one of us. There was a moment of silence. The yellow-and-white tablecloth fluttered at his neck. Then he threw up his arms in disgust and stomped off in the direction he had come.

Vasili's Sea Horse Café, Bar, and Pizza Restaurant was about thirty yards above the shoreline in the seaside village of Skala Eressóu on the island of Lésvos. It was a family-run place with a kitchen and order counter inside. All the tables were set out on the terrace overlooking the sea and a small offshore island where locals said Sappho had often sat to write her poetry. Four iron posts supported a straw roof above the entrance to the café, and smoke from the pizza oven billowed out under it.

The family consisted of Vasilis's enormously fat mother, his silver-haired father, his sad-eyed brother-in-law, Elias, his quiet sister and two hypercharged nephews, Phanos and Kostos. Together they produced scrumptious salads, tasty pizza, and supernaturally slow service.

"You understand business," Vasilis had told me one day when he was especially worried about competing with his bitter enemy, Dimitri, the owner of the café next door. "Come in restaurant and look. Maybe tell me why service so slow."

Flattered, I forgot I understood nothing about business and went in to take charge of things. Five minutes later I had an apron tied around my waist and was frantically washing stacks of dishes. The person who understood business was Vasilis.

My pay was free food and drink, and the love of the family. My schedule was open; I began when I arrived and ended when I left. During the day I also waited tables and broomed sand off the terrace. At night I slept on the beach with the moon and stars for company and the lapping waves for comfort.

Every morning I showered at a spigot above the shoreline and used a small bathroom at the back of the Sea Horse to shave. I had breakfast, a swim, a few minutes in the sun, and then went to my dishwashing post. Vasilis's mother stood next to me making salads and chatting away every minute we were together. She spoke Greek so I never understood a word she said, but she refused to believe it and periodically jabbed a fork into my ribs to get a response. In the afternoon I ate salad and pizza for lunch, read for an hour or two and then took a nap beneath a tree on the beach in front of the café.

On one side of the Sea Horse stood the café owned by Vasilis's enemy, Dimitri. On the other, there was a small general store. About a week after the incident with Yorgos, a crew of three men delivered a refrigerator to the store. It was mid-afternoon and the café terrace was half full. The sky was fiercely blue, the day hot. I sat at the same table with Nikos again. We had just finished our lunch and were drinking coffee and five-star Metaxa. Phanos and Kostos, Vasilis's nephews, waddled about the beach beneath us throwing sand on the tourists. Every so often their mother came down from the restaurant and gave them a spanking. Out past Sappho's island a cargo ship plied up the coast toward the petrified forests of Sígri.

The crew closed the back of the truck and climbed into the cab. The leader put the vehicle into reverse, accelerated and suddenly smashed into one of the iron posts at the entrance to Vasilis's restaurant. There was a tremendous crash. The straw roof over the entrance jumped two feet to the left, shuddered and rustled, seemed about to fall but finally stood still.

A woman seated at a table thirty feet from the accident cried out as if she had been hit, then began wailing. She grabbed her son who was laughing and pointing at the truck, and clutched him to her bosom, where he, instantly confused, started bawling too. Her husband leapt up and shook his fist at the truck.

The driver shrugged, changed gears and began pulling away. Just then Vasilis came rushing out of the Sea Horse, his white pizza apron untied and flying behind him like Superman's cape.

"Watch out now!" Nikos said, translating for me: "Vasilis very mad, He say, 'Wait, Where you go?' Driver-man say, 'To work. Good-bye.' Vasilis say, 'You not go. Look, you crash my café.' Driver-man say, 'Very sorry, but must go—late for work.' Vasilis say, 'You pay money.' Driver-man say, 'My truck is crashed too. We are even—must go now.'"

The driver cunningly moved the truck ahead a few inches every time he finished a sentence, forcing Vasilis to trot alongside. Nikos went on with the live-action report:

"Vasilis say, 'I write truck number—show police.' Driver-man, 'Not worry. Maybe I come tomorrow—talk then.'"

Suddenly the husband ran up to the truck and gave one of the bald tires a vicious kick. Somehow it stopped the vehicle. The three workers reluctantly climbed down and inspected the damaged post with Vasilis. Village men left their tables and gathered around the group. They lit cigarettes, pointed and shook their heads. Across the terrace the remaining people nodded happily to each other—it was a good show—and repositioned their chairs for better views.

Nikos and I could not remain in the audience. Gossip ran around Skala Eressóu like fire set to hay and if Vasilis's friends didn't take a stand by his side, the accident might later be blamed on the iron post. We walked through the crowd and came to the center where Vasilis hopped about, pulling his hair and muttering curses in a potent mixture of English and Greek. Under normal conditions he crackled all over with nervous energy, but now the accident had fused together and short-circuited his already frayed nerve ends: he seemed ready to explode. He looked around through dark, simmering eyes, but then he saw me and his swarthy features brightened; hope lit his face.

He quickly recalled that I had fixed a few broken things in the restaurant and replastered a hole in the wall above the oven. In addition I "really understood business" so I could do damage assessment. I frowned and reminded him I didn't speak Greek.

"You just look," he said. "I tell everybody what you think."

The post was deeply dented two feet above ground level. I kicked it as I had seen the other men do and shook my head. I inspected the ceiling side of the roof structure and made clucking noises with my tongue. I stepped back, surveyed things in general and kicked the post again while Vasilis pointed at me and gave the crowd a detailed description of my thoughts.

The driver clenched his fists and fumed, but one of his helpers gaped at me in admiration. Tourists had wandered up from the beach and filled in the periphery of the circle. Phanos and Kostos waddled about throwing sand on their feet as Vasilis and the driver started shouting at each other.

Suddenly the circle of men cleaved open and Crazy George came stomping toward us. He wore the same khaki shirt and pants as the other day, and again had a rose jammed behind his ear, but this time he used the yellow-and-white tablecloth to wipe his brow. He hurried toward Vasilis and the driver who were still shouting at each other. He placed his scruffy face an inch from Vasilis nose, and a moment later an inch from the driver's. As they shouted, he swung his head back and forth between them, grimacing theatrically. Afterwards he went over to the truck and began wagging his finger at the bumper and scolding it. He gave the same treatment to the post.

Then he began to laugh. But it was mimed laughter, silent and maniacal. He laughed uproariously without letting out a sound. Wiping his forehead, cackling madly, he stepped toward the café terrace and signaled for everyone sitting there to pay attention. He bowed and waved his arm toward us as if he were a master for their pleasure. People chuckled. George pointed to each of us one after the other, laughing silently and heartily while his audience laughed louder and louder.

Nikos skipped into the shadowed alley by the Sea Horse and vanished. I slowly backpedaled toward my table. As the laughter went on, other men caught stage fright too. Within minutes the whole group had broken up. The driver bullied his helpers into the truck to regain some lost pride. They drove off as George shouted after them. Finally he threw up his arms at all of us and stomped off himself.

An hour later Vasilis came out of the Sea Horse with two beers and sat at my table. He was still exasperated. I asked him a dozen questions about the accident. I wanted to know if he would receive any compensation for the damage. He rolled his burned-out eyes and said anything or nothing might happen. He sipped beer and complained about the inefficiencies of Greek life.

"Nothing works," he said, shaking his head, then tightening his lips in despair. "Look my restaurant. People order food and do they get what they order?"

"Not very often," I confessed.

He nodded. "Nothing works in Greece. Everything crazy."

Especially on this island, I thought. It might be famous because of Sappho and because Orpheus's head had washed ashore here along with his lyre, and it may be distinguished for its phenomenal olive harvest, its curious blend of Greco-Turkish culture and the jewel-cities of Molivos and Mytilíni with their Genoese castle and Macedonian-style homes, but what really set it apart was that it was still the old, nutty Greece where the legendary light shone, the crystal-blue sky gleamed, and anything might happen. It had not yet been sanitized and turned into a tourist playground. There were few hotels and definitely none that rated stars or appeared in anybody's guidebook. Men still broke plates in cafés to express their boundless joy (or just to show off)

I find dynamite in the kitchen. There are two large boxes of it beneath the kitchen table. And above the table is a candle stuck precariously on a bottle. Next to the table is a canister of gas for the stove. I have a Lebanese friend named Joseph on the island. He says I shouldn't be the one to talk to the workmen. They will only tell me it is perfectly safe. But, of course, it is not safe…. I talk to the landlord. He says the dynamite is not dangerous. He says he is willing to risk his house and family. I tell him I have only one life. And he says perhaps I should find another place to stay…

Late at night there is a knock at my door. The Lebanese man and the master explain patiently that there is no problem with the dynamite. The Greek has now placed it under his bed so it if blows up he will be the first to die.

—Judith Azrael, "Counting Cats"

and unblinking waiters simply added the cost to their bills. The
original word for theater, *thauma*, still had its original meaning, "a
wonder," and wonders were enacted everywhere. Drama was the
twin soul of tragedy and *tragoidia* still meant the "song of the goat."
Everywhere gods might visit humans at any second. "Nothing
worked" because everything still worked perfectly.

Vasilis took two deep pulls on his beer and looked at his enemy
Dimitri's café next door. At first I thought he was anxiously counting customers but he was just eyeballing Dimitri's twenty-year-old
daughter. Finally he turned around, scratched his head, and admitted he shouldn't get so nervous. We stared out at the sea and
watched people pass by. We talked and drank, smoked cigarettes and
studied the dazzling sunlight on the waves.

"Tell me about this Yorgos," I said after a while. "The one who
yells all the time."

"You mean Crazy George?" Vasilis asked. "He bother you? I
know how to handle him."

"No, no. Nothing like that," I said quickly. Vasilis frequently took
the role of my protector. "I'm only curious."

"He's a crazy person," Vasilis told me. "That all. Nothing more
to say."

"But...tell me how long he's been a priest."

Vasilis laughed out loud. He turned in his chair, shielded his
eyes from the sun and looked at me as if my head were full of air
bubbles. Who tell you Yorgos a priest?" he asked, still chuckling.

"Well, practically everybody," I answered. "Nikos says so and,
really...you can ask anybody."

Vasilis snickered.

"No, no," he said. "Yorgos no priest. Nikos make a big joke on
you. What you call a man who is no good? A man who has no
work and can only sleep somewhere?"

"A bum?"

"Yes. Bum. Crazy George only a bum. He come to monastery
ten years before and no one live there so he move in. He clean a
little and grow a tree and then write a letter to father priest in
Athens. Yorgos say: 'I person who take care of monastery now so

you send money.' Pretty smart idea, yes?"

He raised an eyebrow; a con artist himself, he couldn't help but admire it in others.

"No, Yorgos just a bum," he summarized. "And crazy too. You ask anybody."

Every year the well-heeled, and many of the not-so-well-heeled, families from the upper village of Eressós moved down to their summer houses in Skala Eressóu by the sea. They brought beds, doors, crates, pots and pans, bird cages, wardrobes, and tables with them, and they lugged it all on donkeys, motorcycles, scooters, carts, tractors, cars, trucks, and their backs. The four-kilometer paved road separating the two villages was frequently a scene of accidents, shouting matches and fights, but when the exodus ended, it again became a simple, quiet path buzzing with heat and cicadas.

I set off for the upper village in the late afternoon. The sun was still high and the dry fields bordering the road were golden. A herd of sheep slept in the shade beside a farm-

Harmless lunatics in Greece are regarded today as lucky people to have around, and there is always plenty of work for such mascots. Kostas, after a long career of usefulness, made one bad slip while investigating a car whose petrol-gauge had broken. He hit upon the ingenious idea of ascertaining the petrol level in the tank with the help of a lighted candle. Mercifully the tank was almost empty, but the ensuing explosion was enough to send Kostas flying. He was badly burned and…disappeared from circulation. When he emerged, he had changed his job. The newly born Greek dictatorship of Metaxas had decreed that all the youth of Greece must join the National Youth—a paramilitary organization—for training. It was modelled upon Italian and German equivalents. Judge the amazed delight of everyone when Kostas, clad in uniform, led the first parade, bearing a banner aloft, and goose-stepping fit to kill. All felt that the incident illustrated the mental level of the dictatorship.

—Lawrence Durrell,
The Greek Islands

house. Two curious goats watched me pass from beneath an olive
tree. Most of Lésvos was as dry as this landscape, a rock island of
earth tremors and hot springs, volcanic dust and petrified forests.
Half of the houses were gutted out and had trees growing in them
and sheep wandering through them.

A man bouncing down toward the sea on his donkey motioned
for me to slow my pace. Only a tourist would walk so fast in the heat.

When I arrived in the upper village I went to the café, a pleasant,
tumbledown place on the central plaza beneath an enormous tree. It
was run by a handsome Greek named Spiros and his lovely wife
Thespina. Most of the tables and chairs were outside, but a squawk-
ing black-and-white television watched over a few inside as well.

About thirty donkeys were tied up around the plaza; most of
their owners sat in the café playing cards or telling their worry
beads. Other donkeymen passed by on their way down from the
mountain with bundles of oregano and sage lashed behind their
blanket-saddles.

I went inside and ordered. Few of the few tourists in Skala
Eressóu ever came to the upper village so there was seldom a menu,
usually no food. Thespina told me she might be able to rustle up
some calamari. Off to the right a half dozen donkeymen watched
an American detective show on the blurry television. The cops
were chasing the crooks through a mansion, one so huge they actually had a gun battle in the bathroom.

I looked at the donkeymen. What in the world were they thinking? To get to the "bathroom" in this café you had to light a candle at the back door, trip across a black, foul-smelling inner courtyard, all the while kicking chickens and hens out of the way, and
then fight off the lizards and spiders in the stinky clapboard outhouse so they didn't eat you alive as you struggled to take a pee.

I carried a bottle of retsina back outside and sat at a table. Night
was coming on and a warm breeze up from the sea moved through
the plaza. Children played in the shadows. A vegetable truck pulled
into the center of the square and women in black dresses filtered out
ghostlike from the cobblestone pathways.

Most of the donkeymen stared at me. Anybody who could

order dinner and an entire bottle of wine was as rich as the detectives shooting it out in the mile-long bathroom.

During the hour I waited for my meal, I took the opportunity to ask people about Yorgos. Alexandros the carpenter and two other men told me he was only the caretaker of the monastery. Mikalis the postman and a tableful of his friends said there was no doubt that he was a priest, though definitely crazy. Thespina said she had heard both stories and wasn't sure which to believe. Spiros brought a salad swimming in olive oil, and a large platter of calamari. When I asked him about Yorgos, he rolled his eyes toward a corner of the plaza.

I looked. It was Crazy George himself, just arriving on a magnificent silver-gray donkey with a crude blue cross painted on its side. An equally spectacular long-haired goat with a second cross day-glowing on its brown fleece clip-clopped along behind them. A dozen, smaller crosses shone on the hooves of both animals. It was an astonishing sight, but I was the only person in the plaza looking at it. George tethered the animals, shot an arrogant glance at the café, and swaggered over to the vegetable truck. He disappeared in the crowd of women. As I ate my meal, I kept an eye on the group. After a few minutes, George popped up at the head. He seemed to be ordering a variety of vegetables. The vendor stuffed them into a sack, then announced the price.

George let out a roar and the crowd burst apart. The donkeymen swiveled in their seats. The curtain has risen, the show had begun. As George raged, trying to enlist the support of the frightened women around him, his donkey began braying at the other end of the plaza. The vendor angrily threw the sack aside and pleaded with the women to return. They ran farther away. George stomped around, extreme anguish ravaging his face.

He stopped in the center of the plaza and cried out to the heavens, cupping his right hand up to the sky, imploring that it be filled: the desperate cry of all mankind. Then his arm fell limp and he shook his head in dejection at the earth beneath him, his prayers unanswered.

A second later he rampaged into the café. Somehow he had gotten hold of a cucumber: a large one stuck out of his back

pocket. The yellow-and-white tablecloth was now tied around his
waist as a belt. He roared at several of the donkeymen, yelled again
at the vegetable truck, and suddenly sat down at my table.

For a moment we watched each other in silence. Up close his
scruffy, gunslinger face had a softer look, perhaps only because of
the rose behind his ear, but his eyes seemed to twinkle. I signaled for
Spiros to bring another glass. I poured retsina as George took out a
pocket knife and began peeling the cucumber. He passed a few
wafer-thin slices over to me and I passed back a glass of wine. We
toasted and drank. Using Spiros as a translator, I asked George several questions. He answered most, but vaguely. I learned, for example, that the monastery was forty minutes away, but only thirty if he
beat the donkey. He himself had painted the blue crosses on the
donkey and goat. He had also planted many trees at the monastery.
Spiros seemed to be having a difficult time translating. He muttered
something about George's thick accent. George kept glancing at the
vegetable vendor. All at once he pushed back his chair and jumped
up. I hurriedly asked if I could visit the monastery. George said
something to Spiros and bolted toward the vegetable truck.

"You go tomorrow," Spiros told me. "Tuesday. In afternoon."

At the truck George now held some money in his hand; he waved
it angrily at the vendor. He stomped his feet, shouted at the man, and
yelled back at the café as his donkey started braying again across the
plaza. I glanced around at the other tables. The faces of the donkeymen, normally so dazed by boredom, shone bright as they watched
the show. If George wasn't a priest, he was as good as one.

A moment later he left with the sack of vegetables; in the darkness I couldn't see if he had paid. He mounted his donkey, spoke to
the goat, and rode off into the shadows.

An hour later Vasilis came into the plaza on his motorcycle and
offered to take me down to the beach. I hopped on and we left.
Midway he decided to stop at the Silver Moon, a place that billed
itself as a "disco" but wasn't much more than a shack next to an
open-air terrace where a few colored lights blinked on and off.
Except for a justified reputation for serving lethal ouzo, the Silver

Moon was usually a good place for a nap, but tonight people were crammed onto the terrace, and more and more came pushing through the doors. I ordered a beer and tried to figure out what was going on as Vasilis made a beeline for some tourist girls.

The moon was full and cast a clear, strong light down onto the ramshackle tables and chairs. A crowd of Turks and gypsies started singing, and the girls, a half dozen Scandinavians out for a good time, stomped their feet and clapped their hands. More people arrived. Vasilis wormed his way back and told me why: there would be Turkish belly dancing.

It soon started: three women who gyrated and shook until their rubber limbs turned to dark jelly. Then the Scandinavian girls jumped up to show what they could do, the deadly ouzo began to flow, and the night turned wild. I woke up the next morning on the beach with my head split down the middle and both sides banging together like cymbals. I stared at the sea and Sappho's island and tried to remember what had happened. There had been large blonde women in bikinis, an

---

Then I come to a rotting sign which reads "Disco-Café." It points down a dirt path to where I think the sea should be. At length the sea does materialize, and by it a little shack with three decrepit tables and some chairs — the disco-café. Once upon a time a radio may have supplied the music, but the radio, like the premises, has rusted out and lies in a sad heap on the reedy sand. I admire the Greeks for their ingenuity and wily imagination. With a few letters painted on a sign, they transform reality. If next year the new vogue in Europe is elephant waitresses, the disco master will simply repaint his sign to read "Elephant Waitresses-Café." And when he is asked where the elephant waitresses are, he will shrug. It won't matter. He knows he is operating the only eatery on the beach and can give it whatever fashionable mask he pleases.

— George Galt,
Trailing Pythagoras

ocean of ouzo, and a motorcycle accident. What else? I winced. I had promised to go to the monastery that afternoon.

My hundred-yard walk down the beach to the Sea Horse convinced me I could go no farther that day. The monastery was located in a valley beyond the hills of the upper village and could only be reached by hiking five kilometers on a dirt path running along the side of the mountains. In the afternoon heat, I would end up marking some goat path with my bones.

Vasilis's sister brought me coffee and cleaned the scrapes and scratches on my left arm. She said that Vasilis had been sick all morning. I drank coffee for hours, listened to the cymbals clashing in my head and stared dumbly at Vasilis's motorcycle lying on its side on the beach twenty feet in front of me.

Vasilis joined me in midafternoon. He said that last night he had misjudged where the terrace ended, and we had zoomed out onto the beach and taken a tumble. It was too much to concentrate on. I only wanted to know what would happen with George. Vasilis reassured me. He said nobody ever expected anybody to show up for an appointment in Greece. Making an appointment was just a way of talking. Like discussing the weather, it didn't really mean anything. The important thing was to hide the next time you saw the person who had invited you, that was all.

"It's old Greek game," he said. "Everybody play it."

Nikos had received his papers and would sail in three days on the Aegean freighter with ports of call in Chios, Samos, and the Sporades. I invited him to a farewell dinner Friday night at the Sea Horse and because it rated as a formal affair I warned Vasilis beforehand that I didn't want to serve the meal myself or spend all night waiting for it. He agreed but Friday night came and the first hour of our dinner went by without even a beer appearing at our table.

Eventually I went to the kitchen. Vasilis's enormous mother shook a large frying pan over a fire while her husband stood next to her clunking salad bowls onto a tray. Steam poured out of the huge oven where Elias stood guard over the pizzas. His wife smacked together flour and dough next to him. Vasilis was everywhere, nervous energy shooting around in high gear. He washed glasses. Breaking one for every four he cleaned. He ran to the oven, back to his mother, then grabbed an order pad. He caught sight of me and waved it in exasperation.

"This from last week!" he cried.

Terrific activity and little result. I walked behind the beer cooler and found Kostos and Phanos delighting themselves by smashing tomatoes onto the tile floor. They had been at it for quite a while. A large red puddle extended all the way over to the sink and their legs were dotted with seeds and glistening with sticky tomato juice.

I sidestepped the mess, opened the cooler and took out two beers then decided to take two more in case of further delays. At that moment Vasilis's mother screamed. I looked up. The contents of her frying pan were on fire. Crazily, she grabbed a nearby newspaper and began fanning the flames to put them out. In a moment the paper caught fire too and, doubly terrified, she dropped it just as Vasilis leapt into action. He knocked her out of the way, she crashed into her husband, and six salad bowls hit the floor.

"Water, Vasilis!" I shouted. "Water!"

Vasilis grabbed a bucket of sudsy dishwater from the sink and sent it flying. Half the water squelched the flames and the rest gave the kids a bath. They burst into tears and their parents came running. The family argument convened exactly where I was standing. I held the four beers crushed against my chest as dishwater seeped into my tennis shoes; on my left Vasilis and Elias shoved each other as Vasilis's sister tried to keep them apart. Little Phanos waddled up and sobbed into his mother's skirt, squashing a tomato against her thigh. Suddenly Vasilis yelled the first word I was able to understand: pizza!

The family raced to the oven. Black smoke poured out of it and the stink of burned dough permeated the kitchen. I took my chance, scooped a bottle opener off the counter and hurried back outside. The terrace was full of chuckling locals. One man had enjoyed the show so much he broke two plates. A half hour later Vasilis brought a single salad to our table. He gave it to Nikos and told us with a straight face that the pizzas were on the way.

The moon was no longer full but still cast clear light over Sappho's island and the fishing boats moored at the shoreline. Music drifted down to us from another café farther along where men had begun to dance. Two barefoot teenage girls walked together by the water's edge. In the distance I could just make out a figure strutting across the sand.

"Nevermind!" came a bellowing cry. "Nevermind! Nevermind!"

It was George and he was mad. I remembered that I had to hide. "Look other places!" Nikos told me. "Not see him!" I leaned into the center of the table and munched on the salad. George came up and stood next to us; he stomped his feet and waved his arms; he let out terrifying roars. "Yorgos ask everybody where you are," Nikos whispered excitedly. "He say you make big insult on him."

George went to the center of the café, carried on there for a while, and then strutted off down the beach. Exhausted, I leaned back in my chair and gulped down beer. I had to do something.

The first thing I did was accuse Vasilis of giving me bad advice. I reminded him about the "old Greek game" and how "everybody played it." He denied doing anything wrong and argued that George not playing the game only proved what he, Vasilis, had told me from the beginning: George was crazy.

"I tell you all this before," he said. "Ask anybody."

Nikos and I talked about my problem throughout dinner, consulted Vasilis once or twice and finally decided I should pretend I had misunderstood which Tuesday was the correct one and go to the monastery the following Tuesday afternoon.

When the day came I started out from the beach just after two o'clock. The sun was still high and hot, and the walk on the paved road to the upper village was long and sweaty. I stopped at a café, drank a Coke and rested in the shade for a while. When some of the heat had gone out of the day I bought a bottle of retsina and some goat cheese as peace offerings and stepped onto the dirt path leading to the monastery.

Within twenty minutes I had crossed the first chain of hills and could no longer see the upper village or the farmhouses spreading out from it. The horizon held rows of superimposed mountains. The late afternoon sun darkened the greens of the trees and shrubs. Wandering flocks of sheep, bells tinkling, traversed the valleys. In the distance, through a gap in the hills, lay the dark-blue sea.

I turned right on a secondary dirt path and discovered small blue crosses marking the way. They were identical to the crosses I had seen on the donkey and goat in the plaza, but now painted on rocks, tree trunks and hillsides, painted crudely but glistening in the still harsh sunlight. I followed them downhill, across a small valley, and back up again.

I crested the hill. Far below a dried river bed led to the sea. Directly opposite me, the monastery floated on the side of a mountain like a mirage. I was struck by the air of loneliness and solitude. It was exactly at eye level and seemed close, but I needed another half hour before I ever started up the hill.

George watched my every step from a stone balcony. He had a view of the entire valley and the hills surrounding it. The climb was steep and I reached the outer walls breathing hard. George greeted me gruffly from his position up above and then came down to open the large wooden gates.

I gave him the wine and cheese. He guided me into a kitchen and around the monastery grounds, explaining things as we went with hand signals. He pointed out the grove of trees he had planted twelve years ago, all grown strong now and bearing the ubiquitous blue cross seen on every doorway and corridor. We found his donkey grazing behind the main building next to a vegetable garden. George led the way up the hill and showed me a deep reservoir and the intricate pipe system he had constructed to bring water down off the mountain.

Farther up we came to a well covered by boards and a chair. George nimbly climbed up and demonstrated how he was able to sit there after a hard day's work and view his world.

We went back down and entered a darkened chapel. The smell of incense was overpowering. A hundred votive candles sent shadows playing on the ancient walls. A giant blue cross stretched the length of the linoleum floor; surreal and intense and flickering in the candlelight.

We walked outside onto the stone balcony. George brought out nuts and pears along with the wine and cheese. We watched the approaching sunset; the sky still gleamed like a blue crystal dome above the parched landscape. George raised his hand to the magnificent scene. A sense of solitude and light was pervasive. More than ever the island seemed a place the gods would visit, an enchanted rock gold-ringed by myth and legend, still the nutty old Greece where anything might happen, and as if to confirm it one year later I would receive word of high Greek drama: Vasilis had eloped, eloped not just with any girl, but with the daughter of his worst enemy Dimitri, the owner of the café next door.

Dimitri called together the island police and a band of friends and armed them with clubs and other weapons. The posse had one clear mission: to find and kill Vasilis before nightfall; otherwise the girl would lose her virginity, and there would have to be a marriage. They tore the island apart, racing from Eressós to Mytilíni, from south to north; they interrogated everyone, looked everywhere and found nothing, not even a clue.

Late that night in a small town near Molivos a heartbroken and spirit-crushed Dimitri finally gave up. He took his exhausted posse to a nearby inn and began to drown his great sorrow in a bottle of ouzo. With true dramatic irony it turned out later to be the very hotel in which, one floor up, Vasilis was asleep with his daughter.

But Greek drama is the twin soul of Greek tragedy and married life did not suit Vasilis very well. Before long he started making nightly excursions to the Silver Moon disco to play with the tourist girls. His wife, Dimitri's daughter, cried in the house, cried alone on the beach, at the café with friends, cried through the day and well into the night. It was an old sound on the island, an old sound in Greece, and the ancients called it the "song of the goat."

George raised his hand high, a priest of old summoning the gods to bless all that lay before us. The sun went on sinking toward the sea, still bathing the valley and hills in light. A table and two chairs stood at the balcony edge. We went over and sat. The curtain rose.

We broke open our nuts and ate our pears, sipped wine and stayed there taking in the wonder.

Patrick Pfister was born in Detroit and now lives in Barcelona. This story was excerpted from Pilgrimage: Tales from the Open Road.

PART FOUR

IN THE SHADOWS

STEPHANIE MAROHN

Workers of the World

The risks of working illegally can
outweigh the rewards.

IT WAS IN PLATANIÁS THAT I FIRST HEARD ABOUT THE JOB. I HAD been on Crete for two months; moving from place to place, picking olives to make money, getting jobs easily because olive-picking is women's work. But the low pay and sheer drudgery began to wear on me, and after a bad experience with a boss, I headed for Plataniás, a town in the orange-picking region.

It was the height of the olive and orange seasons, but the winter was a rough one and work was scarce. In every town where bosses came to hire workers, twenty or so foreigners met outside the local café at seven o'clock each morning, in the cold and rain, in the hopes of being chosen to work that day. Ten people might get a job, or maybe only five, or maybe none at all if the bosses decided the weather was too inclement or they didn't feel like working. If we were lucky, a boss arranged with us to work for him on a regular basis. But more often, we suffered through the daily uncertainty of employment. It was a lousy system, but we had no alternative.

Since none of us had a work permit, we were illegal workers and, like illegal workers all over the world, subject to the whims of bosses. When we did get a job, we were paid half of what a Greek would get for the same work—as it was, not many Greeks would

257

do the menial work we did. The going rate for women agricultural workers was 1,200 drachmas (at that time, about $10) per day, plus lunch and dinner. Some jobs paid less; a few, but not many, paid more.

On the rainy night I stepped off the bus in Plataniás, a few days after New Year's, two cafés were still open on the main street. I went into the one on the ground floor of an unpainted gray cement hotel. It was brightly lit and noisy inside. Smoke and conversation and bouzouki music from a jukebox filled the air. All the tables were occupied, mostly by old Greek men dressed in black, but a number of foreigners as well. Nobody paid any attention to me.

After protracted negotiations with the man behind the counter, I had a room—for 350 drachmas (about $3) a night because the "kids" who had stayed there last had broken a window. The proprietor led me up to the room, mentioned the broken window again, and left, shaking his head. After covering the broken pane with a mattress, I crawled into bed.

I woke the next morning at seven, but it looked so cold and windy outside that I couldn't face venturing out to try for work and went back to sleep. When I finally got up, the sun had broken through the clouds a little. Out on the balcony, the air smelled of freshly baked bread and people emerged from a shop farther down the street carrying round loaves. A few doors from the hotel, some scruffy-looking foreigners lounged on chairs on a cement terrace.

I settled in for a Greek coffee at the hotel café and was soon joined by a tall lanky Dutchman named Joss. He and two friends had been picking oranges for two months, and were renting a house in the old section of Plataniás.

"We were lucky," Joss said. "We got here back in November, before all the other workers came, and a boss offered us a steady job. Now, there are too many people and a lot of them aren't getting work. It's not a good year. Are you looking for work?"

"Yes. I've been picking olives and I'm sick of it. I want to try oranges. I hear it pays better."

"It does, if you can get a job." He looked at me apologetically. "The bosses don't like to hire women for the oranges."

"Why not?"

"They think it's men's work, that women can't lift the orange crates."

"Of course. That's why it pays more...Why aren't you working today?"

"The boss gave us the day off. A lot of bosses haven't started back yet from the holidays. It's just as well. It's very hard work and we're tired. Carrying those orange crates all day, your back kills you. And look what it does to your arms." He showed me the insides of his forearms—a mass of scratches. "It's the thorns on the trees," he said. "No matter what you wear, you get scratched."

"And with olives, you get these," I said, displaying the line of multilayered blisters across each of my palms.

He pulled his sleeves down. "Well, you better hide them. The tourist police have been making raids. They come to the disco at night or stop you on the street during the day and make you show them your hands and the insides of your wrists. If you've got these marks..." he jerked his thumb over his shoulder.

I had heard a few deportation stories from other workers, but never this use of the telltale marks as grounds for busting an illegal worker. Of course, we were all illegal, but the farmers needed us, so officials usually turned a blind eye. In the other villages where I had worked, I never saw any tourist police. The towns were too small, and there were never many foreigners, so the problems accompanying a larger foreign presence rarely arose.

But Plataniás was a different situation. It was a seaside town on the northwest coast of Crete. While not exactly a resort, it was on a tourist artery. It was also a center for the orange-growing district and one of the main towns where bosses came for their supply of workers. In the course of filling its dual function, the village had acquired some of the "attractions" of a larger town: a disco, a pizza joint, and a café with video games. It acquired some of the problems too. The town was flooded with young Europeans looking for work. (In my two months of agricultural labor and waiting in cafés between jobs, I never came across a fellow American doing the same.) Since there wasn't enough work, many of them ended up just hanging around. Joss told me there had been fights in the disco between locals and foreigners, and the townspeople had been complaining to the tourist police.

"Watch out in the café in the morning. The tourist police don't usually get up that early, but you never know!" He laughed, then added, "It sounds worse than it is. Sure, they have to do sweeps now and then to make it look good, but they don't really want to send anyone away. We're good for the farmers and for the businesses. We drink a lot of Nescafé."

Joss took me on a walk then, through the old part of Plataniás, up steep and winding streets lined with crumbly, warm-brown stone houses and bright whitewashed stucco ones. Calabashes growing on vines climbed over roofs, and dried ones painted in bright colors decorated front porches. Green leaves from some useful plant draped over clotheslines to dry in the sun. Open doors revealed bent old men and women sitting in tiny rooms. Up past the Greek Orthodox Church and the old graveyard, we walked into the hills where there were no more houses.

> In an Athens-Attica of 300,000 population, the number of slaves seems to have been 100,000, one-third: some estimates of the slave population are much higher. Some slaves worked a ten-hour day, for their keep, in the rich Athenian silver mines at Lávrion. Other slaves were paid policemen (Scythians from north of the Black Sea), public servants, artisans. Slavery was the basis of industry, capitalism, culture. The father of Demosthenes, the orator, had twenty slaves in a workshop making couches and thirty-two in a factory fashioning swords. "Even the poorest citizen had a slave or two." Slaves doing most of the manual work freed citizens for war campaigns and gave employers leisure, which some applied to learning.
>
> —Colin Simpson, *Greece: The Unclouded Eye*

We followed a dirt road through silver-green olive groves. The sky had cleared, the sun was out, and I could see the Cretan Sea in the distance. We came to the top of a rise, and there stretched below us was paradise: a valley with a sparkling stream running through groves of orange trees, thousands of orange globes glowing among shiny green leaves, and not a sign of civilization. We walked through the valley, gathering freshly dropped oranges, and eating to our heart's content. The Edenic setting aside, they were the best oranges I had ever tasted.

After this welcome respite from labor, I got up early the following day and went down to the café to look for work.

"Welcome to the Slave Café," said one of those already gathered. I listened then to dismal stories of unemployment. By 7:30, there were fifteen of us huddled on the chairs outside the café, hugging ourselves to keep out the cold until the café opened and we could go in to warmth and coffee. That is, if we hadn't gotten a job by that time. A handful were taken away by the few bosses who came to look us over, but at eight o'clock when the chances of work became remote, most of us were still there. We adjourned to the tables inside. Old Greek men, gathered for their morning coffee, were already involved in heated discussions. They were used to seeing workers and hardly gave us a look, although a few called out a "*Kali mehra*" [Good morning] to those they knew.

Over cups of Nescafé or Greek coffee, we continued the interminable foreign workers' conversation, exchanging stories of bosses, tourist police, travels, and visions of an easier life.

The next three mornings were the same. I was passed over in favor of men for orange picking. A few olive farmers came looking for workers. One offered me a job, but I turned it down. On the fourth morning, Billy and Franz, a Greek-Canadian and a German who were staying in my hotel, were full of news about the tourist police raid on the disco the night before. It had been a dramatic scene. Two tourist policemen in glittering white uniforms entered the disco and shouted out that no one was to leave. One stood by the door while the other made the rounds of the tables, checking passports. They warned three men to stop work or be deported.

"They didn't do anything to any of the girls," said Billy.

"Of course not. We aren't doing anything illegal—none of us can get jobs."

"Well, there is other work you can do, you know. Greece may be a man's world, but in some cases, that's in your favor. I'd like to be able to make 2,500 drachmas a night for sitting on a barstool."

"What are you talking about?"

"I'm talking about the work you should be doing instead of coming to this lousy café every morning."

"Come on, Billy, 2,500 just for sitting on a barstool? What's that about?"

"It's your ticket, that's what it is. So it's a man's world. So play it their way and get something, instead of knocking yourself out with hard labor. I would if I were a woman."

"So what's the job?" I asked, impatient.

"Like I said, sitting on a barstool. A lure. Bars in Hania pay girls just to sit there to draw men in—servicemen. I know because I met some of the girls."

Hania was the major population center of western Crete, a tourist mecca and harbor city east of Plataniás. There was an American navy base outside of Hania and a port nearby through which German, American, and occasionally Dutch servicemen came on NATO maneuvers.

"I would never do that," I said abruptly, thinking of both the job and the clientele.

"Well, Jesus, you don't have to sleep with the guys," Billy said, piqued at my response to his helpful suggestion.

The next morning when I was offered olive work, I took it, as did a couple with visa problems—one French, the other Spanish. The job included room and board and would likely last for two weeks, so I checked out of the hotel before joining the others in the back of the farmer's truck.

We had no idea where we were going. It turned out to be a nearly two-hour drive to a village in the mountains on the west end of Crete. Costas, our driver, proved to be merely the go-between for his cousin who spoke no English. He introduced us to our boss in whose house we would stay. Katerina, the boss's wife, showed us to the "parlor" where we would sleep. It was obviously the room reserved for special entertaining, but as there were only two other rooms in the house—a bedroom and a kitchen—there was no other place to put us.

Costas later informed us that his cousin was rich. The parlor and the fact that they had electricity were evidence of wealth, but the only running water was a tap outside, shared with the neighbors. There was no toilet, or even outhouse. The dirt plot behind the house served that function. Katerina, her husband, and five children all slept in one tiny bedroom. The kitchen, exposed to the mountain air through an ill-fitting door and a window only partially covered with a sheet of plastic, was freezing cold. Chickens ran in and out, along with two lambs. Katerina periodically shooed them away, screaming at the children to mind them. She was young, perhaps thirty years old, but looked worn out.

I soon saw why. Katerina picked olives all day with the French woman and me, while her husband took the Spanish man to work on building a huge sheep barn. We put in long hours, having to drive some distance to reach their hillside groves. When we returned to the village after the first night of work, it was long past dark. Our boss stopped the truck at the café and invited us in for a drink. Katerina headed up the street to their house. I tossed back a glass of raki and warmed myself at the wood stove. It was bitterly cold and our hands were numb. Old men from the village sat on chairs around the stove, laughing and talking. They were very friendly, urging us to take our shoes off and warm our feet, and including us in the rounds of raki they bought each other.

I didn't stay long, but went up to the house where I knew Katerina would be preparing dinner for us all. And so she was, while the children sat around the stove playing Candyland. When I indicated that I wanted to help her, Katerina looked at me in amazement, then protested that I had worked all day and should rest. When I indicated that she had worked all day too (our conversation was conducted in a combination of pantomime, Greek, and English, for my Greek was not up to these subtleties), she just stared at me, then passed me a bowl of potatoes to peel. As I watched her deft fingers peel and slice three to my one, I felt ashamedly conscious of my urban training in packaged and take-out cuisine.

When we finished, I played Candyland with the children, the oldest of whom was eight. They didn't speak English, but accepted my choppy Greek with good grace. Once tired of the game, they used the board to teach me the names of colors in Greek. Then they quizzed me on my numbers, and moved to items around the kitchen, dissolving into laughter at my woeful answers.

Later, when we were going to bed, Katerina and the eight-year-old daughter came into the parlor where I was unrolling my sleeping bag. They watched in curiosity as I pulled things out of my pack. Katerina, for all her responsibilities as an adult woman with five children and a house to run, suddenly seemed girlish.

"*Posson eton eisai?* [How old are you?]" I asked.

"*Eikosi pende.* [Twenty-five.]"

I wondered if she had any desire to escape from the village and see some of the world. If so, it must be difficult for her to have these footloose travelers coming through her home. We were not the first, nor would we be the last. It was a yearly string of foreigners who came to work in her husband's groves.

I showed them pictures of my family, and then they wanted to know if I had a camera. I told them I was sorry that I didn't, that I couldn't take their pictures. They were looking on with interest as I put Vaseline on my chapped lips, so I extended the container to the girl. Katerina pulled her daughter sharply behind her and shook her head vehemently.

Oh, no, she thinks it's lipstick and that I'm trying to corrupt her daughter with the ways of the West. I tried to explain, but couldn't get my message across.

"*Signomi, signomi* [I'm sorry]," I repeated helplessly.

Katerina shrugged and smiled, seemingly not upset, but Greek responsibility to a stranger went a long way and I couldn't be sure. Soon after, they bid me good night and left the room.

The next day was even colder than the previous. We stayed warm climbing up and down the olive trees and beating the branches vigorously, but our hands and feet became numb as the day wore on. Late in the afternoon, a light snow began to fall. We had to keep working until Katerina's husband came to pick us up. He dropped us off in the morning and came back to get us when he decided it was time to stop his construction work. He came early that day and I was grateful. The European couple and I sat silently in the back of the truck, huddled in our too-thin jackets, trying to forget the cold on the long drive back to the village.

Costas, the go-between, had shown up at the construction site and rode back in the cab with his cousin and Katerina. When we arrived in the village, Katerina went up to the house as before, and the rest of us went to the café. I was too cold to face the drafty kitchen.

Costas acted the magnanimous host to the workers he had enlisted: buying rounds of Metaxa to warm us, making efforts to draw us out, and finally suggesting that we be his guests at dinner and accompany him to hear bouzouki music at a special place outside of Hania. A long drive for a bit of food and music, I thought, but went along with the plan. We would stay at his house in Hania and he would drive us back for work the next morning.

It turned out to be a very

> Crete is Greece magnified. It is to Greece what Texas is, at least in myth, to the United States. Everything is bigger, stronger, better, brighter, darker there. After all, Zorba the Greek and his creator, Nikos Kazantzakis, were from Crete, that largest of Greek islands, situated between Europe and the Middle East/Africa where European civilization began.
> — Andrew Horton,
> *Bones in the Sea*

long night. From the moment we got into the truck, when Costas insisted I sit next to him in the cab, with the French woman on her Spanish lover's lap on the other side of me, it was *kamaki*. *Kamaki* is the Greek word for a spear used by fishermen, but in general parlance, "making *kamaki*" refers to the process of picking up a woman. Artistry, as in the skill of a ladies' man, is implied. And a "*kamaki* boy" is one who practices this art regularly. Groups of *kamaki* boys, usually in their late teens or early twenties, roam the streets of every population center where tourist women are likely to be found.

There is a *kamaki* boy "uniform" consisting of tight black pants, a black dress shirt open at the neck or nearly to the waist according to the seriousness of his intent, black loafers, white socks, and a key chain which is in perpetual play in his fingers (the modern equivalent of the worry beads of the older Greek men).

Costas was old enough to be my father, but *kamaki* is for all ages, so that did not serve as a deterrent. He wooed me over the appetizer and retsina, toasted my health and happiness all through the entrée, and let fall numerous romantic innuendoes with the baklava. The European couple looked on in amusement as I deflected his attentions. Actually, they talked more that night than at any other time, and with the *kamaki* on a lightweight plane, we had an enjoyable evening. Costas was really an excellent host, making us laugh and keeping the conversation and the wine flowing.

There was a sober moment, however. Costas revealed that this night on the town was not as spontaneous as it appeared. He told us that Katerina had said to him on the drive back from the groves, "I'm going crazy. I don't care where you take them, but get these tourists out of here." So he had agreed to remove us for the night and bring us back to work the next day.

I was hurt by this admission, and shocked too, because I thought Katerina and I were getting along fine. I thought of the warm scene in the kitchen, playing games with the children. And then of Katerina shielding her daughter behind her as I offered the Vaseline for her lips. Was that it? Or were we a painful reminder of another kind of life? Or was I so culturally unconscious that I couldn't even see where I was offending?

My face must have shown my hurt because Costas said, by way of apology, "Katerina, she's no good. She makes trouble for my cousin all the time. Always, *fasaria.*" He made the circular hand motion in the air that typically accompanied the word. As he went on, it became clear that he did not like Katerina and only obliged her because she was his cousin's wife.

"She always screams at my cousin. Never just doing her work like a good wife. Always complaining, always yelling. She talks back to her husband right out in the open, in front of the café so everybody can hear. The whole village tells me she is a bad wife. She drinks, too," he said, raising an imaginary bottle to his mouth and winking at us as conspirators in the knowledge of her vice. I saw Katerina trudging up the street to the house to prepare dinner after a long day of work, while all the men adjourned to the café for aperitifs. The cold tongue of village censure touched me and I shuddered.

After dinner, Costas got serious in his *kamaki*. He drove to Plataniás where he summarily deposited my co-workers, saying that there was only room for one at his house. Then he drove all the way back to Hania again, whereupon he suggested a hotel. When I asked about the offer of staying at his house, he answered that his wife would not understand our relationship and therefore the matter must be treated delicately. After further wrangling, I ended up at a hotel—by myself. Despite the failure of his *kamaki* campaign, Costas graciously said he would pay for the hotel when he picked me up at 8:30 the next morning to drive me back to the village for work. I was relieved because I could ill afford the hotel and would have stayed with someone in Plataniás if I had known how the evening was going to end.

The next morning, when I woke up enough to look at my watch in the gloom of my shuttered room, I saw that it was nine o'clock. No sign of Costas, and I knew there wouldn't be. I wasn't surprised, but annoyed that now I would have to pay for my room. As for the job, after what Katerina had supposedly said, I thought my working days in that village were better over. I would have been happy to leave it at that, but I had to make the long trip to that end of the island to pick up my pack. I cursed Costas for stranding me.

But then I opened the shutters and stepped onto the balcony.

The harbor lay before me. The harbor, with its crescent of water-stained stucco and stone buildings, broken by balconies, blank gaping windows, shutters of mauve, washed-out blue, and rust, collapsing sections of brick and red roof tile. The waterside promenade lined with bars and tavernas, most closed for the winter. And across the expanse of green water, at the mouth of the harbor and the edge of the Cretan Sea, the creamy stone lighthouse turned a rosy pink in the morning light. It was enchanting.

Hania had the reputation of a gathering place for expatriate artists, but I had heard conflicting reports as to the kind of environment that produced. Some travelers breathed reverence for the creative process. Others told tales of the coldness of the artistic community. "You could sit in the café every day and nobody would ever talk to you," one disgruntled woman informed me. And another, on hearing that I was thinking of going there, said, "Oh, don't go to Hania. The people are terrible." (By "people," she meant foreigners, which was the narrow circle most travelers moved in.) I was persuaded to go south instead.

None of that mattered, for in my first real glimpse of Hania, I fell in love. Hania, creamy Venetian town, magic of the thirteenth century. Narrow, winding streets with surprise staircases and sudden glimpses of the Cretan Sea—streets made dark by tall houses leaning over them in the preserved decay of their creamy, crumbling stone. Trailing leafy vines and hanging bougainvillea, living green on ancient walls. A city of the old and the new.

From the balcony of my room, I had seen Hania's version of the slave café. As usual, it could be identified by the scruffiness of the clientele. I stopped in and talked to a couple of workers, learning that farmers from the hill towns just outside of Hania came there in the mornings in search of orange-pickers and had been known on occasion to take women. Well, there's always that, I thought, as I left the café. I had already decided I must live in Hania.

Wandering in the old quarter, before hitchhiking to Katerina's to get my pack, I passed a couple of bars. I wondered if these were the ones that hired women and what the job of lure would be like. Having done time as a cocktail waitress, I ought to have had plenty of fuel for my imagination, but somehow my mind stopped short. I could put myself on the barstool and see a crowd of men, but could get no further. What would I say? What would anyone say?

Waiting for a ride on the road out of Hania, I found myself thinking more about the bars. It was one thing to be a waitress, but another to be stripped of the subterfuge of serving. On the continuum of female occupations, I placed lure just short of prostitute. But

I had to admit I was curious. A car stopped, and I thought no more about it.

Back in Katerina's village, I walked up the street to her house. Nobody was there, but a neighbor poked her head out her front door to watch me. She was a widow, dressed in the traditional black. I had met her the first day I arrived in the village. She had beckoned to me mysteriously from her dark doorway and when I followed her into her house, filled my pockets with salt-encrusted peanuts. This day, I told her as best I could that I was taking my pack and leaving, and asked her to thank Katerina for me. She nodded vigorously, and insisted I come in for some cookies.

I didn't get back to Plataniás until late that night, but immediately went in search of Joss and Billy to tell them I was moving to Hania. I couldn't locate Joss, but found Billy in his room at the hotel. I briefly related my experiences with Katerina and in Hania, and then said, "I think I'm going to try to get a job in the bars." It was a surprise to me when I said it, but once I did, it seemed a foregone conclusion. I was a young sailor at sea, and anything that scared me or eluded my understanding had to be conquered.

"I thought you said you would *never* do that."

"I changed my mind."

Billy told me the names of the bars and where to find them. "I should be so lucky to get such a cushy job," he added, with a touch of envy for the easy life of a female.

Billy and Franz saw me off on the bus to Hania, Billy making jokes about me on a barstool. As the bus drove off in a cloud of fumes, I settled back to contemplate my future.

Now living in Sebastopol, California, Stephanie Marohn is currently at work on two books, Crossroads and Awakenings: Turning Points in Lives of Spirit *and* Natural Medicine First Aid Remedies. *This story was excerpted from her forthcoming book,* Feeding the Wolfpack.

Searching for Eleni

The author hunts for the truth about
his mother's final years.

MY MOTHER WAS ONE OF 600,000 GREEKS WHO WERE KILLED during the years of war that ravaged the country from 1940 to 1949. Like many of the victims, she died because her home lay in the path of the opposing armies, but she would have survived if she hadn't defied the invaders of her village to save her children.

I had been her favorite child and the focus of her life, loved with the intensity a Greek peasant woman reserves for an only son. I knew that I was the primary reason she made the choices she did. No one doubted that she died so I could live.

As a boy growing up in the city of Worcester, Massachusetts, living with my sisters and the stranger who was my father, I couldn't talk about my mother and her death the way the rest of my family did, although it was with me waking and sleeping. Every Sunday, in the church full of Greek immigrants, I heard the priest recite a *trisagion* to her memory. My older sisters spoke of her constantly, often reporting dreams in which our mother appeared to them with some message or warning from the land of the dead. In *my* dreams, she was always alive, engaged in familiar scenes from the past, baking bread, harvesting the fruit of our mulberry tree, laughing at my pranks. My sisters had accepted her death, but each time I awoke it came as a new shock.

As a nine-year-old boy struggling with the English language, I felt helpless against the fact of my mother's death. It was not something that I could talk about to anyone. There seemed to be nothing I could do to make up for her sacrifice except to hope that my sisters were right, that God would ultimately punish those who had betrayed, tortured, and murdered her.

Then, in the seventh grade, a teacher assigned me to write about my life in Greece. It was one of the first days of spring. I looked out the school window, remembering our mountainside blazing with purple Judas trees, the Easter kid roasting on a spit outside each house, my mother boiling the eggs in a vat of bloodred dye.

I wrote how, in the spring of my eighth year, I overheard two guerrillas say they were going to take the village children away from their parents and send them behind the Iron Curtain. I ran to tell my mother what I had heard, and she began to plan our escape, setting in motion the events that would end in her execution four months later.

The essay won a certificate of merit, and I realized that I was not as helpless as I had thought. I would learn to write and eventually describe what was done in that ravine in 1948 and by whom. I didn't speak of these ambitions to my father and sisters, who were working in factories and diners to keep us alive.

By the time I finished college I had saved enough money from part-time work on local newspapers to make a return visit to the village which I had left as a refugee fourteen years before. I intended to begin my search for the details of my mother's death.

When I walked out of that village as a boy, I knew every tree and rock of my circumscribed world, but as I followed the new dirt road back up our mountain in 1963, I mistook two villages in the distance for my own before I reached Lia. Clearly, my memory was not as accurate as I had believed. When I finally reached it, the village was no longer deserted; many of the civilians who had been taken into Albania and then dispersed throughout Eastern Europe by the retreating Communists had drifted back since 1954. The guerrillas and their collaborators, however, were still not permitted by the Greek government to return.

I was met by my eighty-three-year-old grandfather, the only male relative I had known as a boy. I remembered him as an aloof, menacing tyrant. He was the one who returned to the empty village to unearth the bodies of my mother and my aunt, then brought the news of their deaths to us children. When he saw me, now twenty-three, my grandfather was the first of many villagers to exclaim over my physical resemblance to my mother. My face seemed to incite the neighbors to pour out details of her torture and suffering. As soon as they began, I discovered that I could not bear to listen. When one man tried to tell me how her feet and legs were swollen to grotesque proportions by beatings, I got up and left the room.

On that first afternoon, when my grandparents were taking their siesta, I left their house and climbed the path up to our old property, now deserted and shunned by the villagers because it had been used by the guerrillas as a military police station, jail, killing ground, and cemetery. I knew that my mother had spent the last days of her life being tortured there, imprisoned in the filthy cellar where we once kept our sheep and goats. I forced myself to enter the front door and look into the room which had served as a kitchen, where my mother, sisters, and I used to sleep on the floor around the hearth. The room seemed to have shrunk over the years. There was nothing inside, no sign that I belonged here. I tried to recall happy times, feast days, but all I could think of were the condemned prisoners in the cellar, my mother among them. I didn't approach the cellar door but left the house, knowing I would not come back....

My sisters had neither the desire nor the money to return to Greece until 1969, when two of them resolved to go back to the village and hold a memorial service for our mother. I decided to go with them, although I knew it would be a painful journey. When we reached Lia, I followed them up the path as far as our land, but when my sisters entered the house, I refused to go with them and waited outside until they emerged, in tears.

The next day the whole village gathered in our neighborhood Church of St. Demetrios for the memorial service. The church was used only on special saints' days, but the village priest agreed to open it and conduct the liturgy. In a small ossuary, divided from the sanctuary by a wall, lay the bones of my mother and my aunt in a small wooden box, mixed together as they had been when my grandfather disinterred the bodies from the mass grave.

Sun slanted through the dusty windows of the crowded church as the priest began to chant and the altar boys swung the censers, the heavy perfume mingling with the odor of decay. Unexpectedly, the schoolteacher stood up to speak. He was the only educated man in the village and he wanted to deliver a eulogy. As soon as he said our mother's name, my sisters began to wail: keening, ululating cries, the Greek expression of sorrow for the dead.

"This woman's death was not an ordinary one," the school-teacher continued over the commotion. "She was executed alone, with her husband far away, because she tried to save her children. She was a victim of her fellow Greeks. This is not an ordinary memorial service for the dead; she was murdered!"

As I stood there, trying to wish myself anywhere else, the air pressed in on me and I was aware of my mother's bones only yards away. Nearly every day of my childhood I had watched her light a candle before this altar. The shrieks of my sisters stripped away the veneer of control I had built up, layer by layer. Even when I was a boy, on the day my mother said good-bye, and again, when I learned she was dead, I had held my grief inside. Now it erupted. Sobs welled up from where they had been hidden for so many years and shook my body like a convulsion. The rush of emotion blurred my vision and then my knees buckled. Two men nearby grabbed my arms and supported me out of the church, setting me on the ground, my back against the trunk of one of the towering cypress trees surrounding the graveyard.

That outburst was the first and last time I lost control and abandoned myself to my grief, but when it passed, I discovered a new strength within me. At last I was ready to learn what the villagers had to tell me and to look directly at the details of my mother's death.

When I began asking questions, I found that many parts of the story were still beyond my reach. The villagers who had betrayed her, who testified against her to curry favor with the guerrillas, were still in exile behind the Iron Curtain. And the witnesses to her last days who were living in Lia gave me contradictory testimony about many incidents, obviously withholding details that might compromise them or their relatives. Those who were willing to talk about the war years openly remembered the guerrillas only by the pseudonyms they had assumed to mask their identities. I spent all the summer of 1969 in Lia, but when I left in the fall to return to America, it was clear that despite my emotional readiness to hear my mother's story, I did not have access to key people involved or the skills to get the truth out of them....

In July of 1974 the collapse of the dictatorial right-wing military junta ruling Greece opened the gates for Communist guerrillas living in exile to return to the country. Many of those I wanted to question about by mother's trial and death would now be accessible to me. In 1977 I persuaded my editors to send me to Athens as *The New York Times*'s foreign correspondent in the eastern Mediterranean. The conditions necessary for me to begin the search for my mother's story were all coming together.

The arrival in Greece in 1977 was a shock to someone who remembered the civil war years. I discovered that the fall of the junta and the establishment of a new civilian government, which legalized the Communist party in an effort to ensure acceptance of Greece in the Common Market, had created a renaissance of Communist power in the country. Posters, movies, books, popular songs, and the youth organizations in the universities were united in celebrating the guerrillas of the civil war as heroes. It seemed that the best talents of Greece were busy rewriting the history of the war, while everywhere Communist leaders were denying that such things as the execution of civilians and the abduction of large groups of children from the mountain villages had ever happened.

As soon as I settled in Athens with my family I hoped to spend every spare moment tracking down and questioning those who had been my mother's interrogators, jailers, torturers, and the judges at her trial, as well as relatives and neighbors who had witnessed her last days. But the volatile political climate in the area left me time for little else but my job. I spent most of my first years in Greece traveling outside the country, covering terrorism in Turkey, battles in the Middle East, a revolution in Iran, and civil war in Afghanistan.

By 1980 it was clear that I had to give myself up entirely to the investigation of my mother's story at once or never do it. I learned that some of the guerrilla leaders responsible for her trial and execution had died in exile. Others were likely to die of old age before I could track them down. Furthermore, Greece has a thirty-year statute of limitation on all crimes—including murder. Anyone who had committed any atrocity during the war years could now return to the country without fear of punishment, and the former leaders of the guerrillas were flooding back in.

In 1980 I was forty-one years old, the same age that my mother had been when she was killed. My son was nine, as I was on the day I learned she was dead. My older daughter, growing out of babyhood, resembled my mother more every day. Seeing my children grow had taught me a lesson that made my mother's story easier to confront.

When I was young I was convinced that her existence was one of unrelieved misery because for the last decade of her life she struggled every day to keep us five children alive, despite war and famine, with no help from anyone. But as I watched my own children I realized that there must have been joy and laughter to reward her while she lived. Knowing that made it easier to face what I would learn.

Finally, clues about the identities of some of her killers began to filter to me in Athens, and I knew I couldn't hesitate any longer. I decided to leave my job with the newspaper to devote all my energy to the search for my mother's story....

Only one thing was clear: I was going back to my village. I had to return to the places where my mother lived and died, to think things through. Heading out of Yannina, I came to a fork in the highway and impulsively turned north. The road on the left led toward my village, but I remembered that the right-hand one led to the village of Mavronoron, the home of the young woman, Despo, who tried to kill herself in the cellar prison by driving a nail into her abdomen. I felt a compulsion to learn if anyone remembered Despo and could tell me at least her full name.

Past ever smaller villages, where storks nested on chimneys and telephone poles, I continued north on a dirt road until I reached a jumble of houses and a large church. I asked a group of women in the churchyard if they knew the name of someone called Despo who disappeared from the village during the war. They clucked and sighed as if it had been yesterday. Her name was Despina Tassis, they said. She left two little motherless boys—grown-up now and living in Athens—but Despo's husband was still around. I could find him outside the coffeehouse playing cards with the other men.

When I spoke to some of the men gathered around the card tables, the tall, unsmiling figure of Stephanos Tassis rose and followed me out of earshot of the others. I told him about my interest in the war and my mother's fate, and said that I had recently talked to a woman who was in prison with his wife.

He showed little interest in my statement, although he told me this was the first concrete news of his wife since her disappearance thirty-two years before. He told me that their two sons had been four and two years old when everyone fled the village of Mavronoron in the wake of the invading guerrillas. But after a while the family, living as refugees in Yannina, had nothing to eat. Despo sneaked back to their village to get some corn she had hidden in their house, and was never seen again. Seven years after Despo's disappearance, Stephanos Tassis managed with much difficulty to find a priest willing to marry him to another village woman, even though there was no proof of his first wife's death.

It wasn't easy wringing answers from the taciturn man in front of me. Clearly, he had no interest in learning about Despo's last days, so I didn't elaborate. I could see that he didn't want the ghost of his first wife intruding on the life he had built for himself since the war. His eyes strayed back to the card game.

If ever he or his sons wanted to learn more, I said, I could put them in touch with the woman who shared Despo's imprisonment. I wrote down my address and telephone number on a piece of paper. Stephanos Tassis scarcely glanced at it as he put it in his pocket and pointedly wished me good-bye.

I felt angry, almost personally injured, by the indifference of Despo's husband. In my uncertainty over what to do about my mother's death, I had sought out someone who was similarly bereaved, only to learn that not only did he intend to do nothing about his wife's murder, he didn't even want to be reminded of it.

Later I would find many more victims of the guerrillas like him. In the course of hunting down the identities of my mother's killers, I uncovered the names and addresses of guerrillas who had killed other civilians, and I confronted many of their survivors with details about the murderers. In each case I was met with apathy and rationalization. "Don't tell me where he is, because I might feel compelled to do something to him," said a postman whose father was shot dead by a guerrilla intelligence officer as he stood in his own field and refused to inform on his neighbors. "Let God punish the guilty," said a man who, as an eight-year-old boy, had watched his mother condemned to death for refusing to give up her children to be sent to the Iron Curtain countries. "The government should bring them to justice," muttered a third, who saw his parents executed in the churchyard of his village while the guerrillas warned him that he would die too if he made a sound.

These excuses kindled in me a growing disgust, rage, and despair. Thousands of innocent people like my mother had been killed during the war, and now their murderers were living in Greece, their sleep untroubled by fear of reprisals. Just one act of vengeance against the men who now bragged of their war exploits would have made all of them feel a little of the anguish they had inflicted on their victims. But not one father, husband, or son had found the will to do it.

My dark mood evoked by the apathy of Despo's husband lifted a little as I drove toward my own village. Whenever I crossed the narrow bridge over the Kalamas River, which isolates the Mourgana mountains, I felt a comforting sense of returning to my childhood, of coming home.

From the river the road leads up, past waterfalls, ruined mills, and white chapels perched on sheer cliffs, around hairpin turns and through tiny villages scattered like pebbles, until the asphalt ends in a bone-rattling path leading ever higher, through the hiding places of mountain goats and wild boar, to the edge of the timberline where the gray slate roofs of Lia become visible nestled among the scrub pine and holm oak of my village.

Bare lightbulbs now hang inside the stone huts, testament to the power lines that reached Lia in 1965, but from the road—another recent incursion of civilization—the village still looks as primitive as the day I walked out of it thirty-three years ago.

As I drove past the Church of Aghia Paraskevi (St. Friday) on the easternmost boundary of the village, the grizzled shepherds surrounded by their goats and the black-clad grandmothers bent under loads of kindling shouted greetings to me.

The pleasure of these familiar sights dissolved when I noticed the stooped, white-haired figure of Christos Skevis at work in his yard. In 1948, when my mother and the others were killed, Skevis was one of the villagers who methodically went around to the houses of the victims and stole the last remaining pieces of food from the survivors, among them my fourteen-year-old sister.

In those climactic days of the war, close relatives and neighbors turned against us. The handful of villagers who had the courage to speak up for my mother at her trial and who tried to console my sister after her execution were not the ones we had always considered our friends. In some cases her defenders were well-known Communists, but they transcended political beliefs and fear for their own safety because they refused to speak against innocent people. But for the most part, our neighbors avoided or betrayed my mother in hope of improving their own chance of survival.

As I drove toward the central square, I kept hearing over the sound of the car's engine a phrase that my sister and my father had repeated a hundred times: *"Tin fagane i horani"*—"It was the villagers who devoured her." To my family, the Communist guerrillas like Katis were an impersonal act of God, unleashed on our village by war, like a plague. It was our neighbors whom they held responsible for my mother's death; the villagers who whispered secrets to the security police and testified against her at the trial.

This was something I had to resolve: perhaps the villagers really were more culpable for her death than the men who passed the sentence and fired the bullets. I wondered if something about my mother incited the people of Lia to offer her up like a sacrificial lamb. Or perhaps the villagers had only been manipulated by the guerrillas, who exploited their moral weaknesses, petty jealousies and fears, because the guerrillas wanted my mother killed for some political purpose. What was the real reason that she was executed?

The beauty of the village all around me, the familiar tang of wood smoke and the music of goats' bells in the air, seemed to refute my suspicions. I passed through the square and stopped near the western boundary of Lia. I left the car at the foot of the path that led up the mountain toward our old neighborhood and the Church of St. Demetrios.

It was August 6th, the feast day of the Transfiguration, one of the three times a year when the church was used for a service. As I climbed, I saw elderly worshipers approaching from all directions.

The sun was high, but inside, the church was dark and filled with shadowy figures in somber clothing. The gnarled faces and the gold of the ancient carved altar screen shone in the candlelight. I stood for a while outside the church door beneath the cypress trees, listening to the priest's chanting and the indistinct voice of an old woman who was seated cross-legged next to a recent grave, carrying on a conversation with the dead.

The door to the ossuary stood open, but I didn't go in. I knew that none of the answers I needed would be found inside the wooden box that held by mother's bones. She was frozen in my memory as I had known her from the perspective of a child; a source of unfailing strength, security, and love. But in delving into the events of her last years, I had begun to glimpse a more complex and ambiguous person, a troubled peasant woman who tried to live

by the rules of the primitive mountain culture that constituted her
world, and when they failed her, defied them.

My mother had scarcely gone to school; she put on the kerchief
at the age of eleven like every other village girl, and from that
moment never dared to speak to men until the day she was handed
over as a bride to a husband she didn't know. The politics that shattered her universe during the last decade of her life made no sense
to her. She never traveled farther than the provincial capital. Her
husband lived half a world away in a country that she longed to see
but knew nothing about, although she was branded, because of her
marriage, with the name "the Amerikana" and all the prejudices
that came with it.

My mother's world was ruled by magic, superstition, ghosts and
devils to be invoked or appeased by holy oil and charms, but these
were not enough to save her and her children from the war that
swept into their mountains. When she saw that living by the strict
village canons was not enough, when it became a choice between
losing her children or her life, she discovered a strength that I now
know is given to few.

Before my search was over I had to find my mother, to see her
with the eyes of an adult, and to uncover her secret feeling about the
world that caged her. I had to do this in order to learn how she
wanted me to deal with her murderers. I had to communicate with
her across the chasm of death to discover if, as she climbed toward
that ravine to her execution, she was Antigone, meeting death with
resignation because she had purposely defied a human command to
honor a higher law of the heart, or if she was Hecuba, crying out
for vengeance. What did she want me to do?

Interrupting my reflections, over the priest's singsong and the
chanter's responses, rose a mechanical roar that I had never heard as
a boy. It came from above, in the direction of my house. I started up
the path leading from the churchyard.

I found the house a complete ruin, overgrown with ivy, deserted
except for lizards; the roof and floor collapsing into the cellar. I
discovered the source of the noise: it was a bulldozer at work,
extending a horizontal path for a road across the lower boundary of

what had been our garden. The low stone wall around the property had disappeared and the remaining walls of the house stared with empty eye sockets at the monster shaving away another great swath of red soil, perilously close to the lone mulberry tree that had been our landmark.

Although the house was a grim monument to the killings that had taken place there, I realized that I wanted that mulberry tree to survive. I motioned to the bulldozer operator to stop and then went over and asked him to cut around the tree, that piece of my childhood.

As the machine set to work again, I walked over to the house, looking down for the first time into the exposed cellar where my mother and so many others had spent their last hours.

The mulberry tree and all the pleasant memories clinging to its branches made me understand that my search

> I'm not speaking to you about
> things past, I'm speaking
>   about love;
> adorn your hair with the sun's
>   thorns,
> dark girl; .
> the heart of the Scorpion has set,
> the tyrant in man has fled,
> and all the daughters of the sea,
>   Nereids, Graeae,
> hurry toward the shimmering
>   of the rising goddess:
> whoever has never loved will
>   love,
> in the light…
> —George Seferis, "Thrush,"
>   *Collected Poems,* translated
>   by Edmund Keeley

would give me as much joy as sorrow. This was the house where Eleni Gatzoyiannis suffered and died, but it was also the house where she was brought as a nineteen-year-old bride, where my sisters and I were born, where we played and fought. The terrace was still there, where my mother would bring her hand-turned sewing machine outside on warm evenings to take advantage of the breeze and look up occasionally from her work to gaze at the valley stretching away below her. We were hungry there but we were happy, too, and our memories would outlast the house. "We have eaten bread and salt together," the Greeks say, meaning that we have shared the most elemental foods, suffered the same hardships, known the same joys, and that nothing can ever break that bond that ties us together, not even death.

I would have to rebuild this house, stone by stone, in my imagination, before I could face Katis and the others. I would have to re-create her lost village—a mysterious world as faded now as a tapestry from the Middle Ages, with only a face visible here, an arm there. When I had remade it, weaving it from the memories of scores of different witnesses, then I would have reached the end of my search for my mother. I would understand what it was that she wanted me to know as she left our gate for the last time to climb to the ravine.

The witnesses to my mother's fate were a generation of leaves scattered by winds of war all over the world—Canada, the United States, England, Hungary, Poland, Czechoslovakia, and every corner of Greece. I had to track them down and use all my professional skill to get the truth from them.

In the course of the journey I would find not only my mother but myself. By re-creating the last decade of her life, I would learn how much I had been formed by that now-dead world. Whatever I decided I must do to my mother's killers, was I capable of it? Others in my place were unable to find the will to claim vengeance. Did I have that will?

When I had uncovered the answer, which lay buried somewhere in the ruins of my house and my childhood, then I would be ready to confront Katis and the rest. But my search had to begin with the discovery of a dead woman and the child who walked out of this mountain over three decades ago. I had to find the story not only of my mother's death, but of her life as well. And to do that I had to go back to the autumn of 1940....

Nicholas Gage was a reporter for the Associated Press and the Wall Street Journal *before becoming chief investigative reporter and later Athens bureau chief for* The New York Times. *He is the author of several books, including the award-winning bestseller* Eleni, *from which this story was excerpted.*

ROBERT D. KAPLAN

⋆ ⋆ ⋆

Farewell to Salonika

What happened to the Jewish city?

I LEFT THE RILA MONASTERY FOR BULGARIA'S SOUTHERN BORDER, from where it was only another fifty miles to the harbor of Greece's second-largest city, Salonika. In Salonika, I sat down at a café table facing the warm Aegean water. On either side of me, stretching for miles along the sweeping, sickle-shaped bay, were dun masses of poured-concrete apartment buildings with rusted balconies, and plastic neon signs advertising fast-food restaurants and video-game parlors. The blue-and-white Greek flag snapped in the dusk from the White Tower, built in the fifteenth century, the only remnant of the decades and centuries before World War II within my line of vision. For the woman who took the chair opposite me at the table, that flag flying over this city represented not the liberating purity of marble ruins on a blue seaboard, but the grim and uncompromising reality of the East.

Greeks are a flamboyant people of gesture: the delicious snap, crackle, and pop of Greek syllables are meant to be punctuated with upward-thrusting jaws and outward-thrusting arms. Greeks spend much of each day talking at café tables. "We Greeks are the most talented of peoples: it is an art to take four hours to finish a small cup of coffee," a writer friend once exclaimed to me in mock-seriousness. But the woman before me now was notably economical in her movements, and, as she coldly pointed out, had only the next forty-five minutes free. She had dark hair and eyes, and a harsh, wounding stare. "Take out your notebook," she said.

Salonika—Thessaloníki in Greek—was named after Salonike, Alexander the Great's half-sister. John Reed, when he arrived here in the spring of 1915, sketched its history:

> Here Alexander launched his fleets. She [Salonika] has been...
> a Byzantine metropolis second only to Constantinople, and
> the last stronghold of that romantic Latin Kingdom, where the
> broken wreck of the Crusaders clung desperately to the
> Levant they had won and lost. Saracens and Franks...Greeks,
> Albanians, Romans, Normans, Lombards, Venetians,
> Phoenicians, and Turks succeeded each other as her rulers,
> and St. Paul bored her with visits and epistles. Austria almost
> won Salonika in the middle of the Second Balkan War, Serbia
> and Greece broke the Balkan Alliance to keep her, and
> Bulgaria plunged into a disastrous war to gain her. Salonika is
> a city of no nations and of all nations.

Then Reed added: "But all the centre of the city is a great community of Spanish Jews expelled from Spain by Ferdinand and Isabella."

According to the British Balkan specialist Nevill Forbes, also writing from the vantage point of 1915: "The city of Salonika was and is almost purely Jewish, while in the country districts Turkish, Albanian, Greek, Bulgar, and Serb villages were inextricably confused." J. D. Bourchier thought the "ideal solution" for the city's future "would be a Jewish republic and a free port under the protection of the Great Powers." Jews themselves, for centuries, referred to Salonika as "the Mother of Israel."

Rena Molho, the woman seated opposite me, was a Spanish Jew, one of 850 Jews left in this city of a million Greeks; the Bulgarian, Serbian, and Turkish communities numbered even less. She was here to speak about a city that no longer existed: the same way that Greeks from Alexandria spoke mournfully of their own multi-ethnic Mediterranean city, also with a sweeping sickle-shaped harbor, that for centuries has been dominated by Greeks, but now was completely Arab. Facts rushed forth from Rena.

The first Jews came to Salonika in 140 B.C. In A.D. 53, St. Paul—Rabbi Saul of Tarsus, that is—preached at the Etz Haim ("Tree of Life") Synagogue on three successive Sabbaths. Jews from Hungary and Germany arrived in 1376. Following the conquest of Salonika by the Ottoman Turks, 20,000 Jews from Spain received permission to settle there in 1492, radically transforming the city's culture and demographic character. In 1493 came the Jews from Sicily. From 1495 to 1497, after the Inquisition had spread from Spain to Portugal, the Jews from Portugal arrived. "In 1913," Rena lectured, "the population of Salonika was 157,000: made up of 80,000 Jews, 35,000 Turks, of whom 10,000 to 15,000 were *Domnes* (Jews who had been con-

In the spring of 334 B.C., Alexander, a Macedonian Greek intent on conquering the Persians, marched with his army to the Dardanelles, which the Greeks called the Hellespont, the great natural divide between Europe and Asia. After conquering the vast empire of the Persians and making his capital in Babylon, he set forth to discover the ends of the earth. He left a wake of destruction and newly Hellenized cities all the way to modern-day Hyderabad in India. His influence on history was nothing less than astounding. Before he died, it is said that he had plans to build a pyramid larger than the Great Pyramid at Giza to honor his father, Philip of Macedonia, and to extend his empire beyond Egypt in Africa and west to what is now France and England. As it was, Alexander's founding of the city of Alexandria in Egypt had a profound cultural influence on generations of Judaic, Christian, and Islamic scholars.

—Sean O'Reilly, "Notes on Archaeology"

verted to Islam in the course of Ottoman rule), 30,000 to 35,000 Greeks, and 7,000 to 12,000 Bulgarians, Serbs, and Albanians."

Rena fired off the titles of books—complete with names of authors and publishers, and dates of publication—to back up her statistics and to say, in effect: *Look at everyone gesturing at the other tables. There you get style, I give you substance. I dare you to dispute any of my facts!*

One book Rena mentioned was *Farewell to Salonica,* by Leon Sciaky, the story of a boy growing up at the close of the Ottoman era in a sleepy city of gardens, minarets, whitewashed walls, green shutters, and red-tiled roofs. I later tracked down a copy of this long-out-of-print book at the British Council library in Salonika. Sciaky refers to the Salonika of that time as the "preponderantly Jewish capital" of Macedonia. In his school class of fifteen, only one student was Greek. The author calls this a "fair cross-section" of the city. It is a memoir laden with historical expectation: "The century was drawing to a close. Stealthily, the West was creeping in, trying to lure the East with her wonders."

At the turn of the century here in Greek Macedonia, the reactionary tyranny of the Turkish sultans was finally collapsing. But fear and uncertainty loomed: in a region of great ethnic diversity, the Jews had carved out a niche. The intolerant—perhaps because it was so long repressed—nationalism of the Bulgarians, who occupied the hinterland around Salonika, and of the Greeks, who occupied all the territory to the south, represented a much more threatening tyranny than that of the imperial Turks. "You have to understand the climate," said Rena. "In 1913, Greeks broke into 400 Jewish shops on account of a rumor that the Jews had poisoned the wells." In *Report to Greco*, Nikos Kazantzakis gives his own account of anti-Semitism in Greece during this period:

> I wanted to learn Hebrew in order to read the Old Testament in the original…my father called the rabbi, and they agreed that I should go to him three times a week to receive lessons…. The moment our friends and relatives heard, their hair stood on end and they ran to my father. "What are you doing!" they shrieked. "Have you no feelings

for your son? Don't you know that on Good Friday those crucifiers put Christian children in a spike-lined trough and drink their blood?"

In 1916, Greek troops occupied Salonika. In 1917, a great fire destroyed the entire Jewish section of the city, along with thirty-four synagogues. The homeless numbered 73,448, of whom 53,737 were Jews. Still, noted Rena, Salonika was "a Jewish city. The lingua franca, and the language of the street kids, was Judeo-Spanish (Ladino). The port closed on Shabbat (the Jewish Sabbath) until 1923, when Greek law forced it open." In that year, 100,000 Greek refugees from Asia Minor—recently overrun by the Turkish army under a new nationalist leader, Mustafa Kemal "Ataturk"—were resettled in Salonika. "The Jews allowed their schools to be used as refugee shelters. For a time after, Jewish children could not attend school," said Rena, anger rising in her voice.

When the Nazis captured Salonika in April 1941, the Jews were the second-largest community after the Greeks. Although the size of the community had diminished, Salonika was still the world cultural capital of Sephardic ("Spanish") Jewry. "It took the Nazis two years, working every day, to loot Jewish Salonika of its artistic treasures," said Rena. "And it took fifteen trainloads over a period of five months to empty Salonika of its Jews. A whole city was moved to a concentration camp. The 500,000 graves in the cemetery, maybe the largest Jewish cemetery in the world, were all destroyed." I was shown a photo of a swimming pool the Germans had built, lined with Jewish tombstones.

Of all the cities in Nazi-occupied Europe, Salonika ranked first in the number of Jewish victims: out of a Jewish population of fifty-six thousand, 54,050—96.5 percent—were exterminated at Auschwitz, Birkenau, and Bergen-Belsen. The successful roundup and deportation of the Jews of Salonika helped make Adolf Eichmann infamous. In the early 1990s, the world's most wanted, still-surviving Nazi war criminal, Alois Brunner (an Austrian, like Eichmann), was being sought from his Syrian hideout specifically for his crimes in Salonika.

When the Nazis occupied Salonika, Rena's mother escaped to central Greece, then under Italian occupation. With false identity papers, Rena's father escaped to Athens, where he sold cigarette paper. "The day Athens was liberated was the greatest day in my father's life, he told me, greater than the day that any of his children or grandchildren were born."

Now Rena came to the heart of her message: "The Jews owned 12,000 houses in Salonika before the German invasion. After the war, they made only 600 claims. The Greek authorities acted on thirty of them. Today, at the university in Salonika, there is not a department, not a course, nothing about the Jews—or about the Turks or other communities either. There is nothing in the historical institutes. Nothing in the city's museums. Hardly a book in the Greek bookstores. Nothing. As if we were never here.

"You know the fairgrounds, where every year there is a trade fair and the prime minister gives a speech? It is built over the Jewish cemetery. There is not a plaque. Nothing."

Rena got up to leave. She had another appointment.

Rena had not been exaggerating. After forty-five years, the Municipality of Salonika had yet to act on a request to name one street in the city—any street—"the Street of Jewish Martyrs." The effacement of the city's multiethnic past had been so total as to be unconscious. The speeches about Salonika throughout the postwar era by Greek politicians, from all shades of the political spectrum, rarely (if ever) contained a reference or a tribute to the non-Greek side of the city's past. In Greek eyes, Salonika and the rest of Macedonia were, are, and always will be purely Greek.

Molho's bookshop, owned by Rena's father-in-law, Saul—opened by his forebears in 1870, and the oldest bookstore in the city, located at 10 Tsimiski Street—is the lone thriving remnant of Jewish Salonika. At the eastern edge of town, past miles of concrete blocks and tacky storefronts, stands the Villa Mozdah, an architectural landmark, named after a prominent family of Spanish Jews whose home it was. The blue-and-white Greek flag flew over its onion-bulb roof and white neoclassical columns and pilasters. There was no plaque outside, no mention of any kind in any local guidebook of the building's non-Greek past. I unburdened myself on the whole issue of Jewish Salonika to a Greek-American friend, Aristide D. Caratzas. Caratzas, a specialist in Byzantine history, is both an active member of the Greek lobby and an academic publisher of books on Greek-related subjects, modern and ancient. Caratzas's firm was soon to publish a book about the Jews of Salonika.

This is what he said: "From classical antiquity through the beginning of the fifteenth century, Salonika was a Greek city. The Greeks were expelled by the Ottoman Turks, who then welcomed the Jews. It's true, for five hundred years, the Jews dominated Salonika; and in historical terms, they preserved the city for the Greeks, who only reclaimed it in the twentieth century—partly due to another Turkish expulsion, this time from Asia Minor to Salonika. But in Greek political mythology, Salonika can only be Greek. There can be no mention of the Jews. The building of a national consciousness in this part of the world sometimes means that what everybody knows privately is what also can never be openly stated or admitted." Caratzas then quoted a sixth-century Greek philosopher, Stephen of Byzantium: "Mythology is what never was, but always is."

In other words, there was little unusual about this story. Just as Serbia, Albania, Romania, and Bulgaria brutally smashed through the undergrowth of Ottoman tyranny and diversity to erect ethnically uniform states, so did Greece. And as the memory of the Albanians was erased by the Serbs, as the memory of Greek northern Epirus was erased by the Albanians, that of the Hungarians by the Romanians, and that of the Turks by the Bulgarians, so too was the memory of Salonika's Jews and other ethnic groups erased by the Greeks. Greece is part of the Balkan pattern, particularly in this city, the former capital of Ottoman-era Macedonia.

And thus I finally come to the matter itself: Greece, the southern dagger point of the Balkan Peninsula, considered the birthplace of our Western culture and value system—what Greece is, has been, and never was.

I lived in Greece for seven years and have visited it often before and since. I speak and read Greek, albeit badly. I met my wife in

Greece, got married in Greece, and had a son born in Greece. I love Greece. But the Greece I love is a real country, warts and cruelties and all; not the make-believe land of the university classicists or of the travel posters.

Because I did not have a "travel experience" in Greece so much as I had a "living experience," my attitude toward Greece is more obsessive than my attitude concerning the rest of the Balkans. My living experience revealed Greece to me as a Balkan country. What made Greece particularly Balkan in the 1980s, when I lived there, was the politics. This is why I will dwell at length on Greece's modern political atmosphere: a subject about which little has been written, compared with all the books on Greek travel.

Before the end of the Cold War, when the existence of the Warsaw Pact enforced an artificial separation between Greece and its northern neighbors, only Westerners like me, living in Greece, realized how Balkan Greece was. Those on the outside were determined to see Greece as a Mediterranean and Western country only: the facts be damned. As I began work on *Balkan Ghosts: A Journey Through History* in 1989—when Macedonia was known only as the birthplace of Alexander the Great, and not as the geopolitical problem it currently is—people advised me to leave Greece out of the story, since it "was not really part of the Balkans." I resisted. Events have borne me out. As the 1990s began, Greece was increasingly making the news in connection with border disputes in Macedonia and southern Albania. And Greece's political behavior in the region, despite a democratic tradition going back to antiquity, appeared no more reasonable than that of its neighbors to its north, whose democratic tradition was generally nonexistent.

The first time I arrived in Greece was by train from Yugoslavia. The second time was from Bulgaria, also by train. A third time was by bus from Albania. Each time, upon crossing the border into Greece, I became immediately conscious of a continuity: mountain ranges, folk costumes, musical rhythms, races, and religions, all of which were deeply interwoven with those of the lands I had just come from. And just as everywhere else in the Balkans, where races and cultures collided and where the settlement pattern of national groups did not always conform with national boundaries, this intermingling was hotly denied.

"No Turks live in Greece," Greece's former Deputy Foreign Minister, Ioannis Kapsis, once told me: "There are only some Greeks who happen to be Muslim and happen to speak Turkish to each other. Nor are there any Macedonians...." Kapsis railed. He was unstoppable. In all the years I lived in Greece, from 1982 through 1989, I never once heard a Greek—outside of a few well-known politicians—bring up the question of the Parthenon (Elgin) Marbles and the British Museum's refusal to return them. And if that issue—which received so much publicity in the West—was brought up by a foreigner, I never heard native Greeks speak long or passionately about it. But hours of my life have been spent sitting quietly at a Greek table, hearing out paroxysms of rage on issues such as the Turks and Constantinople, the Serbs and Macedonia, and the persecuted Greek minority in Albania. When I arrived in Greece in 1990 from Macedonia and Bulgaria, I tried to explain the position of the Slavic Macedonians to a group of Greek friends. They fumed, practically in unison: "Just because those dirty Gypsies in Skopje filled your head with lies doesn't make it true!" To these Greeks, all Slavs who called themselves "Macedonian" were "dirty Gypsies."

That is why, when I arrived in Greece from Bulgaria in 1990, I did not think of myself as having left the Balkans, but as having entered the place that best summed up and explained the Balkans. The icon was a Greek invention. The Greek Orthodox Church was the mother of all Eastern Orthodox churches. The Byzantine Empire was essentially a Greek empire. The Ottoman Turks ruled through Greeks—from the wealthy, Phanar ("Lighthouse") district of Constantinople—who were often the diplomats and local governors throughout the European part of the Turkish empire. *Constantinople* was a Greek word for an historically Greek city. Even the Turkish word for the place, Istanbul, was a corruption of the Greek phrase *is tin poli* ("to the city"). The elite corps of Ottoman soldiery, the Janissaries, included many Greeks, who had been taken from their parents as young children and raised in the sultan's barracks. The Cyrillic alphabet, used in Bulgaria, Serbia, Macedonia, and Russia, emerged from the Greek alphabet when two monks, Cyril and Methodius, left Salonika in the ninth century A.D. to proselytize among the Slavs. The modern Greek race has been a compound of Greeks, Turks, Albanians, Romanians, assorted Slavs, and others, all of whom migrated south into the warm-water terminus of the Balkan Peninsula. The fact that few distinguishable minorities have survived in Greece is testimony to the assimilative drawing power of Greek culture. The peasants of Suli in western Greece, for example, and the Aegean islanders of Spétsai and Hydra, were originally of pure Albanian stock. "The Greece of the classical heritage and of the romantic philhellene has gone, and anyhow has always been irrelevant to the Greek situation," writes Philip Sherrard, a translator of modern Greek poetry. "Greece…never had any Middle Ages, as we understand them, or any Renaissance, as we understand it, or an Age of Enlightenment. That elevation of reason over the rest of life had not taken place."

Greece is Europe's last port of call, where the Balkans begin to be dissolved completely by the East. As such, approaching from the opposite direction, Greece is also where the oxygen of the West begins to diffuse the crushing and abstract logic of the Mesopotamian and Egyptian deserts. This, after all, was the ultimate achievement of Periclean Athens (and by extension, of the West): to breathe humanism—compassion for the individual—into the inhumanity of the East, which was at that time emblemized by the tyrannies of ancient Egypt, Persia, and Babylonia. At the National Archaeological Museum in Athens, I saw this process at work, as the fierce and impersonal statues of the Early and Middle Bronze Ages, bearing the heavy influence of Pharaonic Egypt, gradually, feature by rounded feature, metamorphosed over two millennia into the uplifting beauty and idealism of classical Greek sculpture.

Classical Greece of the first millennium B.C. invented the West by humanizing the East. Greece accomplished this by concentrating its artistic and philosophical energies on the release of the human spirit, on the individual's struggle to find meaning in the world. Meanwhile, in Persia, for example, art existed to glorify an omnipotent ruler. But Greece was always part of the East, albeit on its western fringe. To see Greece in its true Oriental light is to recognize the magnitude of the ancient Greeks' achievement.

Moreover, understanding Greece's historic role as the ideological battleground between East and West lends a deeper insight into the process by which Western democracy and values, in our era, can influence the political systems of the Third World. Greece is the eternal sieve, through which the assaults of the East on the West, and of the West on the East, must pass and immediately deposit their residue.

"Welcome back to the Orient," said Sotiris Papapoulitis, a leading member of Greece's conservative New Democracy party, as he treated me to an expensive seafood lunch at a restaurant in the port city of Piraeus, adjacent to Athens. I had just arrived by bus from Salonika. "But in the Orient," Papapoulitis cautioned me, "you must never confuse an open heart with an open mind."

Papapoulitis was referring to himself. In the fall to 1990, he was engaged in an ultimately unsuccessful bid to be elected mayor of Piraeus. He was flamboyant, sophisticated, and naive, and narrow-minded all at once. He was the kind of fellow who could quote from Descartes and believe a conspiracy theory, while wearing a tight shirt open to his navel. Papapoulitis knew this and relished the fact that his very personality, like the scene around us—yachts, blue sea, sunshine, mountains of seafood, inefficiency, and chaos— constituted the perfect synthesis of the Balkans, the Mediterranean, the European West, and the Levantine East.

"I hate the term *Greek*. It is a corruption of a Turkish word for dog or slave," Papapoulitis exclaimed for all the customers to hear. "Call me a *Hellene*. Call me a *Romios* even. But don't call me a Greek."

Hellene was what the ancient Greek called himself, and it has come to symbolize a Greek (or that part of the Greek psyche) whose roots are in the West. *Romios* literally means Roman, and refers to a Greek of the Eastern Roman Empire (often referred to as Byzantium), whose roots are in the East. Patrick Leigh Fermor, a British travel writer with an unrivaled knowledge of the Greek language and culture, identified more than sixty characteristics and

symbols that distinguish the Hellene mentality from the Romios
mentality. Whereas the Hellene relies on principle and logic, the
Romios relies on instinct;
whereas the Hellene sees
Greece as being part of Europe,
the Romios sees Greece as
lying outside Europe; whereas
the Hellene is a man of
enlightened disbelief, the
Romios believes in the mira-
cle-working properties of
icons; whereas the Hellene
follows a Western code of
honor, the Romios evinces a
lack of scruples for achieving
personal ends; and so on....
Obviously, as was the case
with Papapoulitis and so many
other Greeks I knew, both the
Hellene and Romios aspects
of the Greek personality
could exist side by side within
the same person.

Fermor, like many phil-
hellenes ("foreign lovers of
Greece"), was keenly aware of
Greece's Oriental aspect. A
case in point: Lord Byron, the
nineteenth-century Roman-
tic poet and volunteer in the
Greek War of Independence,
destested scholars of classical
Greece, whom he called
"emasculated fogies" full of
"antiquarian twaddle." Byron's
philhellenic commitment was

Pericles placed the sculptor
in charge of the Parthenon's
construction above the architects
Ictinus and Callicrates. The aim
was not so much an architectural
triumph as a peerless wedding
of architecture and sculptural
decoration—it turned out to
be both.

The marble sculptures were
so many that few if any could
have been carved by Phidias
himself, but he was the director
and possibly the designer of
them all. Apart from the two
great pediment groupings,
ninety-two panels on the
metopes (spaces between
grooved blocks, triglyphs, above
the columns) depicted the over-
coming of Centaurs by Lapiths
(warriors of Thessaly), giants by
gods, Amazons by Greeks. All
but two of the forty remaining
in situ are so eroded the eye can
make hardly anything of them.
Fifteen of the best and best-
preserved are among the Elgin
Marbles in the British Museum.

—Colin Simpson, *Greece:
The Unclouded Eye*

based on a true vision of the country, not on a myth. As for the squabbling Greek guerrilla fighters he encountered in the mosquito-infested swamps of western Greece in the 1820s, the English poet observed: "Their life is a struggle against truth; they are vicious in their defense." Kazantzakis, who was not a foreigner, also had no doubts about the true soul of Greece: "The modern Greek...when he begins to sing...breaks the crust of Greek logic; all at once the East, all darkness and mystery, rises up from deep within him."

For Western tourists and admirers of Greece, the country's crown symbol would have to be the Parthenon, erected by Pericles in the fifth century B.C.— the golden age of Athenian democracy, the period of Greek history with which all of us in the West are familiar. In school, we learned about how the Minoan and Mycenaean civilizations developed over several centuries into the Greek city-states, among them Athens and Sparta, which fought wars against each other and against the Persians, a people who at the time represented the "barbarous East." We learned how Greek culture survived and was spread through the conquests of a Greek Macedonian Alexander the Great. And we are generally aware of the scope and grandeur of ancient Greek history: how the world of Homer's *Iliad* and *Odyssey*, associated with Mycenaean culture of the second millennium B.C., is separated by nearly a thousand years from the world of Socrates, Plato, and Aristotle. Greek history, as we in the West have been taught it, is a long and inspiring saga. Unfortunately, this great saga was just one element in Greece's past, and the past did not end when the Dark Ages began. For what admirers of ancient Greece consider the Dark Ages was, in truth, the beginning of another period of Greek grandeur, that of Byzantium.

Thus, for the Greeks themselves, another building, far from the Parthenon—indeed, standing outside the borders of present-day Greece altogether—elicits far deeper surges of emotion and nostalgia.

The Greeks, like other Orthodox Christian peoples, are fixated on their churches, which are not only places of workship but treasure houses of their material culture that survived the awful cen-

turies of Ottoman rule. C. P. Cavafy, the greatest modern Greek
poet, described this feeling in his poem "In Church":

> ...when I enter a Greek church,
> the fragrance of its incenses,
> the voices of the liturgy and harmonies of sound,
> the orderly appearance of the priests,
> each moving to most solemn rhythm,
> all garbed in vestments most magnificent,
> recall to mind the glories of our race,
> the greatness of our old Byzantine days.

And among Greek churches, one above all stands out: the
Church of Hagia Sophia, or "Divine Wisdom," built in the middle
of the sixth century A.D. by the Byzantine Emperor Justinian and
rising majestically—flat, wide dome mounting a chorus of semi-
domes and flaring buttresses, as though in an act of levitation—over
the scummy waters of Seraglio Point in Constantinople (Istanbul).
Even today, stripped of its gold and silver, with its frescoes faded
and begrimed, there is arguably no building in all the world whose
interior conjures up such a sense of boundless wealth and mystical
power. I visited Hagia Sophia several times in the 1980s. Each time,
I instinctively knew that the political passions of modern Greece
might be explained here—much more than at the Parthenon.
Passing through the imperial door toward the main dome, I always
felt as though I were inside a great indoor city of marble walls,
galleries, and colonnades, and of mosaics, with vast, ambiguous
spaces lurking in the peripheries. Hagia Sophia became the prototype for all Orthodox cathedrals, for St. Mark's Church in Venice,
and for mosques throughout Turkey.

But Hagia Sophia is no longer a church. It is the Turkish
"Museum of Aya Sofya." In place of bells, incense, and priests are
massive round, green plaques hung above the wall corners, that bear
Arabic inscriptions, saying "Allah Is Great." Although Greek tourists
travel to Turkey to visit the "Museum of Aya Sofya," many come
home unsettled by the experience, and the overwhelming majority

of Greeks cannot bring themselves even to go. "The idea of going to our church in what for us was the greatest of Greek cities and seeing those Muslim signs, I cannot tell you how it would make me feel. It is something terrible," an Athenian friend once told me. Istanbul will forever be Constantinoupoli in Greek eyes, even if "Constantine's city" no longer exists. Greeks cannot bring themselves to say the word *Istanbul*. Upon hearing it on the lips of a foreigner, they wince much as Israelis wince at the word *Palestine*, or many Arabs wince at the word *Israel*. His Holiness, Bartholomew, the Patriarch of the Greek Orthodox Church, sits not in Athens, but in Constantinoupoli, in a wood-framed building amid narrow, dirty lanes. This is all that remains of Byzantium, a civilization and an empire created in A.D. 324, as the successor to Rome, and destroyed more than 1,100 years later by an invading army of Ottoman Turks in 1453. During those eleven centuries, the Byzantine Empire was a Greek empire, and Greece then was much more than the classical Mediterranean culture with which the West is familiar: it was a northerly cultural realm of

In one respect the ancient Greeks were always a divided people. They entered the Mediterranean world in small groups and even when they settled and took control they remained disunited in their political organization...Greek settlements were to be found not only all over the area of modern Hellas but also along the Black Sea, on the shores of what is now Turkey, in southern Italy and eastern Sicily, the north African coast and the littoral of southern France. Within this ellipse of some fifteen hundred miles at the poles, there were hundreds and hundreds of communities, often differing in their political structure and always insisting on their separate sovereignties. Neither then, nor at any time in the ancient world was there a nation, a single national territory under one sovereign rule, called Greece (or any synonym for Greece).

—M. I. Finley

unimaginable depth and texture, whose influence spread to medieval Muscovy.

But the Turks smashed it all. That is why Hagia Sophia expresses in stone and marble what Greeks cry out silently in their hearts: *We have lost so much, not one inch more, not Macedonia, not anything more will we lose!*

The pain of this loss was sharpened by the modern experience of war and exile. George Seferis, the Nobel Prize-winning Greek poet, writes in "The House Near the Sea":

> The houses I had they took away from me. The times happened to be unpropitious: war, destruction, exile.

The cause of Seferis's suffering was the Greek-Turkish War of 1922—the final event in the series of Balkan military struggles (beginning with the 1877 Russo-Turkish War in Bulgaria) that dominated news headlines from the last quarter of the nineteenth century through the first quarter of the twentieth, and set the boundaries of the Balkans more or less as they were in 1990, on the eve of the Yugoslav civil war.

The Ottoman Turks had ejected the Byzantine Greeks from Constantinople in the fifteenth century, large Greek communities survived in Istanbul and along the western shore of Asia Minor—particularly in the city of Smyrna—through the end of World War I. The dismemberment of the Ottoman Empire in the wake of World War I provided the Greeks (who had sided with the victorious Allies) an opportunity to regain this lost territory, where over a million ethnic Greeks still lived. But the Greeks wanted even more. For years, the British prime minister and romantic philhellene, Lloyd George, had encouraged them to believe that, whatever Greece did, the Western Allies would certainly support a Christian nation and the heir to ancient Greece against the Muslim Turks. This naive trust, fortified by spreading anarchy in Turkey following the collapse of the Sultanate, caused the Greeks to embark upon their Megali Idea, the "Great Idea": the return of every inch of historic Greece to the motherland. Again there was the same old Balkan revanchist syndrome: each nation claiming as its natural territory all the lands that it held at the time of its great historical expansion.

In 1921, the Greek army, against all military logic, advanced beyond the Greek-populated western coast of Asia Minor, and deep into the mountainous Anatolian interior, only 150 miles from Ankara. This move made the army's supply lines so weak and disorganized as to be nonexistent. A reporter for the *Toronto Daily Star*, Ernest Hemingway, writes that the Greek officers "did not know a god-damned thing," while the Greek troops came to battle in the ceremonial, nineteenth-century uniform of "white ballet skirts and upturned shoes with pom-poms on them."

At that point, in August 1922, the ruthless and charismatic young Turkish general Kemal Ataturk, who was in the midst of whipping together a new Turkish republic out of the anarchic morass of the Ottoman Empire, unleashed his forces. Hemingway writes that the Turks advanced

---

Every time I hear of the Smyrna catastrophe, of the stultification of manhood worked on the members of the armed forces of the great powers who stood idly by under strict command of their leaders while thousands of innocent men, women, and children were driven into the water like cattle, shot at, mutilated, burned alive, their hands chopped off when they tried to climb aboard a foreign vessel, I think of that preliminary warning which I saw always in French cinemas: "Warning to this effect: the public is urgently requested not to display any undue emotion upon the presentation of these horripilating scenes"...

Such was Europe before the present debacle [WWII]. Such is America today. And such it will be tomorrow when the smoke has cleared away. And as long as human beings can sit and watch with hands folded while their fellow men are tortured and butchered so long will civilization be a hollow mockery, a wordy phantom suspended like a mirage above a swelling sea of murdered carcasses.

—Henry Miller, *The Colossus of Maroussi (1941)*

"steadily and lumpily." In only ten days, Ataturk drove the Greek army back to the Aegean coast, where Greek troops deserted to off-shore ships, leaving the Greek population of Smyrna exposed to fire and the Turkish soldiery. The Greek dead numbered 30,000. In the massive population exchange that followed, 400,000 Turks from Greek Thrace marched into Turkey, and 1,250,000 Greeks from Asia Minor went into exile in Greece—homeless, ill-clothed, and starving—increasing the population of Greece by 20 percent. The refugees overwhelmed Salonika and more than tripled the size of Athens.

Concurrently, 3,000 years of Greek civilization in Asia Minor came to an end. Smyrna became a Turkish city and was renamed Izmir. Greece was again small, insecure, reeling with poverty, utterly humiliated, and seething with hate. The dictatorial regimes of the 1920s and 1930s in Athens provided no stabilizing outlet for such emotions. Then came the horrors of the Nazi invasion and occupa-tion, which left 8 percent of the population dead, a million homeless, and the countryside destroyed. Greek resistance against the Nazis was widespread, but the guerrilla movement it spawned was as divided as it was heroic. All of these divisions boiled over in the 1946–1949 Greek Civil War, which saw even more casualties and destruction in Greece than had the war against the Nazis.

The United States backed the royalist Greek government in Athens, while the Soviet Union and its allies backed the Communist insurgents in the countryside. It was the first and last Cold War counterinsurgency that the American-backed side won outright. However, the civil war in Greece was about much more than capitalism versus Communism.

Capitalism had never really existed in Greece, which in the mid-twentieth century was a poor Oriental society of refugees in which a small number of rapacious landowners and ship owners exploited everyone else, and where a middle class barely existed. The American-backed Greek government was characterized by corruption and pointless intrigue. Its supporters had only a vague notion of democracy and a free press, and they numbered more than a few former Nazi sympathizers. They were Western only in the sense that they aspired to be Western. The Greek Communists, meanwhile, had a completely different historical orientation—seeing Russia and the Kremlin not only as beacons of an ideology they supported, but as a second motherland that, since the fall of Byzantium in 1453, had served as the protector of the Eastern Orthodox nations against the Turks. It may be no accident that the first proxy battle of the Cold War, the archetypal East-West struggle, occurred on Greek soil

In the learning centers of the West, however, the most recent 2,000 years of Greek history were virtually ignored in favor of an idealized version of ancient Greece, a civilization that had already died before Jesus's birth. The West would not accept that Greece was more a child of Byzantium and Turkish despotism than of Periclean Athens. As a result, few Westerners could understand what began happening in Greece in the 1980s, an era when Greece's former Prime Minister and President, Constantine Karamanlis, described the country as a "vast lunatic asylum."

Robert D. Kaplan also contributed "Teach Me, Zorba" in Part One. This story was excerpted from Balkan Ghosts: A Journey Through History.

PART FIVE

THE LAST WORD

DONALD W. GEORGE

In Love, In Greece, In the Springtime

In the end, perhaps Greece exists
mainly in our minds.

IT HAPPENS AT SOME POINT EVERY SPRING: I WILL BE DRIVING
innocently along some rural route, and suddenly a certain slant of
sunlight will recall the way the light filtered through the pine
trees along the road that wound up the coast from Athens to the
little taverna no one seemed to know about—no one except
Gisela, the beautiful and mysterious woman with whom I had fallen
ineluctably in love that spring so many years ago.

We would install ourselves in peeling white wooden chairs
around a stolid wooden table on the beach, under the pines, and the
kindly taverna owner would bring us huge chunks of hard, delicious
bread, a salad of feta cheese, tomatoes, cucumbers, and black olives,
and glasses of retsina.

We would eat and sip, but mostly we would watch the shimmering sea and listen to the sighing pines, censing the air with their
tangy perfume.

I re-create this scene, and suddenly that whole mind-opening,
life-transforming Grecian year revives in a sun-flooded succession
of images:

I recall the breath-stopping, time-skipping beauty of just-
blossomed scarlet poppies against white marble ruins at Olympia.

305

I recall the Peloponnese mountain family who insisted on sharing their meager Easter feast with my parents and me.

I recall the ethereal geometry and bony patina of the Acropolis at dawn, before the tourists arrived; and the soul-stirring rite of reading Plato, Socrates, and Aristotle as Apollo's first rays illumined the site.

I recall unfathomable connections on the island of Crete—the magical frescoes and sere splendors of Knossos, and the painter from Chania who showed me the island's harbors and meadows, churches and town squares through his eyes.

I recall the craggy monasteries and worldly monks of sacred Mount Athos, and the sensual abandon of the long, embracing beach at Líndos, on Rhodes, where I communed for a week with a ragtag band of European pilgrims who were all seeking some sort of Aegean answer.

Aegean answers: hungrily, hesitantly, I would unfold for Gisela my despairs and my dreams, but mostly I would talk about Greece: about the clarity of the rock and the light and how it was teaching me to attend to the present; about the earthy kindness I had encountered everywhere; about the sheer *age* of the sites and the accumulation of wisdom and sadness and celebration that seemed to hang poignant in the Attic air.

Summer came and I left—for Africa and then graduate school, a long, winding road. I never wrote to her, never heard from her.

Now, half of my life later, I wonder: do we craft our memories, or do our memories craft us?

Now, half of my life later, I know: I went to Greece seeking the roots of Western civilization, and returned with a rootlessness I have never lost.

And every spring the owner shuffles toward us, bearing a laden tray. The sea shimmers. The pines sense and sigh.

The Attic sunlight gleams again in Gisela's laughing eyes.

⋆

Donald W. George was travel editor at the San Francisco Examiner *for nine years and founder and editor of "Wanderlust,"* Salon.com*'s award-winning travel site, from 1997 to 2000. He is currently Yahoo!* Travel's *writer-at-large, writing a weekly column which appears on Yahoo! and in newspapers throughout North America. He co-edited* Travelers' Tales Japan *and edited* Salon.com*'s* Wanderlust: Real-Life Tales of Adventure and Romance. *He lived in Greece as a Teaching Fellow at Athens College from 1975 to 1976—and returns frequently in his mind.*

Recommended Reading

Davey, Lawrence. *Going After Feta*. Damariscotta, Maine: Nathaniel Austin Publishing, 1994.

Davidson, James N. *Courtesans and Fishcakes: The Consuming Passions of Classical Athens*. New York: HarperPerennial, 1997.

Durrell, Gerald Malcolm. *My Family and Other Animals*. New York: Viking Press, 1979.

Durrell, Lawrence. *The Greek Islands*. New York: A Studio Book, 1978.

Durrell, Lawrence. *Prospero's Cell: A Guide to the Landscape and Manners of the Island of Corcyra*. New York: Marlowe & Company, 1996.

Durrell, Lawrence. *Reflections on a Marine Venus: A Companion to the Landscape of Rhodes*. New York: Marlowe & Company, 1996.

Eisner, Robert. *Travelers to an Antique Land: The History and Literature of Travel to Greece*. Ann Arbor: The University of Michigan Press, 1993.

Fermor, Patrick Leigh. *Mani: Travels in the Southern Peloponnese*. Magnolia, Mass. Peter Smith Publisher, Inc., 1987.

Fermor, Patrick Leigh. *Roumeli: Travels in Northern Greece*. New York: Viking Penguin, 1989.

Gage, Nicholas. *Eleni*. New York: Ballantine Books, 1983.

Galt, George. *Trailing Pythagoras*. Dunvegan, Ontario: Quadrant Editions, 1982.

Graves, Robert. *The Greek Myths*. New York: Penguin Books, 1993.

Greenhalgh, Peter and Edward Eliopoulis. *Deep into Mani: Journey to the Southern Tip of Greece*. New York: Farber & Farber, Inc., 1985.

Halliburton, Richard. *Book of Marvels: The Occident.* New York: The Bobbs-Merrill Company, 1937.

Hiestand, Emily. *The Very Rich Hours: Travels in Orkney, Belize, the Everglades, and Greece.* Boston: Beacon Press, 1992.

Horton, Andrew. *Bones in the Sea: Time Apart on a Greek Island.* New Orleans: Grand Illusion Production, 1997.

Kaplan, Robert D. *Balkan Ghosts: A Journey Through History.* New York: Vintage Departures, 1993.

Keeley, Edmund. *Inventing Paradise: The Greek Journey.* New York: Farrar, Straus & Giroux, 1999.

Keeley, Edmund, and Philip Sherrard., trans. *George Seferis: Collected Poems.* Princeton: Princeton University Press, 1995.

Kizilos, Katherine. *The Olive Grove: Travels in Greece.* Hawthorn, Australia: Lonely Planet Publications, 1997.

Miller, Henry. *The Colossus of Maroussi.* New York: A New Directions Paperbook, 1941.

Pfister, Patrick. *Pilgrimage: Tales from the Open Road.* Chicago: Academy Chicago Publishers, 1995.

Raeburn, Nancy. *Mykonos: A Memoir.* Minneapolis: New Rivers Press, 1992.

Simpson, Colin. *Greece: The Unclouded Eye.* New York: Fielding Publications, Inc., 1968.

Slater, Philip E. *The Glory of Hera.* Boston: Beacon Press, 1985.

Storace, Patricia. *Dinner with Persephone.* New York: Pantheon Books, 1996.

Stumpf, Samuel Enoch. *Socrates to Sartre: A History of Philosophy.* New York: McGraw Hill Book Company, 1999.

Theroux, Paul. *The Pillars of Hercules.* New York: G. P. Putnam's Sons, 1995.

Wood, Michael. *In the Footsteps of Alexander the Great.* Berkeley: University of California Press, 1997.

Index

311

Index of Contributors

Acknowledgments

We would like to thank our families and friends for their usual forbearance while we are putting a book together. Thanks also to Lisa Bach, Susan Brady, Deborah Greco, Raj Khadka, Jennifer Leo, Natanya Pearlman, Tara Austen Weaver, Patty Holden, Tim O'Reilly, Michele Wetherbee, Judy Johnson, and Michelle Snider.

—Larry Habegger and Sean O'Reilly

Heartfelt thanks to my wife, Shelley; Francesca Hayslett and Joyce Davidson for good company; Meredith Pillon who knows Greece as well as anybody who is not actually Greek; and the old man on the Athens sidewalk who bear-hugged me, kissed both my cheeks, and told me he loved America, especially Detroit.

—Brian Alexander

"The Land of Light" by Lawrence Durrell excerpted from pages 16–35 of *The Greek Islands* by Lawrence Durrell (Rainbird 1978). Copyright © 1978 by Lawrence Durrell. Used by permission of Viking Penguin, a division of Penguin Putnam, Inc., and Penguin Books, Ltd., London, UK.

"Marble Girls" by Patricia Storace excerpted from *Dinner with Persephone* by Patricia Storace. Copyright © 1996 by Patricia Storace. Reprinted by permission of Pantheon Books, a division of Random House, Inc., and the author.

Yásas! by Susan M. Tiberghien reprinted from the February 1987 issue of *Resident Abroad*. Copyright © 1987 by Susan M. Tiberghien. Reprinted by permission from the author.

"Sappho's Island" by Katherine Kizilos excerpted from *The Olive Grove: Travels in Greece* by Katherine Kizilos. Copyright © 1997 by Katherine Kizilos. Reprinted by permission of Lonely Planet Publications.

"Hector's Bread" by Rachel Howard reprinted from the September/October 1998 issue of *Odyssey*. Copyright © 1998 by Rachel Howard. Reprinted by permission of the author.

"Teach Me, Zorba" by Robert D. Kaplan excerpted from *Balkan Ghosts: A Journey Through History* by Robert D. Kaplan. Copyright © 1993 by Robert D. Kaplan. Reprinted by permission of St. Martin's Press, LLC.

permission of the author.

"The Apocalyptic Island" by Alan Linn originally appeared as "Patmos" reprinted from the August 1992 issue of *Travel & Leisure*. Copyright © 1992 by Alan Linn. Reprinted by permission of the author.

"The Ravens and the Virgin" by Tom Joyce published with permission from the author. Copyright © 2000 by Tom Joyce.

"Naxos Nights" by Laurie Gough first appeared in *SALON.com* at http://www.salon.com. Copyright © 1994 by Laurie Gough. Reprinted by permission of the author.

"A Breathtaking View" by Robert Peirce published with permission from the author. Copyright © 2000 by Robert Peirce.

"The Marble Island" by Lawrence Davey excerpted from *Going After Feta* by Lawrence Davey. Copyright © 1994 by Lawrence Davey. Reprinted by permission of Nathaniel Austin Publishing and the author.

"The Crones" by Emily Hiestand excerpted from *The Very Rich Hours: Travels in Orkney, Belize, the Everglades, and Greece* by Emily Hiestand. Copyright © 1992 by Emily Hiestand. Reprinted by permission on Beacon Press Boston.

"On the Way Home" by Kathryn Makris published with permission from the author. Copyright © 2000 by Kathryn Makris.

"Embracing the Fates" by Joel Simon published with permission from the author. Copyright © 2000 by Joel Simon.

"Tongue-Tied and Bottoming Out" by Jim Molnar originally appeared as "Tongue-Tied: Bottoming Out in Greece" reprinted from the November 20, 1994 issue of *The Seattle Times*. Copyright © 1994 by Jim Molnar. Reprinted by permission of *The Seattle Times*.

"The Mad Priest of Lésvos" by Patrick Pfister excerpted from *Pilgrimage: Tales from the Open Road* by Patrick Pfister. Copyright © 1995 by Patrick Pfister. Reprinted by permission of Academy Chicago Publishers.

"Workers of the World" by Stephanie Marohn published with permission from the author. Copyright © 2000 by Stephanie Marohn.

"Searching for Eleni" by Nicholas Gage excerpted from *Eleni* by Nicholas Gage. Copyright © 1983 by Nicolas Gage. Reprinted by permission of Ballantine Books, a division of Random House, Inc.

"Farewell to Salonika" by Robert D. Kaplan excerpted from *Balkan Ghosts: A Journey Through History* by Robert D. Kaplan. Copyright © 1993 by Robert D. Kaplan. Reprinted by permission of St. Martin's Press, LLC.

"In Love, In Greece, In the Springtime" by Donald W. George reprinted from the March 13, 1994 issue of the *San Francisco Examiner*. Copyright © 1994 by Donald W. George. Reprinted by permission of the *San Francisco Examiner*.

Additional Credits (arranged alphabetically by title)

Selection from "Athens, Look Closer" by Alan Brown reprinted from the May 2000 issue of *Travel & Leisure*. Copyright © 2000 by American Express Publishing Corporation. All rights reserved.

Selections from *Bones in the Sea: Time Apart on a Greek Island* by Andrew Horton

Selection from "Pie in the Sky" by Roberta Beach Jacobson published with permission from the author. Copyright © 2000 by Roberta Beach Jacobson.

Selection from "The Ravens and the Virgin" by Tom Joyce published with permission from the author. Copyright © 2000 by Tom Joyce.

Selection from "Season's End" by Lisa Moskowitz published with permission from the author. Copyright © 2000 by Lisa Moskowitz.

Selection from "Thoughts on the Apocalypse" by Brian Alexander published with permission from the author. Copyright © 2000 by Brian Alexander.

Selection from "Three Days at the Pink Palace" by Tara Austen Weaver published with permission from the author. Copyright © 2000 by Tara Austen Weaver.

Selection from "Thrush" by George Seferis excerpted from *George Seferis: Collected Poems* translated by Edmund Keeley and Philip Sherrard. Copyright © 1967 by Princeton University Press, 1980 by Edmund Keeley and Philip Sherrard, Greek © 1972, 1976 by M. Seferiades.

Selection from *Trailing Pythagoras* by George Galt copyright © 1982 by George Galt. Published by Quadrant Editions, Dunvegan, Ontario.

About the Editors

Larry Habegger has been writing about travel since 1980. He has visited almost fifty countries and six of the seven continents, traveling from the frozen arctic to equatorial rain forest, the high Himalayas to the Dead Sea. With coauthor James O'Reilly, he wrote a serialized mystery novel and several short stories for the *San Francisco Examiner* in the early 1980s, and since 1985 their syndicated column, "World Travel Watch," has appeared in major newspapers in five countries and on Internet-based information centers. He was a founding editor of Travelers' Tales and currently serves as executive editor. He was born and raised in Minnesota and lives with his family on Telegraph Hill in San Francisco.

Sean O'Reilly is a former seminarian, stockbroker, and prison instructor who lives in Arizona with his wife Brenda and their five small boys. He's had a life-long interest in philosophy and theology, and is at work on a book called *How to Manage Your Dick: A Guide for the Soul*, which makes the proposition that classic Greek, Roman, and Christian moral philosophies, allied with post-quantum physics, form the building blocks of a new ethics and psychology. Widely traveled, Sean most recently completed an 18,000-mile van journey around the United States, sharing the treasures of the open road with his family. He is editor-at-large and director of international sales for Travelers' Tales.

Brian Alexander's understanding of Greece was originally based on the film *Never on Sunday*, and tales from Alexander the Great from whom he imagined he was descended. Disappointed to learn that Alexander the Great was not only not Greek, but never made it to Scotland, from which the editor's forbears hailed, Alexander decided to visit Greece himself. Then to visit it again. And again.

The first thing he learned was to never argue with a Greek. The second was to dribble a little water in your ouzo.

Alexander is the author of *Green Cathedrals: A Wayward Traveler in the Rain Forest* (Lyons Press, New York). His writing has appeared in *The New York Times*, *Wired*, *Esquire*, *National Geographic Adventure*, *Outside*, *Science*, the *Los Angeles Times*, and many other publications.

TRAVELERS' TALES

THE SOUL OF TRAVEL

Footsteps Series

KITE STRINGS OF THE SOUTHERN CROSS

A Woman's Travel Odyssey
By Laurie Gough
ISBN 1-885211-54-6
$14.95
"Gough's poetic and sensual string of tales richly evokes the unexpected rewards—and perils—of the traveler's life. A striking, moving debut." —Salon.com

— ★ ★ ★ —

ForeWord Silver Medal Winner
—Travel Book of the Year

THE SWORD OF HEAVEN

A Five Continent Odyssey to Save the World
By Mikkel Aaland
ISBN 1-885211-44-9
$24.00 (cloth)
"Few books capture the soul of the road like *The Sword of Heaven*, a sharp-edged, beautifully rendered memoir that will inspire anyone."
—Phil Cousineau, author of *The Art of Pilgrimage*

STORM

A Motorcycle Journey of Love, Endurance, and Transformation
By Allen Noren
ISBN 1-885211-45-7
$24.00 (cloth)
"Beautiful, tumultuous, deeply engaging, and very satisfying."
—Ted Simon, author of *Jupiter's Travels*

TAKE ME WITH YOU

A Round-the-World Journey to Invite a Stranger Home
By Brad Newsham
ISBN 1-885211-51-1
$24.00 (cloth)
"Newsham is an ideal guide. His journey, at heart, is into humanity."
—Pico Iyer, author of *Video Night in Kathmandu*

Travelers' Tales Classics

THE ROYAL ROAD TO ROMANCE

By Richard Halliburton
ISBN 1-885211-53-8
$14.95
"Laughing at hardships, dreaming of beauty, ardent for adventure, Halliburton has managed to sing into the pages of this glorious book his own exultant spirit of youth and freedom."
—*Chicago Post*

UNBEATEN TRACKS IN JAPAN

By Isabella L. Bird
ISBN 1-885211-57-0
$14.95
Isabella Bird gained a reputation as one of the most adventurous women travelers of the 19th century with her unconventional journeys to Tibet, Canada, Korea, Turkey, Hawaii, and Japan. A fascinating read for anyone interested in women's travel, spirituality, and Asian culture.

Europe

GREECE
**True Stories of
Life on the Road**
*Edited by Larry Habegger,
Sean O'Reilly &
Brian Alexander*
ISBN 1-885211-52-X
$17.95
"This is the stuff memories
can be duplicated from."
— *Foreign Service Journal*

IRELAND
**True Stories of Life
on the Emerald Isle**
*Edited by James O'Reilly,
Larry Habegger &
Sean O'Reilly*
ISBN 1-885211-46-5
$17.95
Discover the wonder
of Ireland with Frank
McCourt, Thomas Flanagan, Nuala
O'Faolain, Rosemary Mahoney,
Colm Tóibín, and many more.

FRANCE
**True Stories of
Life on the Road**
*Edited by James O'Reilly,
Larry Habegger &
Sean O'Reilly*
ISBN 1-885211-02-3
$17.95
The French passion for
life bursts forth from every
page of this invaluable guide, featuring stories
by Peter Mayle, M.F.K. Fisher, Ina Caro, Jan
Morris, Jon Krakauer and many more.

PARIS
**True Stories of
Life on the Road**
*Edited by James O'Reilly,
Larry Habegger &
Sean O'Reilly*
ISBN 1-885211-10-4
$17.95
"If Paris is the main dish,
here is a rich and fascinat-
ing assortment of hors d'oeuvres."
—Peter Mayle, author of *A Year in Provence*

ITALY
**True Stories of
Life on the Road**
*Edited by Anne Calcagno
Introduction by Jan Morris*
ISBN 1-885211-16-3
$17.95

— ★ ★ ★ —
*ForeWord Silver
Medal Winner—
Travel Book of the Year*

SPAIN
**True Stories of
Life on the Road**
Edited by Lucy McCauley
ISBN 1-885211-07-4
$17.95
"A superb, eclectic collec-
tion that reeks wonderfully
of gazpacho and paella, and
resonates with sounds of
heel-clicking and flamenco singing."
—Barnaby Conrad, author of *Matador*

For a complete list of titles, visit our website at www.travelerstales.com

Asia/Pacific

AUSTRALIA
True Stories of
Life Down Under
Edited by Larry Habegger
ISBN 1-885211-40-6
$17.95
Explore Australia with authors Paul Theroux,
Robyn Davidson, Bruce
Chatwin, Pico Iyer, Tim
Cahill, and many more.

JAPAN
True Stories of
Life on the Road
Edited by Donald W.
George & Amy
Greimann Carlson
ISBN 1-885211-04-X
$17.95
"Readers of this entertaining anthology will be better
equipped to plot a rewarding course through
the marvelously bewildering, bewitching
cultural landscape of Japan." — *Time* (Asia)

INDIA
True Stories of
Life on the Road
Edited by James O'Reilly
& Larry Habegger
ISBN 1-885211-01-5
$17.95
"The Travelers' Tales series
should become required
reading for anyone visiting
a foreign country." —*St. Petersburg Times*

NEPAL
True Stories of
Life on the Road
Edited by Rajendra
S. Khadka
ISBN 1-885211-14-7
$17.95
"If there's one thing traditional guidebooks lack, it's
the really juicy travel information, the personal stories about back
alleys and brief encounters. This series fills
this gap." —*Diversion*

THAILAND
True Stories of
Life on the Road
Edited by James O'Reilly
& Larry Habegger
ISBN 1-885211-05-8
$17.95

— ✦ ★ ✦ —

Winner of the Lowell
Thomas Award for Best
Travel Book—Society of
American Travel Writers

HONG KONG
True Stories of
Life on the Road
Edited by James O'Reilly,
Larry Habegger &
Sean O'Reilly
ISBN 1-885211-03-1
$17.95
"Travelers' Tales Hong Kong
will delight the senses and
heighten the sensibilities, whether you are
an armchair traveler or an old China hand."
—*Profiles*

The Americas

AMERICA
**True Stories of
Life on the Road**
Edited by Fred Setterberg
ISBN 1-885211-28-7
$19.95
"Look no further.
This book is America."
—David Yeadon, author
of *Lost Worlds*

HAWAI'I
**True Stories of
the Island Spirit**
*Edited by Rick &
Marcie Carroll*
ISBN 1-885211-35-X
$17.95
"Travelers' Tales aims to
convey the excitement of
voyaging through exotic
territory with a vivacity that guidebooks can
only hint at."—*Millenium Whole Earth Catalog*

GRAND CANYON
**True Stories of Life
Below the Rim**
*Edited by Sean O'Reilly,
James O'Reilly &
Larry Habegger*
ISBN 1-885211-34-1
$17.95
"Travelers' Tales should be
required reading for anyone
who wants to truly step off the tourist track."
— *St. Petersburg Times*

SAN FRANCISCO
**True Stories of
Life on the Road**
*Edited by James O'Reilly,
Larry Habegger &
Sean O'Reilly*
ISBN 1-885211-08-2
$17.95
"Like spying on
the natives."

— *San Francisco Chronicle*

BRAZIL
**True Stories of
Life on the Road**
*Edited by Annette Haddad
& Scott Doggett
Introduction by Alex
Shoumatoff*
ISBN 1-885211-11-2
$17.95

—★ ★ ★—
*Benjamin Franklin
Silver Award Winner*

MEXICO
**True Stories of
Life on the Road**
*Edited by James O'Reilly
& Larry Habegger*
ISBN 1-885211-00-7
$17.95

—★ ★ ★—
*One of the Year's Best
Travel Books on Mexico*
—**The New York
Times**

For a complete list of titles, visit our website at www.travelerstales.com

Women's Travel

A WOMAN'S PASSION FOR TRAVEL
More True Stories from A Woman's World
Edited by Marybeth Bond & Pamela Michael
ISBN 1-885211-36-8
$17.95

"A diverse and gripping series of stories!" —Arlene Blum, author of *Annapurna: A Woman's Place*

A WOMAN'S WORLD
True Stories of Life on the Road
Edited by Marybeth Bond
Introduction by Dervla Murphy
ISBN 1-885211-06-6
$17.95

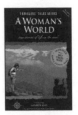

— ★ ★ ★ —
Winner of the Lowell Thomas Award for Best Travel Book— Society of American Travel Writers

WOMEN IN THE WILD
True Stories of Adventure and Connection
Edited by Lucy McCauley
ISBN 1-885211-21-X
$17.95

"A spiritual, moving, and totally female book to take you around the world and back." —*Mademoiselle*

A MOTHER'S WORLD
Journeys of the Heart
Edited by Marybeth Bond & Pamela Michael
ISBN 1-885211-26-0
$14.95

"These stories remind us that motherhood is one of the great unifying forces in the world" —*San Francisco Examiner*

Spiritual Travel

A WOMAN'S PATH
Women's Best Spiritual Travel Writing
Edited by Lucy McCauley, Amy G. Carlson & Jennifer Leo
ISBN 1-885211-48-1
$16.95

"A sensitive exploration of women's lives that have been unexpectedly and spiritually touched by travel experiences…highly recommended."
—*Library Journal*

THE ULTIMATE JOURNEY
Inspiring Stories of Living and Dying
James O'Reilly, Sean O'Reilly & Richard Sterling
ISBN 1-885211-38-4
$17.95

"A glorious collection of writings about the ultimate adventure. A book to keep by one's bedside—and close to one's heart." —Philip Zaleski, editor, *The Best Spiritual Writing* series

THE ROAD WITHIN:
True Stories of Transformation and the Soul
Edited by Sean O'Reilly, James O'Reilly & Tim O'Reilly
ISBN 1-885211-19-8
$17.95

— ★ ★ ★ —
Best Spiritual Book—Independent Publisher's Book Award

PILGRIMAGE
Adventures of the spirit
Edited by Sean O'Reilly & James O'Reilly
Introduction by Phil Cousineau
ISBN 1-885211-56-2
$16.95
A diverse array of spirit-renewing journeys—trips to world-famous sites as well as places sacred, related by pilgrims of all kinds.

Adventure

TESTOSTERONE PLANET
True Stories from a Man's World
Edited by Sean O'Reilly, Larry Habegger & James O'Reilly
ISBN 1-885211-43-0
$17.95

Thrills and laughter with some of today's best writers: Sebastian Junger, Tim Cahill, Bill Bryson, Jon Krakauer, and Frank McCourt.

DANGER!
True Stories of Trouble and Survival
Edited by James O'Reilly, Larry Habegger & Sean O'Reilly
ISBN 1-885211-32-5
$17.95

"Exciting...for those who enjoy living on the edge or prefer to read the survival stories of others, this is a good pick." —*Library Journal*

Travel Humor

NOT SO FUNNY WHEN IT HAPPENED
The Best of Travel Humor and Misadventure
Edited by Tim Cahill
ISBN 1-885211-55-4
$12.95

Laugh with Bill Bryson, Dave Barry, Anne Lamott, Adair Lara, Doug Lansky, and many more.

THERE'S NO TOILET PAPER...ON THE ROAD LESS TRAVELED
The Best of Travel Humor and Misadventure
Edited by Doug Lansky
ISBN 1-885211-27-9
$12.95

— ★ ★ ★ —
Humor Book of the Year —Independent Publisher's Book Award

Food

THE ADVENTURE OF FOOD
True Stories of Eating Everything
Edited by Richard Sterling
ISBN 1-885211-37-6
$17.95

"These stories are bound to whet appetites for more than food."
—*Publishers Weekly*

FOOD
A Taste of the Road
Edited by Richard Sterling
Introduction by Margo True
ISBN 1-885211-09-0
$17.95

Sumptious stories by M.F.K. Fisher, David Yeadon, P.J. O'Rourke, Colin Thubron, and many more.

— ★ ★ ★ —
Silver Medal Winner of the Lowell Thomas Award for Best Travel Book—Society of American Travel Writers

Special Interest

THE GIFT OF RIVERS
True Stories of Life on the Water
Edited by Pamela Michael
Introduction by Robert Hass
ISBN 1-885211-42-2
$14.95

"*The Gift of Rivers* is a soulful fact- and image-filled compendium of wonderful stories that illuminate, educate, inspire and delight. One cannot read this compelling anthology without coming away in awe of the strong hold rivers exert on human imagination and history."
—David Brower, Chairman of Earth Island Institute

THE GIFT OF TRAVEL
The Best of Travelers' Tales
Edited by Larry Habegger,
James O'Reilly &
Sean O'Reilly
ISBN 1-885211-25-2
$14.95

"Like gourmet chefs in a French market, the editors of Travelers' Tales pick, sift, and prod their way through the weighty shelves of contemporary travel writing, creaming off the very best."
—William Dalrymple, author of *City of Djinns*

FAMILY TRAVEL
The Farther You Go, the Closer You Get
Edited by Laura Manske
ISBN 1-885211-33-3
$17.95

"This is family travel at its finest." —*Working Mother*

LOVE & ROMANCE
True Stories of Passion on the Road
Edited by Judith Babcock Wylie
ISBN 1-885211-18-X
$17.95

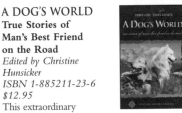

"A wonderful book to read by a crackling fire."
—*Romantic Traveling*

THE GIFT OF BIRDS
True Encounters with Avian Spirits
Edited by Larry Habegger
& Amy G. Carlson
ISBN 1-885211-41-4
$17.95

"These are all wonderful, entertaining stories offering a *birds-eye view!* of our avian friends."
—*Booklist*

A DOG'S WORLD
True Stories of Man's Best Friend on the Road
Edited by Christine Hunsicker
ISBN 1-885211-23-6
$12.95

This extraordinary collection includes stories by John Steinbeck, Helen Thayer, James Herriot, Pico Iyer, and many others. A must for any dog and travel lover.

Submit Your Own Travel Tale

Do you have a tale of your own that you would like to submit to Travelers' Tales? For submission guidelines and a list of titles in the works, send a SASE to:

Travelers' Tales Submission Guidelines
330 Townsend Street, Suite 208, San Francisco, CA 94107

You may also send email to *guidelines@travelerstales.com* or visit our Web site at *www.travelerstales.com*

Travel Advice

SHITTING PRETTY
How to Stay Clean and Healthy While Traveling
By Dr. Jane Wilson-Howarth
ISBN 1-885211-47-3
$12.95

A light-hearted book about a serious subject for millions of travelers— staying healthy on the road—written by international health expert, Dr. Jane Wilson-Howarth.

THE FEARLESS SHOPPER
How to Get the Best Deals on the Planet
By Kathy Borrus
ISBN 1-885211-39-2
$14.95

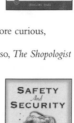

"Anyone who reads *The Fearless Shopper* will come away a smarter, more responsible shopper and a more curious, culturally attuned traveler."

—Jo Mancuso, *The Shopologist*

THE PENNY PINCHER'S PASSPORT TO LUXURY TRAVEL
The Art of Cultivating Preferred Customer Status
By Joel L. Widzer
ISBN 1-885211-31-7
$12.95

World travel expert Joel Widzer shares his proven techniques on how to travel First Class at discount prices, even if you're not a frequent flyer.

SAFETY AND SECURITY FOR WOMEN WHO TRAVEL
By Sheila Swan & Peter Laufer
ISBN 1-885211-29-5
$12.95

A must for every woman traveler!

THE FEARLESS DINER
Travel Tips and Wisdom for Eating around the World
By Richard Sterling
ISBN 1-885211-22-8
$7.95

Combines practical advice on foodstuffs, habits, & etiquette, with hilarious accounts of others' eating adventures.

GUTSY WOMEN
Travel Tips and Wisdom for the Road
By Marybeth Bond
ISBN 1-885211-15-5
$7.95

Packed with funny, instructive, and inspiring advice for women heading out to see the world.

GUTSY MAMAS:
Travel Tips and Wisdom for Mothers on the Road
By Marybeth Bond
ISBN 1-885211-20-1
$7.95

A delightful guide for mothers traveling with their children—or without them!

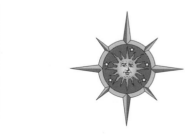